Women, Art, and Literature in the Iranian Diaspora

Gender, Culture, and Politics in the Middle East
miriam cooke, Simona Sharoni, and Suad Joseph, *Series Editors*

Select Titles in Gender, Culture, and Politics in the Middle East

Anxiety of Erasure: Trauma, Authorship, and the Diaspora in Arab Women's Writings
Hanadi Al-Samman

Arab and Arab American Feminisms: Gender, Violence, and Belonging
Rabab Abdulhadi, Evelyn Alsultany, and Nadine Naber, eds.

Arab Women's Lives Retold: Exploring Identity through Writing
Nawar Al-Hassan Golley, ed.

Beyond the Exotic: Women's Histories in Islamic Societies
Amira El-Azhary Sonbol, ed.

The Female Suffering Body: Illness and Disability in Modern Arabic Literature
Abir Hamdar

Mihrî Hatun: Performance, Gender-Bending, and Subversion in Ottoman Intellectual History
Didem Havlioğlu

Unveiling Men: Modern Masculinities in Twentieth-Century Iran
Wendy DeSouza

Words, Not Swords: Iranian Women Writers and the Freedom of Movement
Farzaneh Milani

Women, Art, and Literature in the Iranian Diaspora

Mehraneh Ebrahimi

Syracuse University Press

First Edition 2019

19 20 21 22 23 24 6 5 4 3 2 1

∞ The paper used in this publication meets the minimum requirements of the American National Standard for Information Sciences—Permanence of Paper for Printed Library Materials, ANSI Z39.48-1992.

For a listing of books published and distributed by Syracuse University Press, visit www.press.syr.edu.

ISBN: 978-0-8156-3635-9 (hardcover)
978-0-8156-3655-7 (paperback)
978-0-8156-5482-7 (e-book)

Library of Congress Cataloging-in-Publication Data

Names: Ebrahimi, Mehraneh, author.
Title: Women, art, and literature in the Iranian diaspora / Mehraneh Ebrahimi.
Description: First edition. | Syracuse, New York : Syracuse University Press, 2019. | Series: Gender, culture, and politics in the Middle East
Identifiers: LCCN 2019000538 (print) | LCCN 2019013130 (ebook) | ISBN 9780815654827 (E-book) | ISBN 9780815636359 | ISBN 9780815636359 (hardcover : alk. paper) | ISBN 9780815636557 (pbk. : alk. paper)
Subjects: LCSH: Arts, Iranian—21st century. | Women artists—Iran. | Women and the arts. | Iranian diaspora. | Graphic novels—History and criticism. | Motion pictures—History—21st century. | Satrapi, Marjane, 1969—Criticism and interpretation. | Bashi, Parsua, 1966—Criticism and interpretation. | Neshat, Shirin, 1957—Criticism and interpretation.
Classification: LCC NX574.A1 (ebook) | LCC NX574.A1 E27 2019 (print) | DDC 700.92/520955—dc23
LC record available at https://lccn.loc.gov/2019000538

Manufactured in the United States of America

To my daughter,
Who grew inside me as I wrote this book.
May you live in a world with no monsters and walls;
Its meadows blocked by no borders barring your golden wings.
To my phoenix, my alchemist: my Kimia.

Contents

List of Illustrations · *ix*

Preface · *xi*

Introduction · *1*

PART ONE. Diasporic Iranian Visual Literature in the Form of Graphic Narratives · *27*

1. Marjane Satrapi's *Persepolis* · *37*

2. Parsua Bashi's *Nylon Road* · *64*

PART TWO. Diasporic Iranian Visual Literature Manifested in the Art of Shirin Neshat: *Photo-Poetry and Poetic Film* · *85*

3. Shirin Neshat's Political(ized) Aesthetics · *103*

4. Neshat Moving on to Movies · *135*

Conclusion · *158*

Works Cited · *169*

Index · *175*

Illustrations

1. Relief details of the Achaemenid Empire's Immortal Guardians · *32*
2. Ancient Egyptian sequential images narrate a story on a tomb wall · *33*
3. The end of childhood for Marji · *41*
4. Idealists of the Revolution and their demise · *43*
5. Dichotomies and ambivalence · *45*
6. Torture as envisioned by a child · *46*
7. Not every clergy member is evil! · *52*
8. Categorizing people by their dress code · *55*
9. Revolution was just the start; menace has a way to return · *57*
10. Children perpetuating the violence that surrounds them · *58*
11. Two cover designs of *Nylon Road* for German and English editions · *69*
12. Common Western attitudes toward Muslims, wars, and refugees · *73*
13. Pari training to become a young, leftist guerrilla fighter · *76*
14. Comparing the cults of fashion, religion, and politics · *77*
15. Similar outcomes for teenagers who follow cults · *78*
16. Cults of fashion, religion, and politics produce similarly wealthy leaders · *79*
17. First panel from *Persepolis* · *81*
18. First panel from *Nylon Road* · *82*
19. Miniature scenes from the battles in *Shahnameh* are painted over the subject's body · *95*
20. "Standing in Awe"; an enigma · *119*
21. Neshat displays magic charms · *131*

Preface

> Human beings are as limbs to one whole body
> Created from the same precious essence
> Should one organ be troubled by pain,
> Others would suffer severe strain.
> Thou, careless of people's suffering,
> deserve not the name, "human being"
>
> —Sa'di, 1300 AD

The stock images of violence depicted in war movies have failed to capture and engage the collective imagination of the Western audience (Blackmore 2012). The news media's dehumanizing bombardment of the public with generic, decontextualized violence has desensitized the audience regarding the pain of Others.

Iranian diasporic artists, having faced war, trauma, gender inequality, and racial stigma, can help break what appears to be homogeneity in an indifferent public mind-set. The confluence of poetry, politics, and the visual arts can rechannel compassion fatigue toward genuine curiosity about, and attention to, radical alterity. Whether aesthetics, politics, and ethics can instigate the creation of an aesthetic community, a sensus communis, has been tested in the works of several artists and authors who engage with the question of Otherness. Although their work has been produced in the context of Iran's century-old struggle for democracy, their voice is a broader one, encompassing the whole region and beyond.

From the Constitutional Revolution of 1905 to the Islamic Revolution of 1979; from the internationally aided invasion by Saddam Hussein in the 1980s to the Green Movement of 2009, the struggle in the hearts and homes of the people, especially the women and the abject, have been envisaged in the works of these Iranian artists. Shirin Neshat's photographic collections (such as *Women of Allah*), videographic installations (such as "Mahdokht"), and feature film *Women without Men* (based on a novel by Shahrnush Parsipur; inspired by Forough Farrokhzad's poetry and her documentary film) are specifically in focus. Although Neshat uses orientalized Middle Eastern local colors, it is through political free play that her visual productions create a third space and herald a new understanding of the stories of others.

Before I discuss Neshat's work, I bring into the critical gaze two graphic novels by Marjane Satrapi, *Persepolis I* and *Persepolis II*, and another by Parsua Bashi, *Nylon Road*, especially regarding their treatment of the ultimate villain. Delimiting cartooning technology's potency in fostering empathy, I then turn to the works' ethical spectrum. I specifically look at the systematic manner in which these artists locate and visualize their enemies. Locating the enemy outside ourselves, with no complicity of the self in its creation, is a sure sign of purging and scapegoating in the literature produced by the diaspora.

This research reflects a process of weaving together and tearing apart several apparently disparate threads into Borromean knot-chains of aesthetics, politics, and ethics. Using the triple lens of aesthetics, politics, and ethics in analyzing these works of art allows me to visualize the fissures in the fabric of our torn democracy—not to cover the blind spots and the dead tangles, but to bring their porous texture to touch. I will first delineate the specific definitions of my key concepts: liberal democracy's entanglement with terror and the break, litigation, and dissensus that real art can create. A strategic definition of democracy based on the power of dissensus or disagreement, as suggested by Jacques Rancière, is crucial in viewing aesthetics and politics multifocally. Aesthetic breaks can realize a third space where hierarchies of domination and subjugation are toppled, melted, and subverted.

Borrowing from the medical lexicon, Jacques Derrida refers to autoimmunity as the process whereby the body attacks its own cells for its own survival. Extreme securitarian regimes likewise start attacking their selves—activists, artists, dissidents, and civic liberties—in an attempt to curtail the evil, external enemy. Artistic productions with a fair approach to demonized enemies challenge the axiomatic binary between the comfortable proximity of all who belong to self and the ominous alienness of the Other. A critic treading such a delicate tightrope should heed the polarities of appropriation, incorporation, and projection. Aesthetic revolt happens ethically, where regimes of art challenge regimes of policing. The moment of possibilities looms when a work of art engages in free aesthetic play, dares to say no, subverts and displaces established hierarchies, creates dissensual litigation, and thus aids in midwifing a democracy-to-come.

American Democratic Fascism

> Fascism will come to America in the name of national security.
> —Senator Huey Long

The way democracy today is taken up by politicians as an excuse for territorial hegemony, occupation, or toppling of governments bears uncanny traces to the ancient *mission civilisatrice.* I argue that art and literature have the potential to beckon democracy-to-come by providing a different, relatable, human portrait of the Other that breaks with the policed consensus regarding the evilness of the enemy. These works do more than raise awareness about distant people, lands, and cultures. Raising awareness can be the role of an ideal news media. These works touch the common tissue of our shared life force, bring to audibility and visibility what has been foreclosed from the common political sphere, and playfully mount the walls of dichotomies and fracture their superficial cement ceilings. My aim in the following pages is to bring to attention the seminal role of literature and the visual arts in fostering the democratic process. These texts trace the aesthetics of the different, the inappropriate, and the marginal in an empathic and ethical way.

Although there has recently been a surge in the publication and analysis of exilic texts by Muslim Iranian women, no critic has approached them from the perspective of their contribution to ushering in democracy and countering the war machine against abstract terror. To usher in democracy and counter terror, these texts have been embroidered with the Borromean knots of aesthetics, politics, and ethics. It is with such an understanding and ethical treatment of the enemy that we are invited to take an uncanny, defamiliarizing second look at Otherness. The humanities are the site par excellence for midwifing—in the Socratic sense—of the democracy to come.

It is necessary to unpack my reading of democracy and its relation to literature of the Other in order to deface globalization's march against itself, called the war on terror. The discourse on pop terror relies on a moral binary that considers us (the globalizing powers) as good and them (the generic Muslim Other) as evil. The methods of the war against terror are not terribly dissimilar to the medieval exorcism of evil: "Ultimately, Good could thwart Evil only by ceasing to be Good since, by seizing for itself a global monopoly of power, it gives rise, by that very act, to a blowback of a proportionate violence" (Baudrillard 2002, 11).

While academic critics are rightly quick to point to the shortcomings of the Enlightenment in placing the individual subject at the center of the universe, they are reluctant to see the medieval frames of mind of the current war makers with their stark moral palette. For Baudrillard, terrorism is the globe fighting globalization: "It is what haunts every world order, all hegemonic domination—if Islam dominated the world, terrorism would rise against Islam, *for it is the world, the globe itself, which resists globalization*" (Baudrillard, 10, italics in original). While I find fascinating Baudrillard's shocking categorization of terrorism as a global resistance to globalization, my critical gaze refuses to accept the term *terrorism* as a generic title. Without undermining Baudrillard's theoretical discussions in abstraction, I prefer to avoid generalities and look at case-specific scenarios regarding representation of alterity in the visual and verbal media. In order to understand terrorism, I want to start with its Other: the blanket Western democracy, as an a priori perfect concept. Democracy can be exported to whoever does not share our supremacy and our leadership. Once the antinomies at the crux of the democratic are delineated, the task of the literati becomes apparent: to disalign themselves from real terror by seizing their democratic powers.

With no resistance on the part of the humanist intellectuals, I argue that the liberal democracy of today can easily become a discursive displacement of fascism,[1] with totalitarian[2] ambitions. This argument is not isomorphic with claiming that we are living in utter fascism or with urging people to dispense with democracy all together. Quite the contrary, through a survey of changes in the cultural significance of the term *democracy* across the ages, I argue for an intervention and a rereading of the double-bound term from a fresh, empowering perspective. I will delineate here the intrinsic paradoxes at the heart of the neoliberal concept of democracy that can easily derail it into radicalism.

I begin by outlining the dangers posed by taking democracy as a priori and effortlessly beneficial. Democracy is *a venir*—"to come"—and thus exhibits persistent friction. Breaches of the constitution wrought by the few oligarchs in power who are unanswerable to the public or the law can only lead toward extremism. By becoming silent accomplices, democratic countries have performed genocides in the past. Michel Foucault too, although he concedes that fascism and Stalinism were "responses to a precise and very specific situation," sees these instances of monstrosity as "clearly the heritage of liberal Western societies":

1. The word *fascism* was coined in our current usage by Europe's first modern fascist leader, Benito Mussolini, who based his party's name on the Latin word *fasces*, which referred to a bundle of elm or birch rods bound together (signifying popular unity) and usually containing an ax-head (denoting leadership); it was a symbol of penal authority in ancient Rome. In *The Anatomy of Fascism*, Robert O. Paxton (2004) defines it as a "form of political behavior marked by obsessive preoccupation with community decline, humiliation or victimhood and by compensatory cults of unity, energy and purity, in which a mass-based party of committed nationalist militants, working in uneasy but effective collaboration with traditional elites, abandons democratic liberties and pursues with redemptive violence and without ethical or legal restraints goals of internal cleansing and external expansion" (380).

2. *Totalitarianism* refers to a "form of government that theoretically permits no individual freedom and that seeks to subordinate all aspects of the individual's life to the authority of the government. Italian dictator Benito Mussolini coined the term *totalitario* in the early 1920s to describe the new fascist state of Italy, which he further described as: 'All within the state, none outside the state, none against the state'" (Encyclopaedia Britannica Online).

> it cannot be denied that, in many respects, fascism and Stalinism simply extended a whole series of mechanisms that already existed in the social and political systems of the West . . . [e.g.,] the organization of great parties, the development of political apparatuses, and the existence of techniques of repression such as labor camps. (Foucault 2008, 276)

Apparatuses of mass disciplinary punishment and suppression of dissent are ingrained in the "social and political heritage" of Western liberal societies and all that Stalinism and fascism had to do "was to stoop down and pick it up" (Foucault 2008, 276).

Has the internationally backed American drone empire stooped so low in order to conquer? The anesthetization of citizens confronted by their perpetual responsibility to bring democracy into play, but evading the citizenry's duty of taking turns (*tour à tour*[3]) to govern and be governed aids the engrossment of the militarized, autosecuritarian regime in opting for unilateral consensus as opposed to litigious dissensus. Only through disagreement will "the political" emerge (Rancière 1999). I argue that dissensus prefigures an acknowledgment of the Other and calls for an ethical engagement with it, despite the dangers that such an embrace might entail. The political unfolds as an increasingly more dangerous cry of parrhesia: the courage to voice the truth against the displeasure of others (Foucault 2011).

Quiet, consensual regimes are the ground par excellence for the breeding of fear politics—or rather, policing. Literature that encompasses aesthetics, politics, and ethics flares dissensus. As Rancière and Steve Corcoran (2015) remind us time and again, democracy is not a "static universal mode of representational government" (24); the very idea of a representative democracy would have sounded paradoxical to Athenian ears. According to Aristotle, what distinguishes a citizen from

3. Derrida reworks the concept of *tour à tour* via Aristotle. For Aristotle citizens were those who were ready to govern and be governed in turns. The cyclical, random movement of power in society that works through turns and returns aids him in defining the contours of his argument in *Rogues* (Derrida 2005).

an animal is speech; the former constructs an argument to advance a cause while the latter—an *instrumentum semi-vocale*—moans with grief when plagued by dis-ease. The political is distinguished at the edge of the distinction between an animal cry and a human voice in unrest. It is these tales of suffering and emancipation that can invite a loving gaze at Others. "Ethics are not just a problem of knowledge but a call to a relationship" (Spivak 2013b, 5).

The Paradox of Freedom and Security

In the *Birth of Biopolitics* (2008), Foucault delineates an essential paradox at the crux of what he establishes to be liberalism: it "entails at its heart a productive/destructive relationship [with] freedom," in which individual interest is offset and regulated by the boundaries of collective security on the basis of the economy of power that the government establishes (64). This balance between individual freedom monitored by the police state and the sovereignty of the nation as a whole (in conjunction with other equal or greater world powers) can very well be disturbed through what I recognize as a securitarian, consensual state ruled by fear of abstract terror—what Derrida defines as autoimmunity as an intrinsic organ of democracy.

Michael Hayden, George W. Bush's CIA director, referred to this sensitive security-freedom balance right after the release of the scandalous findings of Edward Snowden; the director called Snowden "the most costly leaker of American secrets in the history of the republic" on CNN. He believed that "the appropriate balance between liberty and security has bedeviled free peoples, including Americans, for centuries" (Hayden 2013). For the former National Security Agency director, speaking up about breaches of constitutional law is a matter of personal "moral judgment," which must be discarded for the sake of consensus with the regime (Hayden 2013). However, in *The Courage of Truth* (2011) Foucault nominates "*parrhesia* (truth-telling, the right to express one's opinion, and the courage to go against the opinions of others)" as one of the fundamental prerequisites of a democracy, but one that even at the time of Plato was becoming increasingly "impossible, or at any rate dangerous," both for the courageous individual who stood up against the system and for the polis itself.

Foucault refers to the threats faced by Socrates as he challenged the Athenians to listen to him despite the bitterness that his illuminations evoked. The US government revoked Edward Snowden's passport, sentencing him to the limbo of international transit, for having the audacity to expose the sabotage of American constitutional law to the world community. The Obama and Trump administrations openly lobbied (that is, bullied) other nations into refusing him asylum.

Hannah Arendt reminds us that the bare human being has no rights outside citizenship. Annulling the passport of a whistle-blower who practices parrhesia, the fundamental prerequisite of a democracy, in the rights discourse is a metonymy for depriving him of his inalienable human rights; it is a civic murder:

> Either democracy makes room for *parrhesia*, in which case it can only be a freedom which is dangerous for the city, or *parrhesia* is a courageous attitude which consists in undertaking to tell the truth, in which case it has no place in democracy. (Foucault 2008, 38)

General Hayden compares Snowden to the "spies"[4] who had given American atomic bomb information to the Soviet Union during the Cold War. The ironic comparison is apt because the paranoia about "Islamist terror" bears an uncanny resemblance to that of the Red Scare with its fear of the atomic bomb. For the likes of Hayden, the civic death of a whistle-blower is justified for the transcendental good of national security: the "democratic state" murders a part of its own body in order to ensure its own survival. Yet I would argue that such a suicidal state cannot carry the prefix of *democratic* any more.

4. Calling Snowden a spy is ironic since it was Snowden who revealed the widespread spying of the US government—not just on American residents, but on people all over the world.

The Fascist Shift

In *The End of America* Naomi Wolf (2007), dockets ten steps that can lead any democratic government toward what she calls a "fascist shift." After a historical survey of the fascist states of previous centuries, she describes the blueprint that modern dictators followed en route to total hegemony. The uncanniness of these ten steps, even years after the book's publication during the George W. Bush administration, still manages to alarm me about our taken-for-granted democracy. According to Wolf (2007), all fascist nations followed these steps on route to total hegemony:

1. Constructing a terrifying internal and external enemy
2. Establishing secret prisons where torture takes place; a gulag
3. Organizing a "thug caste" or paramilitary force that is above law, using security contractors and private armies to deal with emergencies at home and abroad
4. Setting up internal surveillance systems
5. Harassing citizens groups
6. Engaging in arbitrary detention and release
7. Targeting key individuals
8. Controlling the press
9. Equating dissent with treason
10. Suspending the rule of law

She concludes that the US government—which, according to her, was once a beacon of liberty—is rolling down a fascist slope.

I find Wolf's comparative historical research fascinating. Due to changes in the way power disseminates in modern societies since the late-sixteenth and early-seventeenth centuries, I believe, decapitating a single king or government will not necessarily bring about a political movement or grassroots subversion. Democracy is ushered in by citizens' active participation in government *tour à tour*, by people speaking up autocritically, without being crippled by self-immunity. Democracy will be wrought through dissensus, by citizens who dare to speak up loudly and clearly against injustice (practicing parrhesia), creating a break in the policed consensus. The works of art produced by the Iranian diaspora bring the unknown face of the Other into intimate proximity and foster a bond between us and them. This ethical relationship, through an act of disattachment from the chorus of consensual images seen in popular media, is a strong indicator of the power of aesthetics to effect change in the world of perception.

The Pervertible Power of Democracy

Despite the jubilation surrounding the sacredness, uniqueness, and thus exportability of democracy, many Western policies show an aversion to the opinion of the masses about critical concerns, such as the continuation of an illegal war. The lack of public space given to the opinion of the people and adhesion to the expert opinion of a select group of speakers are signs of an oligarchy that is deeply anxious about the readiness of people to lead. The fear that democracy is an unleashing of a beast of public opinion that should be tamed by a pseudo-democratic state is nothing new. However, I do not believe that democracy proper is the nexus of unleashing individualistic desires and unstrapping the spiraling wheel of the market, culminating in the fissure of the social bond.

Rancière contends that it is only by mistaking policing as politics that the irreducible dissensus, difference, and heterogeneity at the heart of community—the very stuff of politics—are reduced to universal, homogeneous consensus in a fascist turn:

> Policing is, essentially, the law, generally implicit, that defines a party's share or lack of it. Policing is thus first an order of bodies that defines the allocation of ways of doing, ways of being, and ways of saying, and sees that those bodies are assigned by name to a particular place and task; it is an order of the visible and the sayable that sees that a particular activity is visible and another is not, that this speech is understood as discourse and another as noise. (1999, 29)

Contrary to the fears of the oligarch, democracy is not the catastrophic unlashing of the masses' desires:

> The democratic process is the process of a perpetual bringing into play, of invention of forms of subjectivation, and of cases of verification that counteract the perpetual privatization of public life. Democracy really means . . . the impurity of politics, the challenging of governments' claims to embody the sole principle of public life and in so doing be able to circumscribe the . . . extension of public life. If there is a "limitlessness" specific to democracy, then that's exactly where it lies: not in the exponential multiplication of needs or of desires emanating from individuals, but in the movement that ceaselessly displaces the limits of the public and the private, of the political and the social. It is this displacement inherent to politics itself that so-called republican ideology refuses to accept . . . [asserting] a strict delimitation of spheres between the political and the social [that] regards the republic as identical to the rule of law. (Rancière 2006, 62–63)

It is only through a half-hearted benevolence of the critics of the policed, securitarian government that democracy—as the count of the uncounted—is being hampered and denounced by the few oligarchs in power. Inherent in the intellectual/artist/critic hybrid's approach to representative regimes of communication is an elitism that presupposes the ignorance of the population who are unable to recognize the current social challenges. Speaking in terms of regimes of representation, such a take corresponds to a mimetic regime that aims at teaching the ignoramus, or at art-preaching (albeit with a postmodern fear of a message).

Plato's exclusion of the "little bald tinker" and those with "disfigured bodies" and "battered and mutilated souls" who "betake themselves to philosophy" in the *Republic* VI is putatively based on the interdiction intrinsic to the reality of their profession; these laborers have no leisure time away from their vocation to contemplate matters of the state as it pertains to the community. According to Rancière, the *dispositifs* that make the subjects lack time, space, and leisure to participate in matters common to humankind still function to police the commonly visible, sayable, and audible. Inspired by the maverick nineteenth-century principle of equality of intelligence introduced by Joseph Jacotot, Rancière came to believe that "one ignoramus can teach another what he himself did not know" (2009b,

1). Hatred and fear of parrhesia in democracies is based on what Foucault calls an ethical differentiation in democracies: the fact that the masses are deemed a homogeneous slum of ignoramuses, and the ruling political elite are the ones entitled to occupy the seat of authority, visibility, and audibility. If masses are ignorant, their rule is to be despised. But how to subvert this belittling binary, even at the level of thought? Art has emancipatory potential to intervene in space-timing, hierarchies, and partitioning of the grievable and the visible. Here, I will look at how, through free play, an artist dismantles the space allocated to the Other.

For me, these uncanonical, apparently indecorous, marginal works of art playfully ignore and surpass the policed mental preconditioning and incite an *aestextasy* that reminds humans of what is shared in the humanity of the invisible, inaudible Other. Nations that build literal, figurative, and metaphoric security walls instead of connection bridges foreclose the possibility of the humanity of the generic enemy. Aestextasy creates visceral bonds that displace and subvert notions of self and other, inside and outside, proximity and distance. It creates joints of connection between the pleasure and pain of one body to that of the world community via a new politics of susceptibility to the shared sensory landscape of life. Aesthetics is etymologically related to sense perception. Aesthetic regimes of art are, as Rancière has argued, political tools for subverting hierarchies of domination. Aesthetics—as that which is derived from sensory perception—perceives the other (the one outside or beside oneself) and forms a point of contact from which egoism transforms into bonding with alterity, connecting individual bubbles with the sensory experience of a common life force:

> Politics begins when those who were destined to remain in the domestic and invisible territory of world and reproduction, and prevented from doing anything else, take the time that they have not in order to affirm that they belong to a common world. It begins when they make the invisible visible, and make what was deemed to be the mere noise of suffering bodies heard as a discourse concerning the "common" of the community. Politics creates a new form, as it were, of dissensual "commonsense." (Rancière and Corcoran 2015, 139)

This research is materially rooted in a certain moment when the individual work of art connects itself to the common song of humanity in the face of war and extinction. Each chosen work reflects on at least two traumatic moments related to the world's present history. These are the turbulent recent history of Iran and the current generic war on terror. Each moment feeds into various other historical sparks and reflects back to the present moment as a witness. The two main images that doubly wound my selected works are the Islamic Revolution of Iran and the war on the Middle East in the name of combating Islamic terror.

The concrete war on abstract terror in the aftermath of the fall of the World Trade Center intensified an already deep-rooted wave of generic Islamophobia. Satrapi, Neshat, Bashi and a plethora of other Iranian artists felt a compulsion to recount, whether verbally or visually, the tales of nuance, of the singularities of each experience and the material effects of terror. These works have been successful in generating an ethical connectivity by remembering the shared thread of humanity, all the while keeping their uniqueness and differences through aesthetics play.

When the world's deadliest iron fist is mobilized to break the fluid concept or metaphor of the Muslim terrorist, the outcome could be a backlash of more terror, a rechanneling of previously immobile forces.[5] The awkward battle between an iron fist and liquid concepts points to the vital significance of enigmatic discursive displacements: our democracy battling their terrorism. If civilians, including women and children, are being murdered by fire from the skies on the basis of a lethal dichotomy between us and them, is it not time to probe the fictitious fabric of that binary further? If wars are supported with appeal to signs, metonymy, and metalepsis, it is a humanitarian duty of the scholars of humanity to deconstruct and reconstruct that worldview. Changing mind-sets will not bring a revolution, according to Gayatri Spivak, but, "without this revolutionary change of mind, revolutionary 'programs' will fall into the same

5. These words were written almost a year before the rise, in Syria, of ISIS, which gained weapons and funds through Western interference in plotting for regime change in the region.

metaphysical bind of idealized and repeatable intention and context" (Spivak 2013b, 88).

In this volume I scan texts that have the transformative power to rearrange desires toward a democracy to come, texts that dare to show a different face of Iranian women to the world. With the grace of their aestextasy, these works remind humanity of the common fabric of life and the palpable danger of unknotting it. I specifically look at the tropes and figures that enable these texts to articulate their aesthetics politically and ethically.

Women, Art, and Literature in the Iranian Diaspora

Introduction

In the age of the war against abstract terror, master words such as *democracy* can become metaleptic[1] alibis for neocapitalistic crusades across the globe. Unlike classical warfare, the frontiers are inhuman/e on one side and invisible on the other.[2]

The excessive brutality of "unmanned" aerial vehicles is in striking contrast with the scarcity of scholarship and public awareness regarding the bombed generic Others. The death-bird, as I call the drone, could be an extension or a metonymy of our perception of the Other. In order to stop the drones' Medusa gaze, we need to change our perception of the Other and learn to risk the extension of an arm or a shoulder.[3]

The enemy, as the Other, has been foreclosed from the fields of sight and sensibility. The suspects are expelled even from the borders of the

1. In *Map of Misreading* (2007), Harold Bloom calls metalepsis a "metonymy of a metonym." In my reading, because the word *democracy* comes to us already abused, and is then doubly misread by politicians, I selected the trope of metalepsis to describe the process.

2. This introduction was written before the rise of ISIS. The unethical treatment of the enemy, even in the realm of aesthetics (which is closely tied to that of politics), can have disastrous effects in our shared experience of the sensible world and lead to the creation of such cancerous monstrosities.

3. The National Security Agency (NSA) often identifies and bombs "terrorists" on the basis of the location of their cell phones. The Central Intelligence Agency (CIA) or US military then orders a drone strike on the basis of the phone's location, but the phone may be in the hand of a friend, a spouse, or a child rather than with the suspect. A former drone operator has leaked the fact that many insurgents deliberately change their SIM cards to confuse the US military: "We're targeting a cell phone . . . in the hopes that the person on the other end of that missile is the bad guy" (Scahill and Greenwald 2014).

nation—as in Guantanamo Bay: outside the rule of law, and treated with extrajuridical measures. Kangaroo courts pass sentences of indefinite detention for subjects outside the condition of being called human. This is while the news media are advised against publishing headlines about civilian casualties on front pages. Even the photographs of war are state-controlled through the use of embedded photojournalists. Jacques Lacan professes that that which is foreclosed from the Symbolic Order will come back haunting the Real. In other words, what we avoid talking about may eventually hit us in the head. The lack of scholarship on our democracies' paranoia toward abstract terror is offset by its prevalence in contemporary political violence. What we are afraid to communicate and engage with in a bilateral, communal way will come and haunt our real, violent world.

This research engages with the humanities' reflections on these mechanisms of foreclosure, invisibility, and Othering, all while thinking of aesthetic alternatives. Sigmund Freud famously defined foreclosure as a process whereby part of an unpleasant reality is erased as if it had never existed: "Here, the ego rejects the incompatible idea together with its affect and behaves as if the idea had never occurred to the ego at all. But from the moment at which this has been successfully done the subject is in a psychosis, which can only be classified as 'hallucinatory confusion'" (1953, 58). The question is, what have we tried to ignore that will come back and haunt our nightmares?

By delving into the question of Iranian Muslim women's agency and struggle for democracy as portrayed in diasporic visual productions, I untangle this "hallucinatory confusion" of Islam with sheer terror. How should the humanities, as an academic discipline, displace and subvert the self-evident facts or epistemes that contribute to the manifestation of a paranoid defense mechanism? I argue that daring authors, including artists, graphic novelists, filmmakers, and memoir writers, have the ability to confuse and complicate set binaries. Their portrayal of the Other not as an enemy, but as someone relatable, perfectible, and human creates a dissensus in the hegemonic discourse circulating against those who are supposedly unlike ourselves. Through this tear in the general imagination, bonds of interrelation and connection are slowly and painstakingly woven, and this is how democracy grows: through litigation, dissensus, and parrhesia (what Foucault calls daring, truthful, yet dangerous critique)—not through silent complicity and consensus. Aesthetics and politics intertwine in the fabrication of our democracy's Other: the semi-mythical figure of the Muslim terrorist. At our nations' checkpoints the fade-outs of our democracy are demarcated by bio-securitarian costumes; the gates gradually extend outward and inward to define the contours of our psychological relationship with the enemy.

The cultural critic's challenge is twofold in representing the Other. Like Georges Didi-Huberman's ropewalker she must be wary at every step not to fall prey to the lethal bipolarities when engaging with the Other. First, she must eschew appropriation and incorporation: she must avoid selfing the Other, appropriating its[4] voice, or exhibiting a "patronizing sympathy" toward it or incorporating traits or symptoms of the victim in the self (LaCapra 2001, 38). Furthermore, she must not practice foreclosure,[5] in which the Other is entirely ignored, expunged from the domain of that which is homogeneously human.

Although we live in times of compassion fatigue, media desensitization, and parochialism, as a student of humanities, I am passionate about, and do not shy away from, the potential of literature to change the world. I believe that it is through an ethical awakening of humanities to the politics of its aesthetics that problematic hierarchies are dismantled. In order to rekindle a fresh vision of a world of perception, the humanities—not as an isolated, precarious discipline, but as a way of life—have to step in and realize that there is no politics without ethics and no aesthetics without both. This is not about committed art standing in a self-defeating posture opposite sloganists of *l'art pour l'art.* This is the humanities remembering the sensory being in a world that can envision a different space and timing in order to alter hegemonic worldviews;

4. I used the pronoun *it* for the Other to highlight the dehumanization intrinsic in Othering.

5. Gayatri Spivak contends that the figure of the subaltern has been foreclosed from the discourse of enlightenment, especially for subject formation in the oeuvre of Kant, Hegel, and Marx, "the last Three Wise Men of the Continental (European) tradition" (1999, 111).

this is about "uncoercively rearranging desires" (Spivak 2013, 375). Art that reaches out can bring to visibility, raise awareness, and rearrange the lethal desires of domination.

I argue that the discourse around terror fueled by neoliberal capitalist crusaders can be interrupted via what I have dubbed aesthetic-ecstasy. In a verbal twist, the word *aestextasy*[6] connects the three concepts of aesthetics, ethics, and politics, all knotted around the text. As in a Borromean knot, removing one ring will disassemble the whole chain. Aestextasy intervenes in the pop-terror discourse in order to create a fresh perspective whence the dangerous Other can be identified as human, as kin, as an extension of the self. It necessitates the formation of that ethical bond without which humanity and life on earth will inevitably perish. Ecstasy or the state of being beside oneself, outside the body with pleasure or pain links excessive sensation with the question of the Other, the one outside or beside the self. Judith Butler contends that the quality of being beside oneself indexes the essential interdependence of humankind: "To be ec-static means, literally, to be outside oneself, and thus can have several meanings: to be transported beyond oneself by a passion, but also to be beside oneself with rage or grief. I think that if I can still address a 'we,' or include myself within its terms, I am speaking to those of us who are living in certain ways beside ourselves, whether in sexual passion, or emotional grief, or political rage" (Butler 2004, 24).

For Butler, disparate bodies are connected via the condition of ecstasis. They are not only connected, but are interdependent and rely on one another for safety. This bodily interdependence is inseparable from the question of ethics and aesthetics. My reading of aestextasy calls for an art that recognizes the relatability of self with the Other, and the precarity of the feeble pulse of life in the world: a web of live throbs that can easily fade away with the press of a red button. Aestextasy is a constant reminder of the ethical and visceral interconnectedness of beings in the world endowed with a sensory constellation. The condition of fluttering simultaneously between the self and the Other, of being oneself and beside

6. Pronounced "es-tex-tacy."

oneself with pleasure or pain, of transcending the self, of perception of the Other as a self—but without the greed of domination—is in a sharp contrast with a solitary aesthetics that commences and terminates in the self. It is impossible for true aesthetics to remain isolated, self-absorbed, completely out of tune with the cycles of politics.

Such egoistic aesthetics leads to formation of partition walls and nuclear weapons to guard them. Aestextasy is a prerequisite for the evolution of humanity from this despicable disposition of Othering, pesticization (imagining those different from us as malignant pests to be crushed), and exploitation that leads completely ordinary modern people to turn into bureaucratic war machines. Such ordinary people-turned-bureaucratic war machines have led the Nazi Party during the Holocaust, the Belgian philanthropic association in the Congo Free State, and the People's Commissariat in the Gulag. With the bloody sectarian civil war in Iraq, the name Mission Iraqi Freedom bears uncanny echoes of other purportedly benevolent military occupations. Civil wars are rampaging throughout the Middle East, self-effacing, cancer-like.

What is the literati's call and contribution in this inhuman reworlding? Who are our intellectuals, and are they responsible for raising awareness, bringing the invisible victims to our fields of vision and hearing? Academic institutions' professed neutrality, consensual recycling, and detached melancholia for lost origins did not stop any of the aforementioned genocides; they are not going to intervene now.

There are, however, artists, authors, and other human beings who have built bridges over cultural estrangement via elements common to humankind: tales of suffering, exile, and reorientation. These artists are beacons of change from within, who break the happy consensus of war machines by offering a different glimpse into the life of the Other. In offering differences, they remind their audience of the similarities between the experiences of pleasure and pain of Others and the self.

The democratic process is made possible through an occupation of the common imagination, through the dangerous endeavor that these artists undertake in hosting different voices and distant figures in the secluded shared space. As Michel Foucault reminds us, there is no democracy without parrhesia—daring truthful talk that can put both the speaker and the audience in danger. Yet speaking truth to power is becoming increasingly dangerous.

Shunning atomization, compartmentalization, and rigid binaries, I have picked texts that meet in the beyond: beyond literature, art, and politics, beyond the visual or verbal. This interdisciplinary approach is part and parcel of the emancipatory reworlding that I continually stress. Each chapter scans an apparently disparate medium of communication, such as the graphic technology, the diasporic memoir, or photo-poetry. These works of art use a political aesthetics to ethically make sense of the trauma of war, revolution, and xenophobia in their different styles. The aestextasy they invoke has the power to move humanity one step closer to a dissensual democracy as opposed to medieval, consensual wars of terror.

I will start with two graphic novels, then move to the oeuvre of Shirin Neshat.

Overview

In the first part of this book, I discuss diasporic Iranian visual literature in the form of graphic narratives. *Persepolis: The Story of a Childhood* (2003) and *Persepolis 2: The Story of a Return* (2003),[7] by Marjane Satrapi, effect a rupture in the corpus of Iranian diaspora writings after the Revolution. The tear opens space for an uncanny intimacy with the trauma of distant Others.

The story is delivered through a triple focus: Satrapi's attention to the playfulness of the medium as she shuttles between cement binaries (tradition/modernity, Islamic/Western, public/private, and so on), her commitment to presenting an ethically balanced narrative about one of the most contested parts of Iranian history, and her use of a Foucauldian subjugated knowledge below the hearts and homes of the people (a knowledge about forgotten struggles and unclassified sciences of intergenerational love and bonding). Satrapi starts with simplified dichotomies such as religion versus science, modernity versus fundamentalism, and freedom versus the

7. Hereafter *Persepolis* 1 and 2.

veil, then complicates and confuses these easy binaries in the second part of her book. It is aesthetic play that adds a third dimension to *Persepolis*'s formal categorizations. Illustrated in a simplified yet amplified black and white comic format, the relatable face of the child avatar transfixes the audience with the trauma of the Other, bringing distant traumas to intimate proximity and upsetting the us-versus-them binary.

Composed in the tradition of *Persepolis*, Parsua Bashi's *Nylon Road* (2009) is a self-reflective, confessional autographic (Whitlock 2006). Ethical engagement with self is the focus of *Nylon Road*, to such an extent that the threads of aesthetics and politics are loosened due to overpowering attention to ethical correctness. The story recounts the experience of a new immigrant in Switzerland who is ambushed by her previous selves. A former left-leaning political activist, she is now living a luxurious life in Zurich, and her past haunts her and drags her into dialectical discussions of her subjectivity between two ideoscapes. Subjecthood is negotiated and constituted in the flux of time and space. The entire book is an ethical autocritique, or an episodic self-questioning.

Without self-criticism, the enemy is externalized, villainized, and made into a justifiable target of attack. Identifying the complicity of the self in the problematic relationship with the Other is the crucial step in engaging in human relationships with enemies and a sure way toward fostering a human bond. However, this self-focus is the axis upon which the entire book revolves. Bashi believes that the youths recruited by fashion cults, religious institutes, and political guerrillas are comparable in that they all suspend their judgment for a transcendental alterity. She introduces ethics as a technology for self-regulation.

Nevertheless, this battle over the creation of a homogeneous, uncomplicated self is doomed to failure. Bashi sees the female body as fraught by the restrictions of class, gender, politics, fashion, and religion. By offering a persistent, ethical "dredging operation" she reminds us that the critics are not free from what they criticize (Spivak 1999, 1). However, her publisher has imposed a paratext onto the book cover that works against all that Bashi has fought to prove. The industry capitalizes on memoirs that "pierce through the veil" to offer a glimpse of the forbidden harem to Western consumers (Naghibi 2007). It is in this context that "shiʿite law" and Iran appear on the dust cover without the author's consent or any corresponding references in the text. The paratext aside, I find Bashi's treatment of the radically Othered quite enlightening. Her dialectic ethics fills an important gap in the writings of the Iranian diaspora.

The second part of this book is about diasporic Iranian visual literature, as manifested in Neshat's oeuvre: photo-poetry and poetic film. Neshat's art achieves a poignant, poetic minimalism that functions through allusions, elision, and collage. As a multifaceted artist, she has access to the "hermetically sealed culture" (Dabashi 2003, 3) of Persia and the artistry to bring it to visibility in the globalizing market of art.

Neshat composed the *Women of Allah* collection upon her return from Iran, after decades of living and studying in the United States. She claims that her gaze is curious, not judgmental. In the context of the Iran-Iraq eight-year war, Neshat is incapable of understanding what propels these women to kill or be killed in order to defend their country, and she stands in awe of them. She says: "I put myself in a place of asking questions but never answering them" (Rondeau 1999). Neshat's oeuvre is dynamic and defies docketing. "The image of women fully veiled but carrying guns on their shoulders or participating in conventionally male arenas contrasts sharply with any traditional or simple definition of womanhood. And herein lies the paradoxical nature of this neotraditionalism regarding women: veiled, but not excluded from the traditionally male domain; silent and obedient, yet at the same time outspoken and articulate" (Milani 1992, 42–43). Such a woman is not the secluded and segregated Other or wife.

Forough Farrokhzad affected the accent, color, and atmosphere of the artistic production of both Neshat and Shahrnush Parsipur. Inscribing the body of her subjects with Forough's poetry in Islamic calligraphy, Neshat sacrileges the poetry and the body of the Muslim woman. Forough (1935–1967) is the most prominent twentieth-century Iranian poet. She is also the most iconic female poet of Iran's millennia-old, male-dominated poetic tradition. Poetry is not a literary form reserved only for the elite or the avant-garde in Iran. It is arguably the most constitutive part of an Iranian sense of identity. Poetry is a way of life, a survival instinct which makes it possible to bear life's fair share of hardship and yet dream of transcendental beauty. Poetry creates a shared community of aesthetics in Iran that helps artists to escape the censors and resist hegemony. The young and the old, the educated and the illiterate, across the social divide, each have a reservoir of memorized verse that they use on a regular basis to make sense of the situation at hand. In the words of Dabashi: "Persian poetry is the pulse of Iranian culture, the rhyme and rhythm of its collective memory. . . . They remember their past as the poetic resonance of their present, in fact, of their presence in history" (Dabashi 2007, 13).

Through her "political free play," Neshat's visual productions create a third space that breaks with simple, policed representational regimes and heralds a multivalent and playful aesthetic configuration. Neshat's cinematic palette is colored by several transnational influences. The most prominent of Neshat's muses is again Forough, who was also a filmmaker, theater actor, and translator. Along those lines, more than half of Neshat's artistic career has been devoted to translating into cinematic personages and a feature film.

The most intimate motif prevalent in the works of the women studied in this book is the possibility that space politics allocates to the female characters and their embodied resilience, resistance, and revolt. Neshat maneuvers smoothly between the feminine and the intimate, on the one hand, and the political and the public, on the other. She self-consciously resists demonizing her alleged enemies. She chooses to ask questions instead of answering them. Her film *Women without Men* was released in 2009 right after Iran's Green Movement, with its march of millions in the streets. The film refers to the lives of four women who find shelter in a magical garden that mirrors the psyche of its inhabitants as well as the political atmosphere of the country during the coup of 1953. With the rise of democracy and the nationalization of Iran's oil industry, the garden flourishes, and the deserts around it bloom. After the coup against Mohammad Mossadegh, the garden starts to hover and fall. These four women have been the subject of numerous videographic installations for Neshat. A prominent concept that aids in such acrobatic movement between the aesthetic, politics, and ethics is that of free aesthetic play.

Free Aesthetic Play, the Cornerstone of Aesthetic Revolt

The connections in my proposed Borromean knot are made through the concept of free aesthetic play. Jacques Rancière's reading of free play is founded on those of Immanuel Kant and Friedrich von Schiller. For Rancière, free play generates a new "art of living," a new form of "life in common" because it "defines that which comes within the province of art through its adherence to a sensorium different to that of domination" (2009a, 30). In my understanding of his concept of free play, the lack of volition when one stands in the presence of art, the circle of inactive activity of the faculties, the suspension of desire to dominate the idle work all educate the human sensorium in a promising new aesthetic regime, a new humanity. Free play has the power to disarm the audience and foment a new sensorium of being: a novel *aisthēsis* or an aestextasy. This subversion, suspension, and disarming are the very stuff of a system of aestextasy that I have so far devised.

Kant bases his *Critique of Aesthetic Judgment* on the human cognitive ability to perform a twofold suspension of the faculties of imagination and reason—via free play. For Kant, free play consists in a relationship of the faculties that is a "requisite for cognition in general" (2007, 218). This suspension of the faculties of imagination and understanding can "suspend the power of form over matter, of intelligence over sensibility" (Rancière 2009a, 31). A few decades after Kant, Schiller elevated the concept of free play so far as to say that persons are fully human only when they play: "For, to speak out once for all, man only plays when in the full meaning of the word he is a man, and he is only completely a man when he plays" (1967, 22). Schiller anthropomorphized the Kantian propositions of free play in the context of the French Revolution. For him, "The power of form over matter is the power of the class of intelligence over the class of sensation, of men of culture over men of nature" (Rancière 2009a, 31). By suspending the domination of the faculties over one another, free play reaches out to social classes and heralds change to the vision of the community: "If aesthetic play and appearance found a new community, then this is because they stand for the refutation of this opposition between intelligent form and sensible matter which, properly speaking, is a difference between two humanities" (31).

The Post-9/11 Iranian Memoir Boom

The surge of Iranian diasporic memoirs that glance back at the experience of 1979 Revolution and the ensuing invasion by Saddam Hussein in 1980[8] is a curious phenomenon in the wake of 9/11. In "The Generic Fix of Iranian Exilic Memoirs" Gillian Whitlock contends that memoirs of Iranian diaspora are pushing Chinese scar literature off the shelves at bookstores, apparently because the Iranian memoirs are speaking to the present moment's traumas in a more direct way (2008, 9). What has triggered the memoir boom after more than two decades of relative silence by Iranians living relatively comfortably in the West?[9] Although the United States is trying hard to sell the image of a violent, sexualized Islam that picks and preys on women, there are a few groups in the Iranian diaspora who can perform the role of victims of the Islamic government and can directly or indirectly advocate regime change. These groups include bourgeois Iranians whose only preoccupation with the regime is its public restrictions on women's attire and bans on alcohol consumption, and active members of armed guerrilla forces who think solely of overthrowing the government

8. A nonexhaustive list could include: Nesta Ramazani, *The Dance of the Rose and the Nightingale* (2002); Firoozeh Dumas, *Funny in Farsi: A Memoir of Growing up Iranian in America* (2003); Azar Nafisi, *Reading Lolita in Tehran: A Memoir in Books* (2003); Farideh Goldin, *Wedding Song: Memoirs of an Iranian Jewish Woman* (2003); Roya Hakakian, *Journey from the Land of No: A Girlhood Caught in Revolutionary Iran* (2004); Farah Pahlavi, *An Enduring Love: My Life with the Shah—A Memoir* (2004); Azadeh Moaveni, *Lipstick Jihad: A Memoir of Growing up Iranian in America and American in Iran* (2005); Marjane Satrapi, *Embroideries* (2005); Afschineh Latifi, *Even after All This Time: A Story of Love, Revolution, and Leaving Iran* (2005).

9. This is a question asked by Gillian Whitlock, Nima Naghibi, Julie Rak, and other memoir critics. What specifically interests me is the boom in publication of visual memoirs of Iranian diasporic subjects in the context of war against the so-called Muslim terror.

with no clear plan for an alternative. However, there are exceptions in the popular voices heard from Iran, such as those of economic immigrants and students.

The stakes are high in the circulation of witness accounts regarding the Islamic Revolution of 1979. In *Soft Weapons: Autobiography in Transit* (2007), Gillian Whitlock takes a contrapuntal glance at the popular genre. On the one hand, some autobiographies are "soft weapons" in the New World Order, while others can create a space for human rights and a shared community:

> We need to ask old questions about these autobiographical acts, which are implicated variously in contemporary culture wars, liberation movements, and armed conflict. Which bodies are breathed into life, and which lives are being brought into view by autobiography? . . . The stage for contemporary life narratives is framed by the war on terror that dramatically shapes their jurisdiction. This includes events such as the attacks on New York and Washington in September 2001, the subsequent campaigns of armed intervention and insurgency in Afghanistan and Iraq. . . . It also includes the renewal of fundamentalisms, the ideological shifts to patriotism and homelands, the renewed vigor of Orientalism and Occidentalism in the constructions of self and the other, and a pervasive strengthening of modes of state power that operate diffusely to regulate populations and reproduce subjects in relation to strategic policy. . . . Life narratives are "soft weapons," but what follows is a series of essays on how the war on terror ripples in and through life narrative, a sign of contraction in the public sphere that is mediated in the private domain to political effect and emotional affect. (2007, 9)

The war of the world's superpowers drives publishers' demand for native informants.[10] Taking advantage of paratext for marketing, some publishers

10. I will later elaborate on the concept of native informant as introduced by Antonio Gramsci and incorporated into the discourse of Gayatri Spivak. Suffice it to mention that people who are considered experts merely because they belong to a minority group are native informants. They receive tokens by reiterating the discourse of power.

induce stereotypes without the consent of the author.[11] It is as if the only way to sell memoirs is by clinging to the "victimized Muslim woman" or the despotic Islamic Iran fantasy. However, Whitlock does not forget that the genre is capable of relaying affect toward the Other. It is with this potential of the less canonical genre of comic or visual memoirs to "be used to describe experiences of unbearable oppression and violence across a cultural divide" (2007, 55) that this monograph engages.

In this chapter I explore, through graphic memoirs, the possibility of creating a shared community of humanity and an opportunity for alternative viewpoints to freely occupy the public space. To this end, I closely scrutinize the memoirs' twin engagement with political concepts and aesthetic sensitivity, all the while keeping a third eye on their ethical engagement with enemy Others. *Nylon Road* is the most self-critical and ethically balanced of the collection. However, it loses sight of aesthetic appeal in presenting the intimate personal story of oscillation between East and West. The *Persepolis* books manage to keep an eye on each element of the trio of aesthetics, politics, and ethics.

All the works selected for this book have a visual as well as a literary element. It is important to clarify that the genre of autobiography or memoir,[12] in itself, is not the focus of this research. I am interested in how the authors use new media such as the comic form, photo poetry, and even avant-garde film to find a different space for engaging with age-old questions regarding the connection of Muslim and Iranian women with the Other, the location of the enemy in diasporic Iranian artistic production, artists' self-positioning regarding the Iranian revolution and the current

11. Please see Julie Rak's *Boom! Manufacturing Memoir for the Popular Market* (2013) for the publishing industry's investment in the memoir book market.

Bashi claims that her American publishers have not respected her wish to avoid the word *Iran* in the title or on the back cover of *Nylon Road* (2009). Not only do they include Iran in the title, they also criticize "Shiʿite law" on the dust cover—a concept that is nonexistent in the book in that context.

12. *Autobiography* and *memoir* are used interchangeably in this monograph, due to the way that (mostly) women have challenged the claims of objectivity and centrality of autobiographies with their groundbreaking memoirs.

government, and their ethical engagement with alterity in order to create bonds of connection and community. Many authors find that they have to observe severe auto-critical standards in order to keep their narratives from falling into the marketable yet perilous traps of victimization, exoticization, and demonization of a complex, rhizomatic governmental system.

The Islamic Republic of Iran: A Heterogeneous Political Entity

Although the Islamic Republic of Iran carries in its short history several unforgivable violations of human rights,[13] it is not a dictatorial fundamentalist theocracy, argues Serge Michel, who has lived in Iran as a *Le Monde* correspondent and has studied the system for years (Michel and Woods 2010). The country witnesses wide turnout for presidential and parliamentary elections on a regular basis.[14] Those who call it a fundamentalist dictatorship might be confusing Iran with Afghanistan under the 1996–2001 rule of the Taliban, Iran's number one enemy at the time. The characterization would also be degrading to the people of Iran, who enjoy a certain political literacy and sophistication that is unique in the region. I would call Iran a fundamentalist dictatorship only if it becomes common practice to call the United States a fascist state. It is not that the leaders do not want to dictate; they do. In both countries, the opposition to consensus is working hard against efforts to turn the country toward totalitarianism.

The Islam of the 9/11 terrorists and the Islam advocated by the Iranian government are completely different entities. No Iranian is associated with suicide bombings anywhere in the world, much less with the attacks of 9/11. Those events and the ensuing war on terror in 2001 jolted the Iranian diaspora after decades of relative silence regarding their own

13. The most notable is the imprisonment and massacre of hundreds, if not thousands, of left-leaning intellectuals in the 1980s during the war with Iraq, under the pretext of national security.

14. In 2009 millions of people took to the street because they thought the election was rigged. This shows a general belief that votes are counted. Although none of the candidates believe in toppling the regime, they do represent different sectors of society, and election time is taken seriously in Iran.

national Revolution and the eight-year war with Saddam's Iraq. Iran's Revolution of 1979 has roots in centuries of battle against imperialism, colonization, forced modernization and monarchial tyranny. For the majority of Iran's 2,500 years of civilization, either its territory has been invaded by foreign occupiers who sought to drain it of its resources,[15] or it has been ruled by fierce, unrelenting leaders who have paid little attention to the well-being of the population. The country became dismembered as a large portion of land and water rights were severed from it by foreign occupiers. Iran's first democratically elected prime minister was ousted in 1953 in a joint British-American coup d'état that incited more mistrust against the West among the religious elite. Oil theft continued under the Shah. With the advent of the current government, efforts for nationalization of the oil industry were challenged by internal corruption and external sanctions.[16]

The popular uprising that ousted a puppet king brought to power the dispossessed partisans as well as the tortured and exiled clergy. But this new clan of rulers, mostly youths, had no formal training in democratic governance. They relied on favoritism, corruption, trial and error, and an iron fist to advance their causes. Soon Saddam, armed to the teeth with international aid, attacked Iran. By that time, Iran had become internationally isolated.

The Iranian Resistance

In order to combat the ruthless invaders, Iranians developed survival skills that are exemplified in the common proverbs: "to cut throat with soft cotton" or to "to kill with silk." Historically, after being defeated at

15. The invading Greek army ravaged the country in 500 BC, burning and looting the Persepolis palace, as well as libraries, schools, and Zoroastrian temples. The invading Arab army followed suit between 633 and 651 AD. The Mongol invasion was among the bloodiest, and it still lingers in popular imagination. Continual battles with the Ottoman Empire and the Soviet Union over the map of the new Iran dismembered much of the soil. The indirect colonization of Iran by the British, who pumped free oil from the South, and the Russians, who controlled the North, left the country in famine during World War II.

16. Iran now manages to export its own petroleum, but it imports gasoline in return.

war, Iranians welcomed the invaders with an extended bow but wove their nooses behind their backs. They accepted the Islam of the Omar dynasty but turned it into a militant Shiʿism: an underground antimainstream reading of Islam that is based on *Ijtihad* (interpretation of original Islam in accordance with the mandates of the present moment by the *mujtahed*, or Islamic scholars), as well as fighting against injustice, primarily inspired by Imam Hussein's revolt in Karbala. Like those who embrace Derrida's concept of democracy *a venir*, Shiʿites battle for a justice to come, through their last immortal imam, Mahdi, who is absent yet present. Shiʿites were a peripheral force that always worked against the tyrannical stream. Their rare accession to power, once in the Safavid dynasty and again in 1979, marked a paradox that undid their complex philosophical identity. Shiʿites gaining political power has proved counterintuitive so far in history. In the words of cultural theoretician Hamid Dabashi:

> Precisely the same insurrectionary disposition that inaugurates Shiʿism into history constitutes its Achilles Heel. Shiʿism is predicated on a paradox: It fails upon success, just like the Sisyphus. Shiʿism is a religion of protest. It can never succeed. As soon as it succeeds politically, it negates itself metaphysically. Its material success is its moral failure. . . . Shiʿism cannot be turned into an official ideology of repression without immediately negating its own very reason for being. The key operative concept constitutional to Shiʿism is that of *mazlumiyyat*, "having been wronged," or "having been tyrannized." . . . So far as Shiʿism is on the side of the oppressed it is in its full revolutionary blossoming. The instant that it becomes fully institutionalized into an apparatus of power it ipso facto mutates into a most brutal theocratic tyranny. All its revolutionary zeal now comes back to haunt and turn it into a monstrous negation of itself. (Davison and Muppidi 2017, 59–60)

To think of the Islamic government of Iran as a homogeneous fundamentalist theocracy is a great fallacy sold by the Western media as well as by sectors of the Iranian diaspora who fail to see that the majority of the population actually supported the Islamic leaders at the dawn of the Revolution. They have turned their backs on their leaders now. The support began to decline from the start. Religion, even in name, has a strong influence in the political arena, but Iran is not a theocracy. The function of state and religion cannot unite. Although the country has a supreme leader who lobbies behind the curtain of law—and is arguably the strongest man in the complex system of power—the president and the members of the parliament gain their seats through votes. Although they have to uphold the mandates of the Islamic Republic, the political arena is witness to intense political disputes that mark a thwarted yet live democracy.

As Rancière reminds us time and again, democracy is not a static, universal mode of representational government (that is, it is not about voting only); the very idea of a representative democracy would have sounded paradoxical to Athenian ears. Democracy consists in the people's process of becoming politically conscious; taking up the space for litigation, dissensus, and disagreement; and taking turns in leading. Even within the government, the reformist left and the conservative religious right, a plethora of in-between political agendas, and the suprapolitical military mafia of Sepah (the guardians of the Revolution) compete over the drafting of Iranian foreign and domestic policies and the management of its oil wealth. Members of parliament, the cabinet, and the judiciary form different alliances with the advent of each presidential and parliamentary election.

Democracy is never a finished process. Derrida talks about the cyclical nature of revolution. Before the Revolution, the Islam of Iran was boldly colored by the politics of anticolonization. After the Revolution, religion became so marginal that it seemed nothing more than a performance, a means of struggle for power and riches. However, there are policy makers, parliamentary members, and politicians who are still struggling to shatter the quiet consensus by standing up against injustice. To call the government a religious dictatorship is to overlook the long march of the Iranian population toward freedom from external and internal bondage. Despite their sometimes weak, sometimes cruel, sometimes opportunist leaders, the Iranian people, including the few members of the ruling elite, have fought for justice and equality, the overlooking of which only leads the way to inhumane sanctions or foreign military intervention.

Aestextasy demands a second look at the painting of an absolute-evil picture of one solid Iranian regime, which ironically ascended to power via the sacrifices of people fighting internal and external hegemony. The government's breaches of human rights against Kurdish and leftist activists at the beginning of the Revolution, as well as dissidents such as journalists, artists, and intellectuals throughout the years, demand a trial so the culprits in the government are brought to justice. However, this does not call for foreign intervention through sanctions on all Iranian trade, or for externally orchestrated regime change.

The battle is not one between Islam as barbarian and the civilized West as the saviors. The battle is in the arena of politics, of control of wealth, public opinion, and the nation's borders. The most effective opposition to the right-wing, so-called Islamist fundamentalist faction of the country has come from within the circle of power itself. Grand Ayatollah Montazeri, the official successor to Ayatollah Khomeini, severely criticized the killings of dissidents during wartime. For this reason, he was removed from his influential post and remained under house arrest until his death. However, even from his home, he led a generation of critics of injustice. Many high ranking government officials became dissidents after the reign of President Mohammad Khatami. These include Ali Akbar Ganji, Mohsen Sazegara, Ebrahim Nabavi, and Ali Abtahi (Rahimi and Gheytanchi 2008, 50). In 2009, the oppositional presidential candidate Mir-Hossein Mousavi and Islamic cleric Mehdi Karroubi were both put under house arrest for openly criticizing the rigged reelection of Mahmoud Ahmadinejad. They also called for reform and the curbing of corruption.

This is not to say that every dissident of the regime is imprisoned. The dissatisfaction is widespread, especially among those in power. Ever since the dawn of the Islamic Republic in 1979, critics, dissidents, and reformers have been fighting a battle against hegemony, and that is what democracy mandates: creating space for litigation, for alternative voices of dissensus to be audible. No matter the restrictions imposed by the Iranian government, Iranians within and outside of the country have won battles against dictatorship in the past through very intricate aesthetic and political battles. War and revolution, as violent fissures in the fabric of society, bring radicals to power.

The 9/11 hijackers and a host of other Western terrorists were second-generation, relatively assimilated immigrants who had little knowledge of

Islam, or the Qur'an for that matter, argues Doug Saunders. "All of them are integrated, Westernized and educated." He quotes Oliver Roy on terrorists grown in the West:

> They do not have any particular social background that would explain their political radicalization because of poverty or exclusion. Most of all, almost all of them become "born again" in the West. . . . The source of radicalization is the West and not the jihad or the conflicts in the Middle East. None became a radical after attending religious studies completed in a Muslim-majority country. Finally, for almost each of them, the time between their return to religion and their transit to political radicalization has been very short, which shows that they are as much, if not more so, interested in politics as in religion. (Saunders 2012, 110)

As unrelated as the two events appear (Iranian Revolution of 1979 and the destruction of the World Trade Center), 9/11 incited a blind fury against anything Islamic or Middle Eastern. The diaspora coming from wealthy, avant-garde, nontraditional families clung to the sole common denominator between the cause for their displacement from Iran and the cause for their subjugation in the West: Islam!

Romanticizing All Diasporic Narratives as Exile Literature

Even astute critics of memoir sometime fail to distinguish between the literature of voluntary émigrés and the memoirs of exiles who carry a sense of isolation due to "banishment" (Said 2002). I prefer the designation *ghorbat* literature, with its strong poetic and milder political connotations. *Ghorbat* refers to the state of being outside one's home and longing to return. But it does not connote that one has been forcefully removed from one's home, with a threat to one's life. It also lacks the political implications that *exile* carries. Whitlock, who studies life narratives in the context of postcolonialism, subtitles her article on Iranian life-writing narrative "The Generic Fix of Iranian Exilic Memoirs" (2008). She considers all writings of members of the Iranian diaspora to be exile memoirs, disregarding the volunteer nature of some departures from Iran.

In an interview with the BBC, Azar Nafisi said: "I lived in Iran until I was thirteen, and then my parents sent me to England—to Lancaster—to finish my studies. That was when I first tasted the pangs of exile. I finally returned to Iran in 1979 . . . and stayed for eighteen years in the Islamic Republic" (2004). The acclaimed author experienced living as an international student in Britain as throbbing with "pangs of exile." Such an educational trip to England was, of course, a luxury, afforded only to few at the time. In her case, her father, the mayor of Tehran before the 1979 Revolution, funded the trip. She immediately conceded that she was able to live in Iran for eighteen years after the Revolution.

By calling authors who float freely between Iran and abroad exiles, we are doing an injustice to the true exiles who have no possibility of returning to their homeland due to their specific occupation of public attention. The Jewish population fleeing fascism in the World War II would be considered exiles, the Armenians fleeing genocide were exiles, as are the Palestinian refugees living in impoverished camps and across the Arab world, dispossessed and having no home to which they can return. Nevertheless, rich Iranians who left the country fearing Saddam's invasion or the imposition of the veil cannot be called exiles just because they are Iranian emigrants. The title gives them an aura of rebelliousness and intellectuality but vilifies an already vilified government. They can always return to their homeland without facing legal constraints.[17]

Using the word *exile* for all immigrants who fled poor economic conditions during war or feared the onset of a revolution elevates a certain stratum of well-to-do Iranians to the position of native informants. By untagging the title of exile from their literature, I do not propose to humiliate them or ridicule their plight. Rather, I caution against romanticizing

17. This is, of course, before they gain popular recognition as opposition leaders against the Iranian government. Satrapi traveled regularly to Iran even after the publication of her books. However, the movie caught the attention of Iranian authorities. She then decided not to return. Bashi, who published two books about Iran in Switzerland, has returned to Iran permanently. As long as their books do not create an anti–Islamic Republic buzz in the world, authors have managed to freely come and go.

all immigrant literature as exile narratives. Edward Said distinguishes between exiles, refugees, expatriates, and émigrés: "Exile originated in the age-old practice of banishment. Once banished, the exile lives an anomalous and miserable life, with the stigma of being an outsider" (2002, 181). Refugees, however, are a creation of the twentieth-century state, according to Said: "The word refugee has become a political one, suggesting large herds of innocent and bewildered people requiring urgent international assistance, whereas 'exile' carries with it, I think, a touch of solitude and spirituality" (181). Expatriates voluntarily choose to live in another country, "usually for personal or social reasons." According to Said, "expatriates may share in the solitude and estrangement of exile, but they do not suffer under its rigid proscriptions." For him émigrés "enjoy an ambiguous status" (181). Anyone who decides to live in another country with the possibility of choice is an émigré. Life narratives contribute to the sense of identity, and the opportunity to imbue their identity with romantic concepts of intellectual rebellion causes many authors to opt for exile instead of émigré status. This would have been innocent in itself had there not been an international war for regime change against vilified countries, based on the hunches of politicians.

Members of the Iranian diaspora who left on the eve of the Revolution or during the war with Iraq mainly come from upper-middle class bourgeois families with little or no connection to the religious traditions of the country. Even the word *diaspora* has been used strategically in this book. What these literatures share is not exile but a sense of *ghorbat* ("غربت"; estrangement, with a sorrow that eats or gnaws at one) in living outside one's homeland. This sense of estrangement can be internal as well. Imam Ali has described *ghorbat* as the loss of a beloved. The word *ghorbat* clearly alludes to the state of being outside one's native land, whether poetically or physically, and yet it does not carry the politically exploitable tag of banished exile. *Ghorbat* is a physical as well as a psychological state; exile is also both, but has a strong political aftertaste too. In Rumi's *Masnavi*, a lover seasoned by his travels in *ghorbat* is asked about his preference regarding his dwelling place. Instead of picking his homeland, he claims that his favorite city is wherever his beloved resides:

گفت معشوقی به عاشق کای فتی
تو به غربت دیده ای بس شهرها
پس کدامین شهر از آنها خوشتر است
گفت آن شهری که در وی دلبر است
(Book 3 of *Masnavi*)[18]

As opposed to a generalized literature of exile, *ghorbat* literature would be an apt—though difficult—way to describe the writings of the Iranian diaspora. *Exile* does have poetic connotations, but its historio-political strings make it a distasteful choice for describing all the literature written outside Iran by Iranians, as is currently in fashion. *Exile* connotes a grand political accomplishment that resulted in banishment, giving unmerited grace to economic-immigrant authors who wish to access a wider audience. As soon as the prime source of existential angst in a memoir is the author's inability to wear a miniskirt in public while drinking alcohol, it is a relatively sure sign that the memoirist comes from a luxurious family of bons vivants who commonly do not concern themselves with economic inequality or political independence. Such authors, who insist on their condition of exile while reacting only to the loss of their class luxuries, generally recognize emancipation as adoption of a Western liberal lifestyle. Obsession about the veil and the ban on alcohol as the only main troubles with Iran are red flags indicating that the author is quite distant from the agonies of impoverishment, foreign invasion, unemployment, skyrocketing inflation due to sanctions, and so on.[19]

The detached immigrants' sole anxiety regarding Iran usually concerns women's imported notions of sexual liberation. This may be acceptable and

18. My literal translation reads: A beloved asks her lover: "Brave man, you have resided in different cities outside your homeland in *ghorbat*, tell me in which one of those lands have you found joy?," and the lover replies, "in the city that lives the beloved." This adds a poetic dimension to the concept of home and complicates modern binaries. An English expression was suggested by Dr. Tim Blackmore: home is where the heart is.

19. I do not endorse the forced veiling laws of Iran or its ban on alcohol consumption. However, I believe that there are worthier causes for rebelling against the government, including human rights, women's rights, and justice.

innocent in itself, and cause for due critical attention. However, once these émigrés, unconcerned about social equality and economic hegemony, occupy the position of native informants, they sit on the thrones of experts to elaborate on the condition of women in the Middle East. They are then consulted about anything ranging from the Israel-Palestinian conflict to the prices of oil in the region. They channel their personal grudges against the Islamic Republic of Iran in international arenas. It is then that the sole problem of Iran becomes the veiling of women. They disregard the long historical rally against colonization and globalization, and their detached, alienated viewpoint is indispensable for Western warmongers who jump at every chance to invade the resource-rich, strategic region under the pretext of liberating the women: "White men saving brown women from brown men" (Spivak 2010, ii). It is here that the choice of a title becomes the marker of war strategy. For democracy to come, it is necessary that the current Iranian government acknowledges its crimes, especially those committed during the heyday of the Revolution and its own reign of terror. However, the emigrant authors, whether exiled, in a state of *ghorbat*, or in a voluntary economical migration, have to observe autocritical ethics as well. Even in the less polemical writings of the political refugees, there is a foreclosure of the terrors and political assassinations performed by their own factions during the Revolutionary days.

The Veil

In a country where social class, politics, and religious beliefs go hand in hand, it is condescending to read unveiling as the obvious sign of modernization and elitism. The diasporas have symptomatically fixated on the veil while Western readers are captivated by reading about narratives that pierce the veil (Naghibi 2009, 80). Whitlock prefers to call the veil one of "the most intractable symbols of cultural difference between Muslim societies and the West" (2006, 974). For me the veil is a fetish object; it points toward the symptom, not the cause of the unease. It is a synecdoche that stands in place of the Muslim societies, but in itself it is quite devoid of such significations. Fetishizing the veil to the level of a cultural demarcator risks overlooking the sociopolitical struggles of the nations over material resources for survival. Randa Farah, who has closely studied the demands of Palestinian refugee women for years, believes that the Western fixation on the veil is drawing attention away from the true sociopolitical needs of Muslim women:

> There is an obsession with Arab women's bodies both in the "East" and the "West." Debates, books and articles on the hijab or the veil, titled "beneath," "beyond" or "behind" the veil, may be found in almost any library. Female genital mutilation, such as in some parts of the Sudan and Egypt, is another favourite topic in the West, including among others women's rights groups. Although these issues are important, the emphasis and lopsided attention these topics are given at the expense of the larger political, historical and cultural context and other dimensions of women's lives and struggles reproduces the Orientalist and essentializing view of Arab women as victims of a "tradition" (Islam and Muslim men), juxtaposed against the "modern." (2002, 93)

Clothing becomes significant for people whose security and wealth are already satisfied. The veil vogue conceals the battle against oppression. It brings to focus, like a magician's left hand, only the visible differences. I am very troubled by the continuous readings and misreadings of the veil that look at it as a "symbol of cultural difference," but do not take into consideration Middle Eastern nations' struggle for survival. The veil is documented to have aided the struggle. The veil has become the most significant trivial object of analysis in the discourse on the Middle East, and one that has overshadowed other, more vital concepts. While Whitlock's discussion of the veil in *Persepolis* is ahistorical, her analysis of the Afghan burqa is much more nuanced and contextual. This might be because:

> Afghan feminist activists do use the burqa strategically. Quite literally so—messages, weapons, and banned publications were transported beneath its folds during the Taliban regime. Feminist activists in Afghanistan were quick to adopt the burqa as a shroud of anonymity and disguise. For these reasons, the burqa is a complex symbol. It is a reminder of an oppressive regime, but it is also an icon of brave and successful resistance. (2005, 57)

While Afghan activists see beyond the veil to its sociopolitical implications, members of the Iranian diaspora who have not suffered from the same fundamentalism as their Afghan neighbors see the veil as the last obstacle on the way to total Westernization. However, Reza Shah's forced unveiling act of 1936 proved traumatic and catastrophic for women of Iran who were publicly stripped by soldiers. It defeated its purpose by bringing more physical segregation for women: they stayed indoors to avoid public humiliation. Only a few authors among the plethora of memoir writers have dared to weigh the possibility that veiling is not the ultimate symbol of Islamic fundamentalism.

Marjane Satrapi starts with the veil, but moves well beyond it. With the aid of the free play of the comic medium, she creates a space for dissensus in the writing of Iranian diaspora.

Part One

Diasporic Iranian Visual Literature in the Form of Graphic Narratives

Political in their toppling of text-image hierarchies and subversive for their indecorousness in dealing with traumatic topics through a putatively juvenile genre, graphic narratives take a fresh look at old wounds to imagine new possibilities of encounter with the Other. In this part I closely read three works of graphic narrative—the *Persepolis* books by Marjane Satrapi and *Nylon Road* by Parsua Bashi—to visualize the workings of the comic technology in negotiations of identity. For Edward Said, comics are a rebel's tools for subverting policed mind-sets: "Comics seemed to say what couldn't otherwise be said, perhaps what wasn't permitted to be said or imagined, defying the ordinary processes of thought" (2005, ii).

However, this medium is not without its critics, who have a hard time taking it seriously.

> Comic books are what novels used to be—an accessible, vernacular form with mass appeal—and if the highbrows are right, they're a form perfectly suited to our . . . collective attention deficit. Comics are also enjoying a renaissance and a newfound respectability right now. In fact, the fastest-growing section of your local bookstore these days is apt to be the one devoted to comics and so-called graphic novels. (McGrath 2004)

Charles McGrath's much quoted *New York Times Magazine* article goes on to mention that a slow, pensive reading and looking practice is necessary for understanding a graphic narrative. To master the skill of looking carefully and reading along requires more concentration than skimming a book quickly.

Graphic memoirs as a contemporary form of sequential art loom as one of the most appropriate media for reimagining an Other that can be identified as human, as kin. In our age of scopophilia and terror, many factors contribute to the recent widespread appeal of graphic memoirs for recounting traumatic historical moments from a refreshingly playful and subversive perspective:

- The contingency of the visual and the verbal planes foster a "bi-ocularity," or double vision (Hirsch 2004) that constantly causes attention to fluctuate from the center to the margins, allowing for multiple readings, perspectives, and speakers at once. This movement from the center to the margins and back breaks the hegemony enjoyed by words over images. Bi-ocularity gives priority to neither the word nor the image but sees both as contributing elements to the formation of the overall affective relay of the graphic narrative.

- Graphic memoirs defamiliarize us with, estrange us from, and refamiliarize us with grave events through their cartoon avatars. The abstraction of the faces of these avatars allows for identification on an intimate, personal level. The more abstract the face, the easier the identification (McCloud 1994).
- Graphic memoirs' scattered frames parallel the fragmentary nature of human memory after an encounter with trauma or loss.
- Graphic memoirs' contemplative "aporetic" quality (Naghibi and O'Malley 2005) involves pauses between the panels, invites audience interpretation, and demands interactive personal "closures" (McCloud 1994).
- Images have an inherent "excessive expressivity" to them. They leave a direct imprint on the "sense memory," the "memory residing in the body" of survivors (Hirsch 2004, 1211).
- "Words can be put into the service of sense memory," but "vision has a very different relationship to affective experience, experience which whilst it cannot be spoken as it is felt, may register visually. The eye can often function as a mute witness through which events register as 'eidetic memory' images imprinted with sensation" (Jill Bennett, quoted in Hirsch 2004, 1211–12).

With their direct affective dimension, images are potent vehicles for transmitting visceral sensations of the pain or pleasure of others. Sequential images, in turn, form an interrupted, staccato narrative that moves with the drive of the reader's imagination.

Sequences of still frames and words interrupted by the aporetic silence of gutters can create a magical convergence for a unique sense of personal interpretation, identification, and closure. Scattered frames need a participatory contemplative imagination to keep the narrative flow. The apparent cohesion between the word, the image, and the silence cannot be forced upon the hybrid form, but is co-"laborated" between the reader and the graphic text. *Persepolis* uses these fecund pauses strategically when narrating enigmatic private and historical events in which the audience's judgment is decisive. The unique, perplexing sense of closure invited by the comic form seems indispensable in personalizing distant dilemmas that may be irrelevant to our daily concerns. Satrapi gives a unique, relatable face to generic, vague stock images of distant Others. The relatable faces, along with quiet spaces for contemplation in the margins, become the nexus for creating ethical bonds of connection through aesthetic and political means.

History of the Graphic Genre

Sequential art forms, or the craft of telling a story through scattered images, have had a mythical allure for humanity since the dawn of civilization. Scott McCloud defines comics broadly as "Juxtaposed pictorial and other images in deliberate sequence, intended to convey information and/or produce an aesthetic response in the reader" (1994, 20). In an attempt to move comics out of the isolated corner into which the superhero cult has moved, McCloud locates comics in the origin of art itself. Biblical narratives on church windows, the 2,500-year-old stone reliefs in the ancient palace of Persepolis in Iran (figure 1), and Egyptian tomb paintings (figure 2) can all be considered art forms that lay bare their narrative spatially with a series of related images.

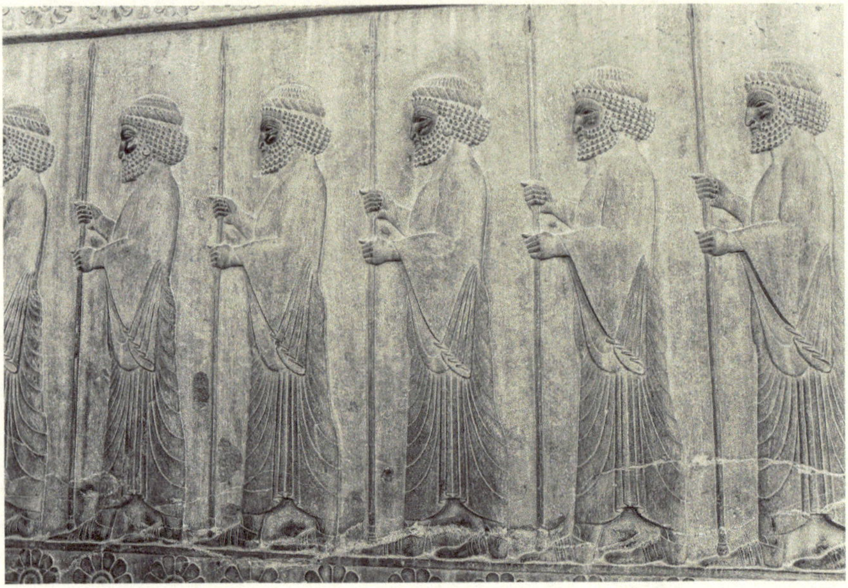

1. Relief details of the Achaemenid Empire's Immortal Guardians on the stairway facade of the Apadana at the old city of Persepolis. © Dbajurin, Dreamstime.com.

The graphic medium's immediate accessibility and ease in communication, as well as its mystery and beauty, have made it a favorite for public dissemination of the discourse of power to the semiliterate population. The inherent vigor and violence in images make them a suitable vehicle in the service of the elite in power as well: the church, the state, and the police. Although images have been used and abused by power, as a property of the people, public sequential images can never be fully appropriated. The colorful tales of the holy scriptures and epic narratives of the Achaemenid conquest of Babylon and the life achievements of great leaders told with the binding magic of the medium have produced immortal works of art that carry with them an aura of transcendence, power, and holiness. Although comics have been abused in the service of institutions of power and control in the past due to their accessibility to a wider population, recent comics also use their ancestral popularity to reach out to a wider reading public.

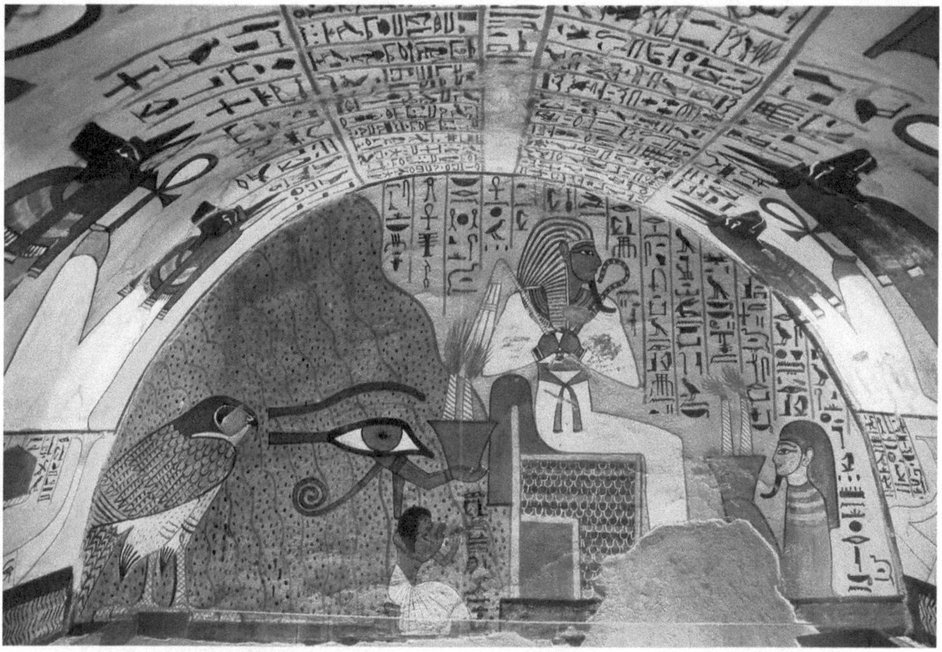

2. Ancient Egyptian sequential images narrate a story on a tomb wall in Luxor, Egypt. © Vladimir Melnik, Dreamstime.com.

Beginning in the nineteenth century, comic books—as a modern form of sequential art—carried that aura of transcendence that transports the audience from the mundane to the realm of fantasy. Comic shorthand has allowed for an outlet of escapism, erotica, superhero cults, utopic visions, depictions of violence, and the Othering and stereotyping that are prevalent in popular comics. Though at times abused by institutions of power or used as an outlet for violent expression, the enchanting medium has the potential to produce aestextatic masterpieces that benefit from the interrupted contingency of letters and images, of past and present depicted simultaneously. Comics lend themselves well particularly to contested histories. They are fragmentary, and they shuttle between past, present, and future with a spatial ease unparalleled in other media.

The zenith of historical comics is unquestionably the two volumes of *Maus: A Survivor's Tale*: *My Father Bleeds History* (1986) and *And Here My Troubles Began* (1991) by Art Spiegelman. *Maus* does not provide Western readers with an unfamiliar denouement. What it does do is present a story of a central trauma of the twentieth century in a subversive, playful, and accessible format; one that, like the format of *Persepolis*, requires active, participatory readers/viewers with multiple focalities and points of reference—readers who are comfortable with facing voids in the midst of a dual narrative and are imaginative enough to fill them with their own cross-cultural translations.

In portraying Jews as mice, Spiegelman uses the self-same rhetoric of Nazis against Jews. It is commonly accepted that mice are vermin to be demolished because they spread diseases and steal from people's crops. However, through the work of identification in cartooning, Spiegelman converts and unsettles that dichotomy. Satrapi, too, starts with infantile stereotypes and then skillfully subverts, reverts, and displaces them. The Shoah as a grave, untouchable event has rarely been handled lightly by its survivors. Adoption of a comic genre for the depiction of this tragedy points to a playful twist in its rendition. Not only does Spiegelman treat the serious event in an apparently indecorous medium, he also adopts a very autocritical stance regarding his link to the event: his father. His honesty regarding the fuzziness of his father's memory as well his father's acute survival skills in times of abundance give the book an ethically balanced and credible tint. Satrapi has always referred to *Maus* with reverence as a source of inspiration for her career in comics.

Comics and Chronology

A point of comparison between *Maus* and *Persepolis* is their adoption of a significant historic moment: the Shoah and the Iranian Revolution and the ensuing war. With the use of comic techniques, these historical traumas become fluid and meaningful on a personal level:

> Comics can help constantly play with chronology and return to the past to re-explore old narratives by opening up new ones within them. The point here is that with comics, the characters are never finished developing, the story is never over. Unlike other media, one of the defining characteristics of comics is that narrative structure is infinitely malleable, and earlier points of narrative may be reopened, added to or altered. (McCloud 1994, 24)

There are many characteristics that make comics an ideal medium for recounting tales of trauma: their ability to play with chronology, to shuttle easily between multiple speakers and perspectives, to provide personal identification with the avatars, and to give space for personal translation of the panels. These are especially useful for personalizing contested histories. In order to reread the highly contested histories that *Persepolis* narrates, Satrapi draws beautifully from what Michel Foucault calls subjugated knowledges. These are systematic knowledges from below, in the hearts and homes of the people, as well as knowledges regarding repressed battles that have been foreclosed from the official collective memory of the nation. These knowledges map out the lines of confrontation in the national memory. They will eventually open space for critique, dissensus, possible reconciliation, and the people's sharing in the power of the government: democracy.

1

Marjane Satrapi's *Persepolis*

Though comics were once considered a marginal, lowbrow art form, their interstitial position in comparison to well-established canons of literature give them the strategic advantage enjoyed by Foucauldian "subjugated knowledges"—a genealogy that makes criticism of hierarchies of domination possible (Foucault and Ewald 2008). Both facets within which Michel Foucault contextualizes his concept of subjugated knowledges apply directly to *Persepolis*: Many critics have alluded to *Persepolis*'s treatment of both the public and the private dilemmas of the cartoon avatar and her country.

Satrapi skillfully blends the personal with the political, the private with the public, and the juvenile with the mature. The collection flows between the lowbrow and the philosophical, the intimate and the obscure, the traumatic and the humorous. All the while she keeps a third eye fixated on the ethical balance of the book. The historical struggle of a nation at its pivotal moments of political revolution and foreign invasion is dotted with a personal affective dimension. *Persepolis* destabilizes formal and generic docketing: a graphic novel, a children's book, a political witness account, and a private coming of age story. The arc of aesthetics, politics, and ethics is built by the interlocking of historical trajectories and personal, local knowledges. The relatively unreliable child narrator and the voice of the adult speaker have a keen autocritical filter that prevents them from judging according to stereotypes and hierarchal dichotomies.

Satrapi does not recirculate an image of an Iran ripe for invasion or a West overflowing with freedom and democracy. Judgment is suspended, multiple speakers claim their histories, and the reader is left with meaningful fragments to sift through according to her own political, aesthetic, and ethical palette. Even violence is not seen only in the institution of the government. During the turbulent days of revolution and war, violence is witnessed in children's games and the domestic sphere as well, highlighting the effects of the political on the personal lives of people. For Satrapi, extremism is not endemic only to post-Revolutionary Iranian politics. She offsets the troubles in Iran with the experience of religious bigotry in an Austrian boarding school, the rise of the new extreme right with its explicit racist inclinations and xenophobia in Europe, and finally her experience of alienation and utter helplessness as a young émigré.

Satrapi weaves the knowledge of the people from below with the history of masked and buried political struggles in a new medium. I see in *Persepolis* a genealogy of Foucauldian subjugated knowledges. These are personal, local histories, the systematic savoir faire of the people that is "masked in formal systematizations" (Foucault and Ewald 2008, 7): the knowledges from below the hearts and homes of the people that are disqualified as nonconceptual or insufficiently elaborated. They prefigure a range of affective resilience that drives the intimately political story forward. These include the wisdom of the grandmother that transcends religious or secular dichotomies.

Although these experiences from the hearts and homes are below the level of conceptualization, they create moments of empathic connection, defamiliarization, and intimacy. A significant dimension of *Persepolis* that has gained little critical attention is the history of repressed battles. Marji's uncle Anoosh, as well as family friends Siamak and Mohsen, could be among those fighters for freedom who have been victimized under both the regime of the Shah and that of the Islamic Republic. Their efforts have been foreclosed from the official collective memory, yet *Persepolis* writes them back into the disputed narrative. The war martyrs and the wounded are also celebrated for their sacrifices in *Persepolis*. These stories from inside Iran are less known in the West. Whether below the level of scientificity or disqualified as nonconsequential, the graphic witness account revives these subjugated knowledges, and in so doing it creates an affective, intimate fracture in the dominant, universal narrative of war, revolution, and exile.

Foucault explains:

> When I say, "subjugated knowledges," I mean two things. On the one hand, I am referring to historical contents that have been buried or masked in formal systematizations. . . . Historical contents alone allow us to see the dividing lines in the confrontations and struggles that . . . systematic organizations are designed to mask. Subjugated knowledges are, then, blocks of historical knowledges that were present in the functional and systematic ensembles, but which were masked, and the critique was able to reveal their existence by using, obviously enough, the tools of scholarship. (Foucault and Ewald 2008, 7)

The contested and concealed histories outlined in *Persepolis* map out the rift between the dominant discourse of the Islamic Republic and the unofficial yet highly popular account of the diaspora circulated widely in memoirs in the West. *Persepolis* does not see the root of the antagonism in the divide between the religious and secular factions competing for power. Satrapi's autocritical lens sees violence that exists at a quotidian level during the turbulent days of the Revolution. Othering is widespread on a rhizomatic scale in the Iran of 1979 and the war of the 1980s: parental cruelty, torture games of children who gang up on an outcast, and the xenophobia of Iranians living in secure cities against migrants from borderline provinces in wartime. Not only is the history a casualty of the warring factions; times of war beckon rising levels of aggression within society. And *Persepolis* does not stop in Iran. Satrapi visualizes symptoms of soft aggressions in the West as well, dismantling the claim that immigrants reach utter freedom by traveling to the West. Time and again, the trauma repeats itself in the West through racism, political consensus, and atomization.

Here I start at the root of the conflict between the diaspora and the Iranian government. I delineate a violent political regrouping between two pre-revolutionary allies that fought together against oppression of the Shah: Islamists and leftists.

As a hybrid book that draws from history but does not rely solely on it, *Persepolis* brings up histories of forgotten dissidents who lost their lives fighting for Iranian democracy—personal narratives of freedom fighters who have been brutally suppressed by both secular and religious institutions of power, by those of both the Shah's monarchy and the Islamic Republic. Wiped clean, or rather, masked from the official national discourse of both political systems, their untold stories resurface and haunt the writing of the leftist Iranian diaspora. Mapping these buried histories will clarify the dividing lines in confrontation and struggle between the Islamic Republic and the left-leaning diaspora and also between Iran and the West.

Persepolis starts with a quick tour of Iran's revolutionary history over the past century, not through a historian's distant gaze, but via a relatively unreliable child narrator, Marji, who witnesses the sufferings of her friends and relatives. From this perspective, the historical narrative has been made intimate and its scars fresh through the comic techniques. The most historically complex parts of the book unfold during Marji's early childhood. These are events relating to the Shah's atrocities, the Revolution, and the tortures suffered by her communist uncle Anoosh under both regimes. It is only after his execution that Marji loses the comfort provided by her imaginary friend "God" and leaves her childlike avatar behind. The end of Anoosh marks the termination of Marji's childhood. This deep tear in her moral constellation is painted in a panel in which she is floating aimlessly in space, with no firm ground to support her (figure 3).

After the loss of Anoosh, Marji's avatar metamorphoses into a more physically developed, less idealistic preadolescent. Presenting the most complex historical narratives through a comic child narrator opens space for doubt, double-checking, and dissensus—the very stuff of democracy.

Nima Naghibi and Andrew O'Malley see the subversive qualities that the child narrator and the comic medium provide as a strategy dubbed trivialization. Quoting Dana Heller, they write: "The employment of a form—a mode, a genre, etc.—that is considered by the dominant culture to be unimportant, innocuous, or irrelevant . . . allows comics to 'camouflage' potentially subversive messages or ideas by conveying them in a medium generally considered unthreatening" (2005, 234). *Persepolis* destabilizes the common fiction of accessibility, childhood simplicity, and innocence. If anything, it would be a costly luxury to afford a childhood untainted by direct or second-hand exposure to violence. The unreliable

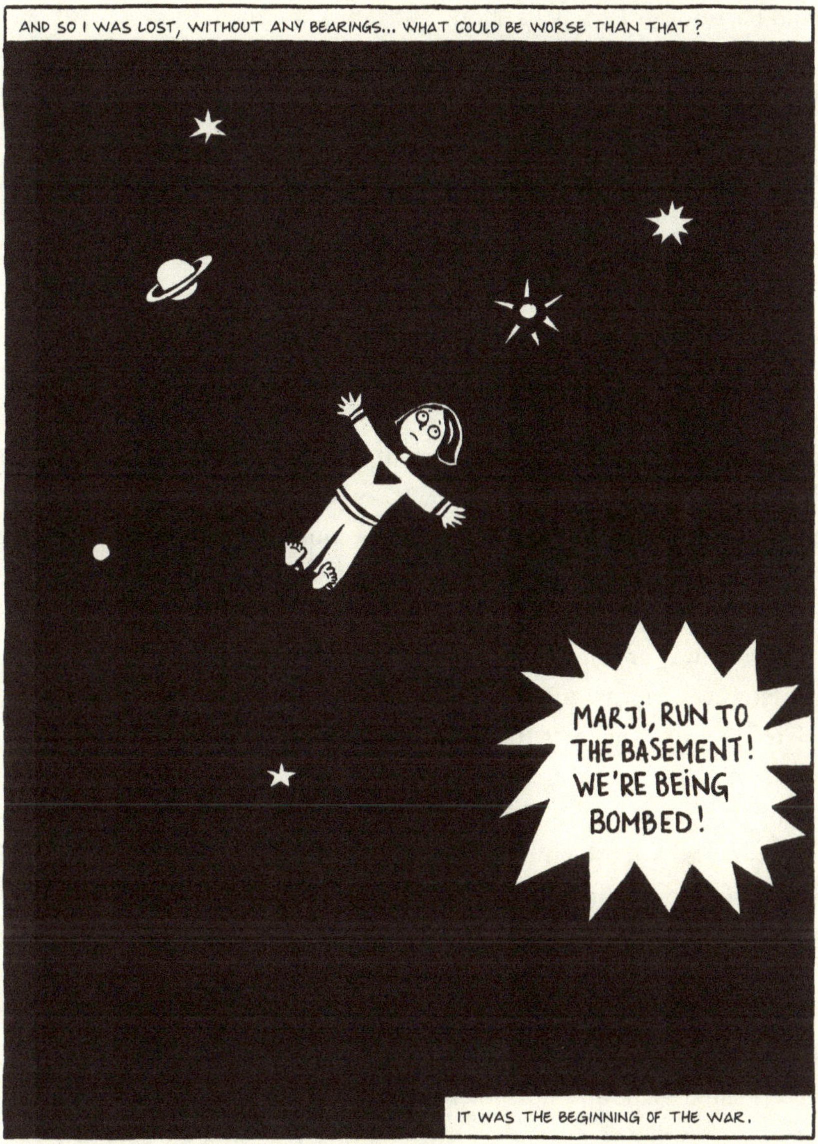

3. The end of childhood for Marji. From *Persepolis: The Story of a Childhood* by Marjane Satrapi, translation copyright © 2003 by L'Association, Paris, France. Used by permission of Pantheon Books, an imprint of the Knopf Doubleday Publishing Group, a division of Penguin Random House LLC. All rights reserved. P. 71.

child narrator in *Persepolis*, along with the simplified yet amplified black and white drawing style, all create a playful space for questioning of the offered narratives and imagining differently.

One of the most palpable contrasts between the child and adult point of view on political matters is mapped out in the chapter named "The Sheep" (figure 4). Comics facilitate the oscillation between several speakers. Here the three perspectives offered include that of the idealist Marxist uncle Anoosh, who, in the dreamy days following the overthrow of the Shah, can fantasize about the "hegemony of the proletariat." Marji, on the other hand, repeats the propaganda of the Islamic Republic as broadcast on TV: "People have voted Yes 99.99% to the Islamic Republic." (The official Yes votes were announced as an undisputed 98.2%. Ironically, it was the Soviet Union that produced 99.99% votes for its one-party government.) It is the father who tries in vain to consolidate the two viewpoints. The father's double standard regarding his political philosophy and lifestyle is introduced earlier. He is outraged at his daughter's lack of tact and sends her away crying.

However, Marji's quickly dismissed reporting proves prognostic. After the referendum, the interim Islamic government becomes the official government of Iran. At a time when everyone is boasting of their scars in the battle against the Shah to gain popular recognition as well as governmental posts, Anoosh embodies a true idealist who eventually dies for his beliefs. Before the Revolution, Anoosh has been active in the democratic liberation of the province of Azerbaijan, but the city falls to the monarchial army. He has to escape by walking through snowy summits toward Moscow, where he becomes a student, marries, and receives a doctorate in Marxism-Leninism. After his divorce from his Russian wife, Anoosh feels isolated, so he attempts to cross back to his hometown unrecognized. The Shah's military, however, identify and arrest him. He spends almost a decade of his life in the Shah's prisons. At the dawn of the 1979 Revolution, all political prisoners are set free, and Anoosh can finally reunite with his family members. The spring of freedom does not last long. As the gang fights over occupation of seats of government reach a bloody pinnacle in the anarchist heyday of the revolution, Anoosh is sent back to prison, where he is executed under allegations of being a Russian spy.

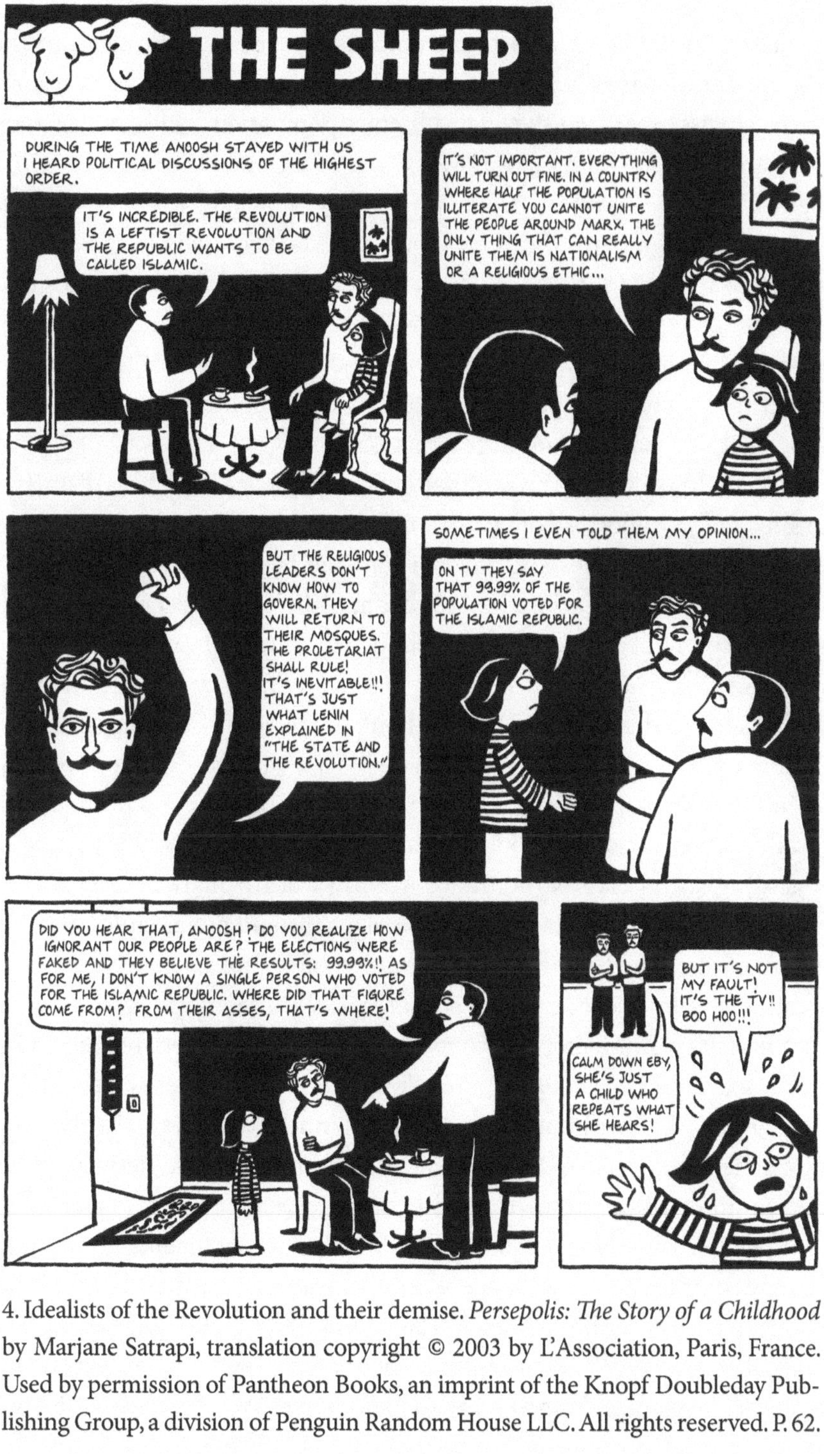

4. Idealists of the Revolution and their demise. *Persepolis: The Story of a Childhood* by Marjane Satrapi, translation copyright © 2003 by L'Association, Paris, France. Used by permission of Pantheon Books, an imprint of the Knopf Doubleday Publishing Group, a division of Penguin Random House LLC. All rights reserved. P. 62.

From Anoosh's raised fists and optimistic demeanor, his idealism and blindness to what is going on around him is apparent. An elitism lurks in his chants regarding the "half-illiterate population," who, due to their ignorance, choose religion over Marx. The equation of the religious with a class of illiterate, ignorant people who do not know how to govern or what to vote for was perhaps the blind spot of the Marxists, who ironically were supposed to fight for those so-called ignorant masses. It was the sacrifices of those same people that brought the Revolution to fruition. If the majority are Muslim, they will choose what they believe in. The government sometimes abuses the power invested in it through the people. Even in hindsight, it is hard to judge the situation.

When Marji warns the adults about state propaganda, she is dismissed immediately. Anoosh's convictions do not change even after he is cut off from his civic liberties and thrown into the Islamic Republic's prisons, where he awaits execution. He still chants "the proletariat will rule," but this time without a raised fist or a confident gesture. His murder under the rubric of being "a Russian spy" breaks Marji's long-standing relationship with "God" and leaves her "lost, without any bearings" (Satrapi 2003, 71). This is not the Marji who is caught between avant-gardism and religion as in the first chapter—the one who dreams of becoming a prophet, forbidding all injustice, and doing away with her father's double standards regarding social classes (figure 5). Anoosh's death marks the end of all such dichotomies for Marji, and also marks the end of her childhood.

According to Naghibi (2016), a point of comparison with Satrapi's treatment of political prisoners is Shahla Talebi's memoir *Ghosts of Revolution: Rekindled Memories of Imprisonment in Iran*. Talebi recounts tales of the extreme physical and psychological suffering of leftist revolutionary fighters, but without succumbing to annihilating despair or hatred of a generic externalized enemy. She offers bright and sometimes blinding glimpses of the aesthetic and ecstatic resistance of prisoners under extreme hardship; a resistance that celebrates human agency even under regimes of internal surveillance and punishment. We learn about Talebi's incarceration over the span of a decade under the two regimes preceding and following the 1979 Revolution. She recounts her tales of torture and aesthetic resistance from the first-person perspective of an adult victim.

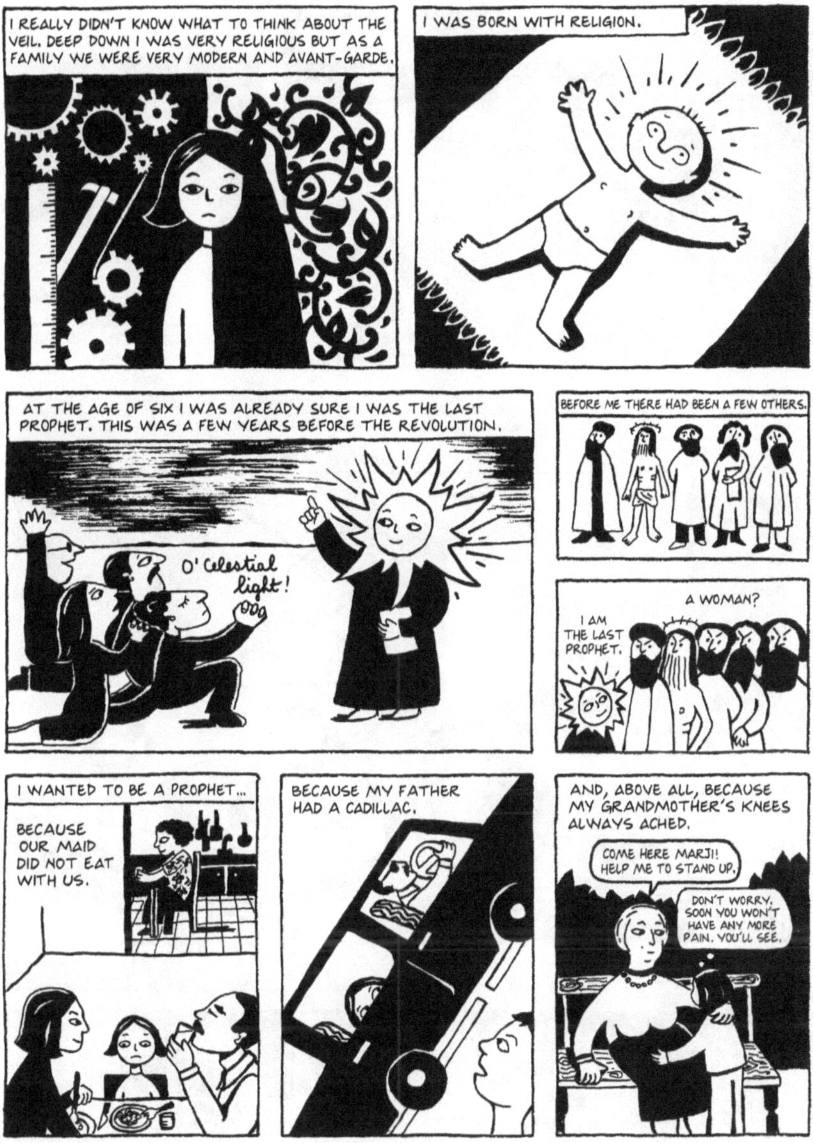

5. Dichotomies and ambivalence. *Persepolis: The Story of a Childhood* by Marjane Satrapi, translation copyright © 2003 by L'Association, Paris, France. Used by permission of Pantheon Books, an imprint of the Knopf Doubleday Publishing Group, a division of Penguin Random House LLC. All rights reserved. P. 6.

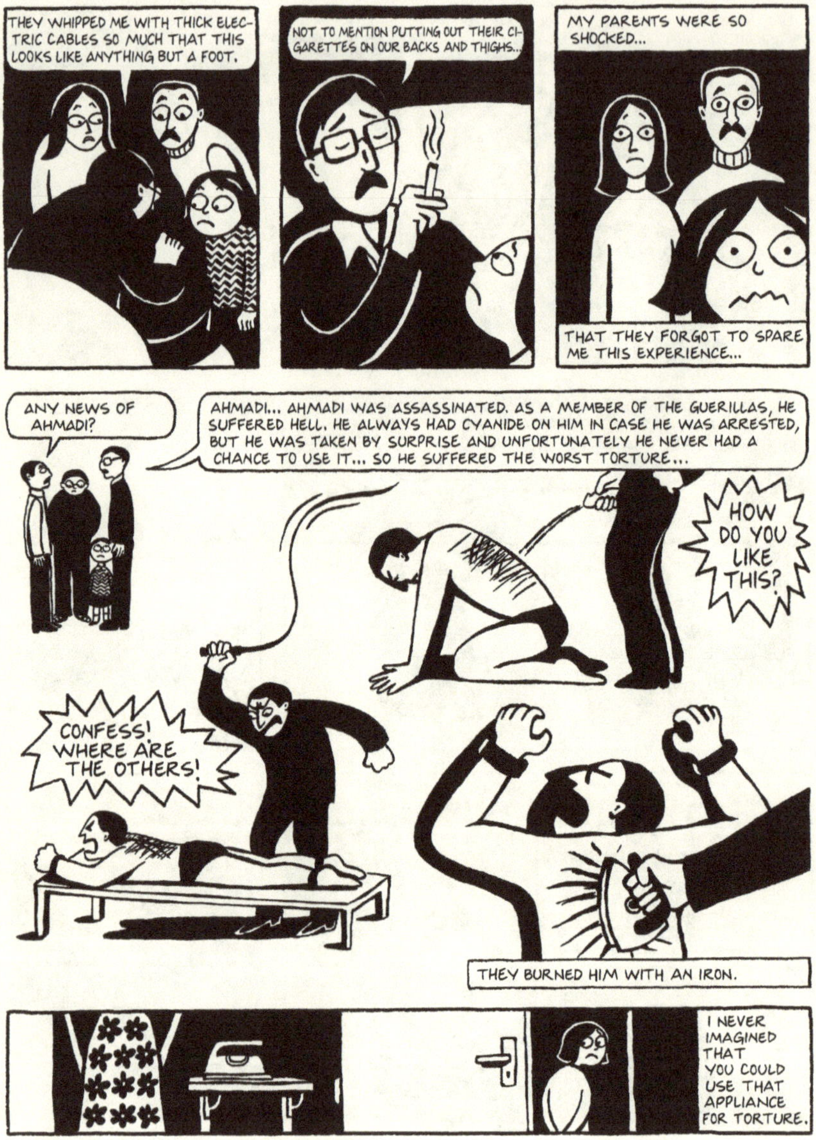

6. Torture as envisioned by a child. *Persepolis: The Story of a Childhood* by Marjane Satrapi, translation copyright © 2003 by L'Association, Paris, France. Used by permission of Pantheon Books, an imprint of the Knopf Doubleday Publishing Group, a division of Penguin Random House LLC. All rights reserved. P. 51.

Marji, on the other hand, is a cartoon avatar who witnesses torture vicariously through the accounts of her uncle Anoosh, her grandfather, and their friends Siamak and Mohsen, all left-leaning intellectuals under the Shah (figure 6).

The Genealogy of Iran's Leftist Movement Resurfacing in *Persepolis*

Iran's leftist rebellion occupies a double-blind riddle in the country's "functional and systematic ensembles" (Foucault and Ewald 2008, 7). Those who believe in the Islamic Revolution of 1979 as a Shi'ite uprising contend that it was founded on social democratic ideals that struggled to bring justice and equality to the deprived population. Both the left and the Shi'ite Islamists had suffered torture and prosecution under Shah. They had both called for an end to the internal and external oppression of the people during the monarchy, although some factions of the left had ties with the Soviet Union. Once the Shah fled the country the two allies, who had previously shared a common enemy, became new archenemies. The left carried out targeted assassinations, bombings, and a guerrilla war against the Islamic Republic. In retaliation, the latter, which now enjoyed hegemony, executed activists from the left en masse. Despite its socialist roots, the Islamic Republic foreclosed the national histories of leftist rebellion from its official discourse. In its place, the government launched a major propaganda campaign to enlighten the population regarding the utter inhumanity of the previous regimes' torturers. Aided by the CIA, which used the latest neuropsychological research on human pain tolerance, torturers in the intelligence ministry of SAVAK, the Shah's secret police, were infamous for extracting vital information regarding insurgencies.

Although the Islamic Republic valorizes certain religious prisoners of the Shah and the war as heroes or martyrs, it denounces the efforts of combatants connected to competing factions from the left or to the military of the Shah, who also fought against Saddam. In retaliation, the left formed a strong systematic opposition campaign against the Islamic Republic outside Iran. Their propaganda ranged from a call for regime change with the aid of West, a push toward crippling sanctions, and sincere humanitarian activities. Only recently a more acceptable, aesthetic technique of resistance became widespread: memoir writing and provision of a public podium for witnesses and victims of the Islamic Republic.

Many bourgeois diaspora narratives about Iran's contested history of the Revolution are also very elitist. They are detached from the population and traditions and rely heavily on neo-orientalism. In certain diasporic renditions (now best-sellers in North America), Iran fits within Western axioms of normativity. For these well-to-do writers, the real Iran has no regard for Islam or traditional moralities. Those few families who lived comfortably during the Shah's reign almost unanimously refuse to accept the fact that the majority of the population are deeply traditional Muslims. Not only the people but the religious insurgency that aided the Revolution and defended the country against eight years of international invasion by Iraq disappears from their accounts. The Islamic Republic and the diaspora, each by erasing from visibility the other's contribution to the wars against the Shah, Western imperialism, and Saddam, risk providing a radicalized review of Iran's contested history. Villainizing the Other and making the Other disappear from master narratives are both unethical acts. They tear open the Borromean connection of aesthetics to politics through ethics. Foreclosure of the enemy from the field of visibility is a violent act that leads toward fanaticism and perpetuation of the circle of hatred.

"Ethics are not just a problem of knowledge but a call to a relationship" (Spivak 2013b, 5). Engagement and relationship with the Other who has been excluded from visibility creates a response and a responsibility. Gayatri Spivak's notion of ethical responsibility is reminiscent of Mikhail Bakhtin's answerability. Here the act of response that completes the call between a speaker and a listener is not the only concern.

> We all know that when we engage profoundly with one person, the responses come from both sides: this is responsibility and accountability. . . . The object of ethical action is not an object of benevolence, for here responses flow from both sides. . . . The ideal relation to the Other, then, is an "embrace, an act of love." (Spivak 2013b, 270)

Satrapi and Talebi are careful regarding the treatment of their enemies. Satrapi does more than retell the stories of forgotten tortured prisoners of the Shah. She also turns her autocritical gaze toward local knowledges of what people know and considers how this informs the ethical palette of politicians and governments in general. To continue with Foucault's elaboration on genealogy:

> When I say "subjugated knowledges" I am also referring to a whole series of knowledges that have been disqualified as nonconceptual knowledges, as insufficiently elaborated knowledges: naive knowledges, hierarchically inferior knowledges, knowledges that are below the required level of erudition or scientificity. And it is thanks to the reappearance of these knowledges from below, . . . the knowledge of the delinquent, what I would call, if you like, what people know (and this is by no means the same thing as common knowledge or common sense but, on the contrary, a particular knowledge—a knowledge that is local, regional, or differential, incapable of unanimity . . .), it is the reappearance of what people know at a local level, of these disqualified knowledges, that made the critique possible. (Foucault and Ewald 2008, 7–8)

Satrapi uses both manifestations of subjugated knowledges in her work of art. The historical content of *Persepolis*, whether masked, forgotten, or marginalized, gains an affective dimension through a cartooning strategy that plays with the presence and absence of contested narratives. The comic form makes the abstract face of an imprisoned hero, Anoosh, as relatable as that of our own kin; his plight identifiable as our own misfortune: "when you look at a photo or realistic drawing of a face—you see it as the face of another but when you enter the world of the cartoon—you see yourself" (McCloud 1994, 36). Comics tend to escape the radar of policed mental preconditioning, and in so doing they become aesthetico-political media for reimagining significant events. Of course, they are slowly losing their power to escape the radar as they are becoming mainstream in many countries, such as France, Belgium, Italy, and Spain.

The comic techniques draw on the human ability to familiarize ourselves with abstract shapes by finding human faces on disparate objects in order to relate with them. *Persepolis*'s rugged history is interwoven with intimate personal stories. It marks the site where masked and buried historical narratives are interlaced with personal knowledges that fall below the accepted levels of scientificity, and it empowers a critique that cannot be homogeneous, unanimous, and consumable for warmongers. Many narratives from the diaspora can be used as evidence for the hawks in politics. But *Persepolis* cannot be read as a black and white tale. A girl's universal coming-of-age story is contrapuntally depicted alongside the tears in the social fabric of a nation at the crossroads of political unrest, religious fervor, and globalization. Her adolescence is accompanied by the modernist tunes of war sirens, with its marches for lost causes, air raids, and the pure experience of loss. Everything is understandable, but not quite, not right, leaving space for aesthetic uniqueness.

In "Estranging the Familiar" Naghibi and O'Malley pinpoint the fact that *Persepolis*, despite its apparent simplicity and accessibility, evades easy docketing and consumption. Although the general liberal humanity critique tries to look beyond minute political differences and focus on the wider experience of childhood rebellion and coming of age traumas, *Persepolis* offers moments of slippage and aporia that demand more complex historico-political lenses:

> *Persepolis* is a disruptive text on many levels. It delivers, for example, comfortable liberal notions of our common humanity in its representation of the universal desire for personal freedom. At the same time, it demonstrates liberalism's need for an abject or menacing other that is excluded from the common humanity by allowing the reader to reconfirm stereotypes of, for example, subjugated, veiled Muslim women and of post-revolutionary Iran as a threatening and alien place. However, *Persepolis* upsets the easy categories and distinctions that it appears to endorse: between the secular West and the threatening religious East; between the oppressed and liberated woman (i.e., veiled and unveiled); between domestic and political/public. (Naghibi and O'Malley 2005, 245)

In "Out of the Family: Generations of Women in Marjane Satrapi's *Persepolis*," Nancy K. Miller draws attention to the relation between Marji, her mother, and her grandmother. Marji's relationship with her mother, "represented as one of sporadic struggle as well as underlying complicity, is supplemented by crucial encounters with the grandmother" (2007, 23). The wisdom of the grandmother transcends religious or secular dichotomies. It falls in the pond of love and ethics. Marji's very last night in her homeland is spent in the arms of her grandmother: an original *heim* (home). The last advice of her grandmother is: "In life you'll meet a lot of jerks. If they hurt you, tell yourself that it's because they are stupid. That will help keep you from reacting to their cruelty. Because there is nothing worse than bitterness and vengeance, . . . always keep your dignity and be true to yourself" (Satrapi 2003, 150). Although Miller zooms in on the last phrase: "be true to yourself" (in French: *intègre*), I believe that the first part, delivered in broken syntax, is more telling of grandmother's ethical demand on Marji: abstain from rash reactionary revolt. It also outlines the frame of reference of *Persepolis* as a whole. Despite the stupidity of governments or dogmatic people, whether in Iran or Austria, Marji abstains from painting a black and white picture of the multifaceted human condition at the junctions of historical turning points.

The aesthetic break that allows for a turning of the judgmental tables occurs with the slippages in common frames of reference. Although Marji is troubled by public mourning of martyrs, aversion to signs of capitalism, the Iranian laws regarding dress code, and so on, she shows gratitude to the Muslim clergyman in charge of the university entrance ideological exam. He is the only clergyman with a voice in the book, although he has no face; he is completely drawn in black except for his glasses and a line that shows his turban (figure 7). The clergyman is the enigma of a book that comments on the Islamic Republic and may personify one of the many slippages in common stereotypes that Satrapi uses skillfully. Although the book is full of angry, bearded revolutionary guards who are full of nonsense about a literal reading of Islam, the "one true religious man" (Satrapi 2003, 130) saves Marji twice: once after she is honest regarding the fact that she does not pray and does not wear the veil in Austria, and another time when he rescues her from expulsion after she vents her rational anger at the revolutionary guards' propaganda in the university.

On both occasions, the clergyman is a masked figure. The audience is not allowed a glimpse of his expressions. He is denied a relatable face, but his mystery makes Iran a more complicated place than the common

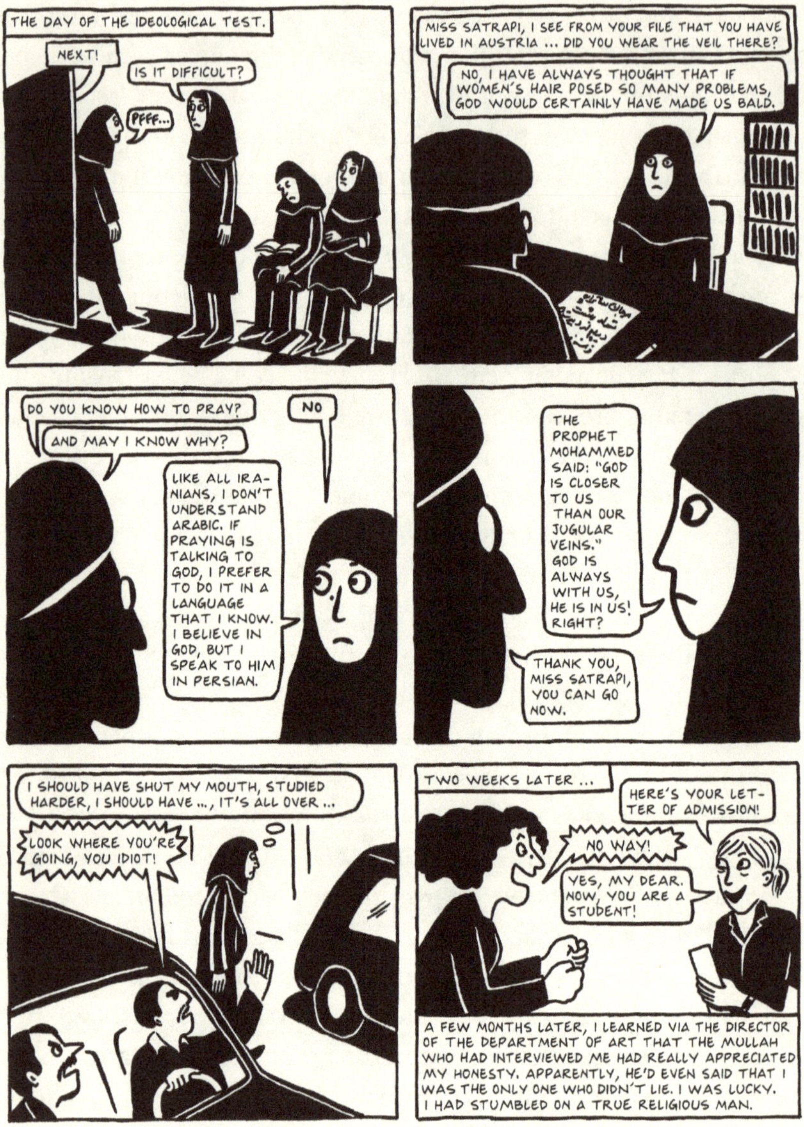

7. Not every clergy member is evil! from *Persepolis 2: The Story of a Return* by Marjane Satrapi, translated by Anjali Singh, translation copyright © 2004 by Anjali Singh. Used by permission of Pantheon Books, an imprint of the Knopf Doubleday Publishing Group, a division of Penguin Random House LLC. All rights reserved. P. 130.

stereotype as a country of oppressive mullahs. Not only does the mullah pass her on the ideological exam despite her lack of familiarity with Islam, he calls her the only applicant "who didn't lie" (Satrapi 2003, 130). Marji's reading of Islam is a personal reading that is based on honest self-interpretation. If she does not speak Arabic, she does not feel the need to pray in Arabic. She is content about talking with God in a familiar language. She even cites a Hadith from the Prophet Muhammad to prove her point: "God is closer to us than our jugular veins" (130). Thus, if God is close, she does not feel the need for the external performance of mainstream prayer to connect to an internal being. Her reasoning appeals to the clergyman as honest. She demonstrates how a true believer is supposed to be.

Despite the frankness with which Marji talks to the clergyman about her connection with God, on the very opposite page Satrapi draws one of the most hypocritical acts of the whole book. In a chapter named "The Makeup" Marji tells on a bystander to the revolutionary guards in order to save her own neck before meeting her boyfriend in the streets. She is afraid because of her heavy makeup and indecent hair coverage, and thus decides to deflect the guards' attention to an innocent bystander. The police take the confused man away because she complains that he has "said something indecent to me!" (131). The spatial composition of the two pages that open together but are in sharp contrast with one another is aporetic. Marji risks the future of her education by being honest to her beliefs. However, in order to meet her date on the streets and evade the revolutionary guards' temporary burden, she lies and puts another man in danger of fines and possibly a good beating. Here Satrapi distinguishes between true religion and a fake empire of the revolutionary guards who boast of religion yet repel people from any religious beliefs.

Marji's "survival instincts" are unacceptable according to her grandmother's sense of ethics. She yells at Marji for the first time in a speech that is not contained in a bubble; maybe it is not just addressed to Marji, but is a wake-up call to the audience. After this chastising Marji regains her rebellious spirit. She reasons with the propaganda machine at the university and disagrees with their rule of a modest dress code. She once again relies on a personal interpretation of religion: "Now, I ask the question: is religion defending our physical integrity or is it just opposed to fashion?"

(143). She is summoned by the same clergyman who accepted her on the ideology exam earlier. He is frank: "Miss Satrapi, . . . always saying what you think. . . . It's good! You're honest, but you are lost" (144), to which she replies "Yes!" Not only does the clergyman not punish her, he rewards her with the task of producing the official dress code of her department: "I'm going to give you a second chance. This time you're not expelled. In exchange I am asking you to imagine the uniform adapted to the needs of the students in your college. Nothing extravagant, you understand" (144). She commits herself to design a fashion that will "please both the administration and the interested parties" (144).

Iranian people win their rights from authorities like that: through battles that are heartfelt, rational, and planned. *Persepolis* shows the agency of the people of Iran who suffer through their government's lack of experience with ruling and its reliance on the force of obscure laws, but at the same time, it is the agency of the people that wins them their rights. Both sides compromise, but victory is always on the side of those who rebel against injustice.

Marji designs an acceptable new fashion for the Department of Art and agrees that "Though subtle, these differences meant a lot to us" (144). Afterward, the approving love of her grandmother returns: "It's fear that makes us lose our conscience. It's also what transforms us into cowards. You had guts! I'm proud of you!" (145). Just as a clergyman can become the source of artistic inspiration that enables peaceful coexistence if not reconciliation, the so-called modern, Westernized, emancipated Iranians can be the pillars of either traditionalism or oppression (figure 8). *Persepolis* does not just look for an external enemy: the Islamic Republic. It delves honestly and deeply into the lives of Iranians and Austrians to touch the chords that vibrate with dissonance and discord. Satrapi does start with generalization and easy dichotomies that can categorize people according to types. But her ethical glance moves her past her prejudices to enable a balanced relationship to crystalize via aesthetic and political means.

Marji calls a woman in chador a fundamentalist, a statement that, if not based on sanctioned, commonly acceptable ignorance, is utterly mistaken. She then refutes and complicates the stereotype in several instances. Women who loosen their veil, smoke, go skiing, and try to avoid

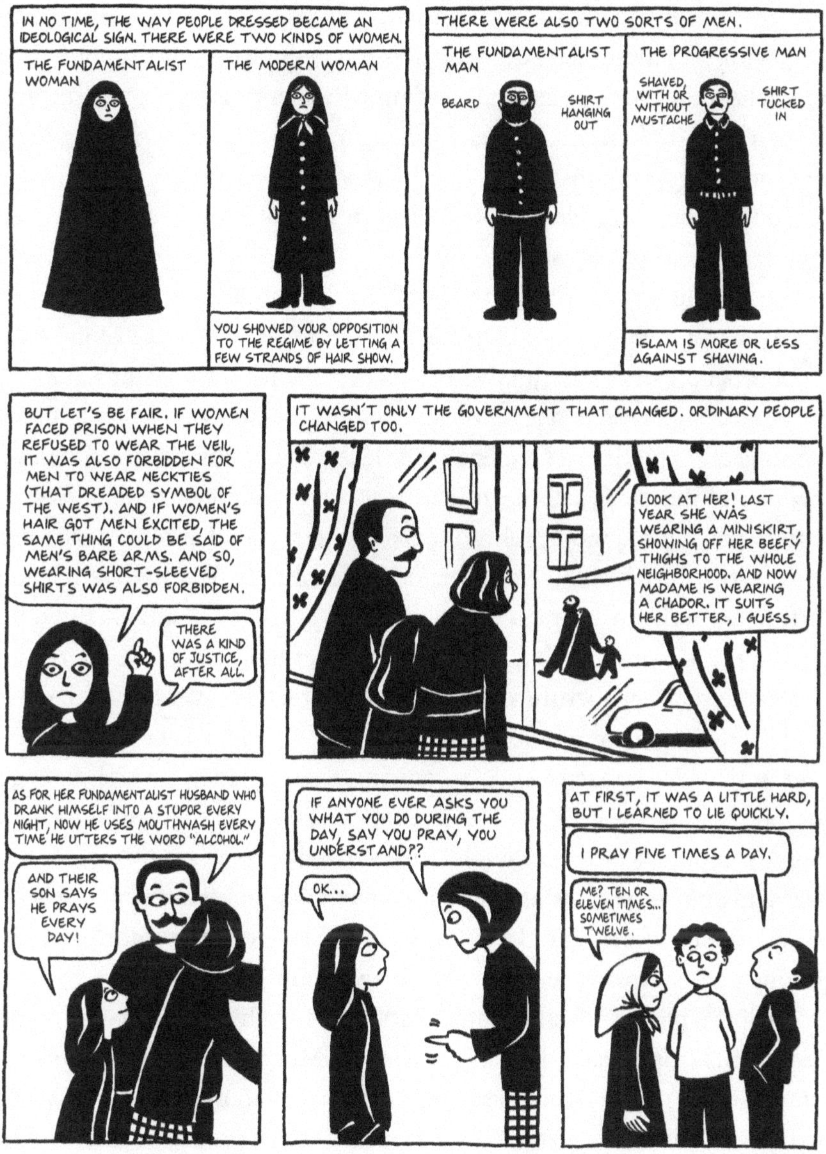

8. Categorizing people by their dress code. *Persepolis: The Story of a Childhood* by Marjane Satrapi, translation copyright © 2003 by L'Association, Paris, France. Used by permission of Pantheon Books, an imprint of the Knopf Doubleday Publishing Group, a division of Penguin Random House LLC. All rights reserved. P. 75.

any ties with the mandates of the Islamic Republic gang up against Marji for having had multiple sexual partners. The man who was the epitome of an intellectual warrior against the Islamic Republic's censor over the press is not a hero in domestic circles. He has no respect for his wife's opinions and interrupts her constantly. University students, who are generally believed to be open-minded, regard Marji in a negative light after discovering her contraceptive pills.

So the binary Marji creates between the fundamentalist and modern woman on the basis of their fashion crumbles in the face of modern-looking people who hold rigidly to their convictions. As Winston Churchill once said, "a fanatic is one who can't change his mind and won't change the subject." Fanaticism happens at the level of convictions, not clothes. A member of the clergy can negotiate an appropriate dress code for women with Marji, but à la mode Tehrani female skiers cannot accept Marji's sexual practices. In *Persepolis* the location of malice is in a state of tension, in transit, between inside and outside. The enemy is channelled from a beast outside to an instinct inside, and vice versa. It is not just the regime that carries out the torture and execution of prisoners. With the fall of the Shah, retribution commences. Although there is much cause for celebration in the "departure of evil," in one interesting panel, Satrapi manages to draw its long serpentine tail encircling the domestic space, almost grabbing the mother's face. Although Marji's parents have happily closed their eyes and appear to be relieved, evil seems to have its claws firmly set into the quotidian space. Marji is nonplussed, and evil looks unwilling to leave, glaring at them from the corner of its eye (figure 9).

Is it the heated social debates that affect the children, or is it spontaneous calls from inside the gang of friends? Marji and her friends plan to attack a child whose father has allegedly been collaborating with SAVAK's torturers. Marji organizes the gang attack, equipping her friends with sharp nails to hold between their little fingers. Luckily Marji's mom taps into their vicious plan and manages to stop them by evoking empathy: "What would you say if I nailed your ears to the wall?" to which Marji responds with "Wow! It would hurt a lot" (Satrapi 2003, 45). The moment of revelation is the moment of imagining the self in the same pain that

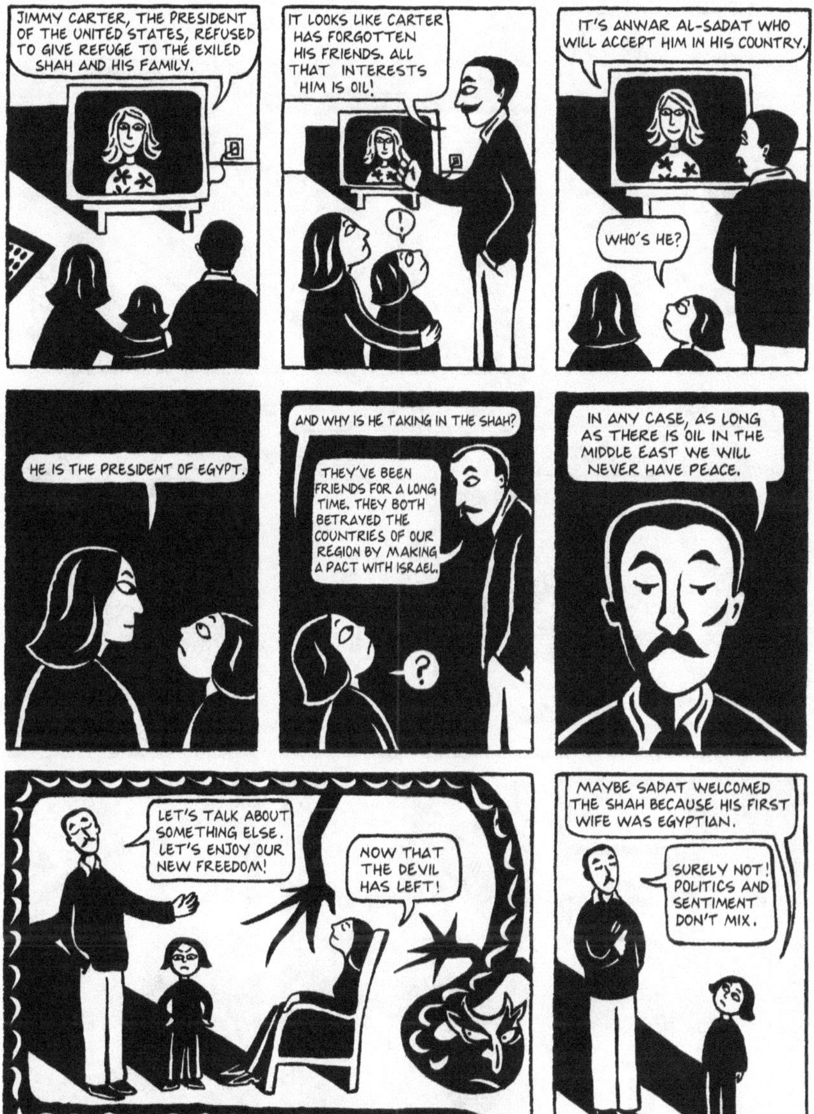

9. Revolution was just the start; menace has a way to return. *Persepolis: The Story of a Childhood* by Marjane Satrapi, translation copyright © 2003 by L'Association, Paris, France. Used by permission of Pantheon Books, an imprint of the Knopf Doubleday Publishing Group, a division of Penguin Random House LLC. All rights reserved. P. 43.

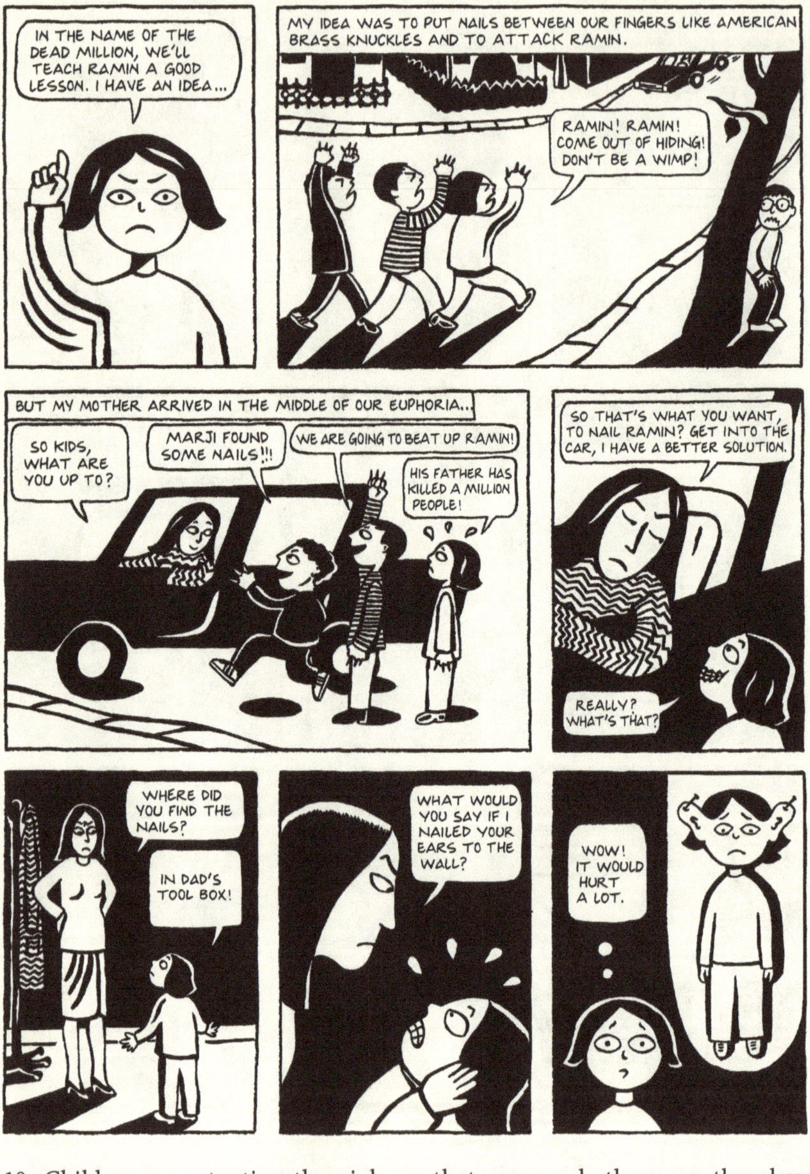

10. Children perpetuating the violence that surrounds them, on the playground. *Persepolis: The Story of a Childhood* by Marjane Satrapi, translation copyright © 2003 by L'Association, Paris, France. Used by permission of Pantheon Books, an imprint of the Knopf Doubleday Publishing Group, a division of Penguin Random House LLC. All rights reserved. P. 45.

was supposed to be inflicted on the Other. Marji imagines herself hanging with her elongated ears fastened to the wall with two nails (figure 10).

It is then that her mother preaches: "it is not for you and me to do justice. I'd even say, we have to learn to forgive" (46). The imperative turns into a refrain for Marji, repeated in front of the mirror over and over again: "you have to forgive, you have to forgive" (46). However, as all else in *Persepolis*, forgiving is not easy when the personal scars are deep. The selfsame mother who talks of forgiveness screams for vengeance after hearing about the Shah's torture of the family friends (figure 3), "all torturers should be massacred" (52). The double standard confuses the child. Now instead of ganging up on an outsider, Marji comes up with torture methods for the "losers" of the clan: "The mustache-on-fire consists of pulling on the two sides of the upper lip," "the twisted arm," "The mouth filled with garbage" (53); Marji is depicted eating garbage, pulling her own upper lip, and twisting the arm of an agonized little boy with a vicious smile on her face. And when Marji accosts her mother regarding forgiveness, she conveniently turns to the argument that "Bad people are dangerous but forgiving them is [dangerous] too. Don't worry. There is justice on earth" (53).

Common Misreadings of *Persepolis*

Hillary Chute (2008) and Jennifer Worth (2007), in their different publications, have alluded to *Persepolis* as the only means of visibility for a subaltern, or visually "effaced" Satrapi. Despite her well-grounded research on graphic narratives, when it comes to women of Iranian descent, Chute falters. *Persepolis*, for Chute, marks an ethical call to bring the invisible subject with no other chance of visibility to the attention of Western readers. Her ethics contain an elitist mission of re-facing, retracing, or, rather, "repeating":

> I am interested in this notion of ethics as it applies to autobiographical graphic narrative: what does it mean for an author to *literally* reappear—in the form of a legible, drawn body on the page—at the site of her inscriptional effacement? Graphic narratives that bear witness to authors' own traumas and those of others materially retrace

> inscriptional effacement; they reconstruct and repeat in order to counteract. It is useful to understand the retracing work of graphic narratives as ethical repetitions (of censored scenarios). (2008, 93)

Although I am all in favor of an ethical approach to autobiographical graphic narratives, I do not believe that the author has "reappear[ed] . . . at the site of her inscriptional effacement" or that the act of visual representation, with all its shortcomings, is a moment of repetition or mimicry. Chute's question of effacement is absurd in the case of Satrapi, as Satrapi is not a subaltern who would be "effaced as she discloses herself" (Spivak 2010, 21). Why would Satrapi need to "reappear . . . at the site of her inscriptional effacement"—if not by assuming that had she not reappeared, she would have been inscriptionally effaced. It is as if Satrapi had no method for self-disclosure other than her text—the site of her inscriptional effacement. Cloaked in flowery adjectives, the argument is offensive to women authors of Iranian diaspora, who have strong voices. Chute indirectly labels them as subaltern, supposedly because of their Iranian origins, and despite their social position.[1] She is just as vague regarding the Satrapi's drawing style: "Satrapi's choice of pared down techniques, of line and perspective—as with modernist painting such as Cezanne's; as with German Expressionism; and as with abstract expressionism" (Chute 2008, 99).[2] The three art examples are very different, general, and unspecific.

Chute is not alone in her generic categorization of literature written by women of the Iranian diaspora. Worth's far less rigorous reading, "Unveiling: *Persepolis* as Embodied Performance," relies heavily on generalizations, half-digested theoretical interpretations, and stereotypes. After enumerating a handful of autobiographies published by women of the Iranian diaspora including renowned authors, university professors, and journalists such as Azadeh Moaveni, Farzaneh Milani, and Azar

1. She also labels all her choice comics written by women as feminist only because of their attention to the body.

2. Using these three examples is analogous to saying a book's writing style is similar to that of Margaret Atwood, Canadian indigenous authors, and American postcolonial texts.

Nafisi, she remarks: "Clearly, the subaltern has learned to speak" (2007, 143). Had she known the usage of the word *subaltern* as circulated by Spivak or Antonio Gramsci, she would not have called relatively well-off Iranian women living in the global North subaltern. For Spivak, the subaltern is "outside the mode of production, narrative" (2010, 1), having no access to discourse except through effacement or death. Whether the subaltern can learn to speak is outside the question here. Worth's unprofessional usage of theoretical terminology is widespread when it comes to the marginal genre of diasporic literature. Considering any woman of Iranian or Islamic background as subaltern—who may or may not learn to speak—is reminiscent of what Spivak calls "sanctioned ignorance."

The astonishing flourishing of post-revolutionary women in all walks of social life in Iran is not accounted for due to the same sanctioned ignorance that relies on "knowledge passed down" (Said 1978). And these are among the better fallacies. Stacey Weber-Fève thinks that the reader is following Satrapi's coming of age in the "Islamic Revolution of 1978" (2011, 324)! In her own somewhat autobiographical article "Out of the Family," Miller sees Marji's taking up of the book *The Second Sex* as "turning theory into practice: peeing standing up" (2007, 19)! Stretching the panels to accommodate her vision of Marji's feminism, Miller forgets the utter failure of this act, which is denounced quickly afterward by the protagonist. Theory does not turn so easily into practice for women who negotiate the borders. The panel that depicts Marji's failure at peeing while standing up may, instead, be read as a critique of the inapplicability of the Western framework of feminism to Iranian women.

Many have alluded to *Persepolis*'s connection to Persian miniatures. I accept that miniatures and *Persepolis* both lack perspective and a vanishing point. Miniatures also tell a story through conjugations of words and images. But miniatures function within a tradition of classical poetry with strong mystical connotations. Elements of the divine and transcendental take precedence over the material and the mundane. The delicate line is not just a line, but the manifestation of an ecstatic state, an amorous dance with the lover, a mystic state. There are many other art movements that shun linear perspective and vanishing points. The fact that the works both originated within the same country does not necessitate their relationship. Such a classification is based on a lack of knowledge regarding Persian art history movements, as well as the general lack of visual literacy among literary critics of comics.

Persepolis Conclusions

Although Satrapi starts the English edition of the first book with a statement of authorial intent, the complex book's lack of explicit volition is what arms it with free aesthetic play, a political tool for subverting hierarchies of domination. The playfulness of the comic medium that allows for identification with the face of the cartoon avatar at the same time that it creates an uncanny moment of difference is pivotal in this subversion.

The comic medium leaves small aporetic gaps for contemplation in an interrupted verbal-visual narrative. The reading pace moves with *ritmo lento*, proceeding slowly and multifocally: an eye on the image, an eye on history, another on politics, aesthetics, ethics, and so on. Satrapi intricately sews intimate personal knowledges from below into a web of histories of masked battles to complicate the process of finding an easy enemy whose elimination will heal the traumatic scar. The position of the Other as the evil enemy swirls from kin to the state, from homeland to the West, and returns, always with similitude, always with a difference. The torturer is affiliated once with the Shah, another time with the Islamic Republic, but it is also channeled deep within the quotidian circle of parental brutality, playground cruelty, and Iranians' intolerance toward one another. The beloved leftist father can also be the enforcer of class segregation; the loving mother who preaches forgiveness can scream for the "execution of executioners."

In *Persepolis* upper-class Westernized Iranian women renouncing the Islamic veil can become traditionalists regarding women's sexual affairs, while Islamic clergy can accept arguments regarding interpretation of Islam and reconcile themselves with the desires of the youths. There is tension and a delay in the apparently easily communicable text. Iran at war is not favorable for an artist, but Austria at peace is hostile to Marji. She is subject to xenophobia and suffers from a lack of profound bonds, to such an extent that she exclaims to her husband: "but in the west you can collapse on the street and no one will give you a hand" (Satrapi 2003, 126). Iran is not ripe for invasion, and the West is not overflowing with freedom. *Persepolis*'s aestextasy, which consists of its visual aesthetic, political subversion, and ethical landscape, engulfs a text that is dissensual and challenging, yet paradoxically accessible.

2

Parsua Bashi's *Nylon Road*

While *Persepolis* provokes an immediate, visceral connection with the audience, using its intrinsic free play, Parsua Bashi's *Nylon Road* appears to be more mediated, somewhat keeping a critical distance, and more philosophizing. Regarding aestextasy, Bashi[1] is concerned mainly with positioning herself on ethical ground between Iranian and Western negotiations of identity. The double-sided connection between the aesthetic and politics is overshadowed by her overt attention to a certain dialectical ethics. This ethics is an internal sense of responsibility that she kindles via internal dialogues as she revisits herself at pivotal points in Iran's turbulent modern history.

Bashi's narrative style is interrupted by spats of intellectual self-argumentation regarding the protagonist's current beliefs and past convictions. The explicit auto-critique takes up a majority of the panels, turning the book into a manifesto on ethical thinking instead of a graphic memoir as the title suggests. When it is read in conjunction with other memoirs about Iran, this poses no problem. It fills a very important ethical gap.

Bashi challenges the easy binaries that most Iranian memoirists draw between a free West and a fundamentalist Iran. She looks at the threats to world peace posed by regarding Islam as the cause of all that went wrong with Iran and the world. She contrapuntally glances at extremism in Iran

1. I will use Bashi to refer to the author and Pari for the cartoon avatar of the protagonist as her present self in Switzerland. Her past selves will be introduced later. The narrator and the protagonist remain unnamed throughout *Nylon Road*. The only name in the entire book is in its dedication: "To my daughter Abi."

and radicalism in the West. However, on its own *Nylon Road* lacks the intimacy of a memoir. It leaves abrupt gaps in the personal story starting from the first page. The book opens with a full-length self-portrait of Pari, who appears to be modern, relatable, and candid. The first panel reads: "I've been living in Zurich since the 23rd of April 2004" (Bashi 2009, 1). But then in the second panel we encounter Pari talking on the phone across the years with a mystery man whose face is not fully disclosed. It is, however, similar to that of a companion of hers whom we meet further on in the book. She writes, "The reason why I came here is another story that I won't explain now" (1), but she doesn't explain it later either. She will explain the sociopolitical situation in Iran and negotiate her own identity constructions between these territories. However, in this enigmatic panel she is referring to a romantic relationship with a Swiss man who will later become her husband. This is never clarified in the book.

I agree that the choice of omissions in a personal narrative is with the author. The continual lapses and abrupt ends to chapters steer attention away from the life story and toward the intellectual personal debate with the author's selves. According to Jacques Rancière's politics of aesthetics, she does create a space to imagine what was not supposed to be imagined before. For Rancière, politics is a *repartage*, a redistribution of the tribune to vent a dissensual argument, to break new ground, to say something against the quiet consensus. To this end, Pari tries to combat her past dogmatic conventions—for example, as an astute communist teenager. This shattering of the consensus is a moment of possibilities that functions like an aesthetic intervention; it rearranges the set frames of mind and hierarchies of domination. Dissensus prefigures an acknowledgment of the Other's stance and calls for an ethical engagement with it, despite the dangers that such an embrace might entail. When, with the help of the comic medium, this Other is a self, the outcome could be an aesthetic break. Nevertheless, Bashi's push to police a reconciliation prevents the break.

Nylon Road's English translation appeared in North America in November 2009, a few months before the Green Movement against Mahmoud Ahmadinejad's rigged reelection. Despite the international attention to this spontaneous popular revolt, *Nylon Road* did not trigger a wave of critical acclaim in English, as was enjoyed previously by *Persepolis*.

The reviews and interviews were mostly in German, the book's original language.

Composed in the tradition of Satrapi's works, *Nylon Road* poses challenging questions about Iranians' and Westerners' problematic understandings regarding one another. Instead of relying on a few rudimentary internal monologues, Bashi conducts extensive external dialogues between her different selves: the happy-go-lucky child avatar, the communist adolescent, the fashionista youth, the drowned-in-sorrow divorcee, and the independent artist and intellectual. These different versions of her past alternatively accost the current-day immigrant Pari in Zurich, Switzerland, at moments that intensify the contrast between Iranian and Swiss lifestyles and frames of mind.

Bashi takes full advantage of comics' potential to have several speakers from different points in time appear simultaneously in a dialogue. They appear at pivotal moments in the new immigrant's adjustment to her life in the West. Bashi attempts to internally reconcile her traumatic experiences with her apparently happy and quiet life in Switzerland. The criticism she offers is dialectical, self-critical, and less playful than Satrapi's. Bashi's voice lacks the immediate intimacy of Satrapi's. Her characters—mainly her different selves—are not as easily identifiable as Satrapi's, say, child narrator.

Satrapi's characters are not quickly consumable either. Satrapi produces an arguably universally identifiable rebellious child and teenager, but then marks her with an intrinsic enigma that prevents the book from being ideologically cornered or docketed. Satrapi's art starts with the known and moves toward the destabilizing unknowns as the book progresses. Her aesthetic is unique for its inexplicable yet striking feel of honesty as she gains the trust of the readers while recounting personal as well as political traumas.

The phantasmagoric apparitions of Pari's younger selves, ambushing the current-day self of the protagonist, contest the nonfiction or memoir tag. The English translation of *Nylon Road* is subtitled "A Graphic Memoir of Coming of Age in Iran." However, the coming of age happens in Switzerland, through Pari's critically and physically distant process of looking back at her episodic self. It is by looking her past selves directly in the face and holding rigorous dialogues with them that she comes of age in

Switzerland. After all, the main audience of this book is the author herself, as she claims in an interview:

> The main audience of the work was myself, just as in diary writing or memoirs that an individual writes for herself. Then I had in mind my close friends and people I lived with. Now that the book has been published, I believe its audience is among the intellectual spheres, the curious, and mostly people with an open mind, and probably Western left-leaning subjects who are deeply interested in learning about Middle Eastern societies. (Kuzegar 2007)

Bashi acknowledges that her intended audience has been primarily herself. She is set on a therapeutic mission of diasporic self-discovery, a project of comparing the social values of Iran with those of the West. The feisty conversations are to reconcile the self—removed from Iran's intellectual circles with all its dilemmas—to a rather isolated, yet trouble-free self as an immigrant.

In the midst of this battle between her present and past selves, Bashi introduces and analyzes bits of controversial history and concepts. The lengthier speech balloons provide the required space for textual analysis while reducing the effect of an immediate response to the images. Bashi's forte is this strong, ethical critical analysis, which she accomplishes masterfully by presenting juxtaposed panels consecutively—a technique widely used by Satrapi but mostly not for critical analysis of a concept. One of the most controversial topics that Bashi takes up skillfully and fairly concerns Islam. While Bashi's theoretical arguments regarding religion are surprisingly accurate, the graphic narrative of her life experiences belies a balanced approach to religion. In words, her battle is fair. However, it is interesting that she is battling herself.

Paratext

The original Swiss publishers consented to Bashi's wish that the word *Iran* not be flashed on the book's front or back cover for commercial gain. The American publishers of the English version did not. The US edition relies on an irrelevant but catchy script on the dust cover: "a young Iranian woman's struggles with growing up under Shiite law," despite the fact that neither Shiʿite nor Sunni laws are mentioned in the entire narrative. Pari's older self does distinguish between government and religion, but that rich analysis is never carried through to the book covers. As an experienced book cover designer herself, Bashi expresses aversion to catchy book covers that surf the waves of cultural stereotypes: "I wanted my audience to choose and read the book based on its content; not for example based on the cover photo depicting a woman in burqa, a camel, a desert and so forth" (Kuzegar 2007).

The New York–based St. Martin's Griffin even changed the original cover, designed by Bashi herself, against her wishes:

> I intentionally avoided picking a title with any direct reference to Iran, let alone subtitle or back cover. As you know, not all Iranian memoirists are famous for the quality of their work. Many gain visibility because of the vogue of Iran in Western media. This makes the memoirs about Iran "in fashion." To procure this marketability, the publishers need a name of an Iranian landmark, or an Iranian symbol and the like. I was strictly against this and wanted the book to be read for the quality of its content and not based on marketability. That is why I picked the mysterious word "*Nylon Road*" which has a paronomasia with the ancient "Silk Road." In the English edition the New York publisher correctly knew that the chance for selling more books will be increased with the addition of a subtitle containing the word "Iran." The back cover was entirely written by the publishers themselves. (Parsua Bashi, email interview with author, December 2014)

In chapter 11, young Pari shows aversion regarding the "burqa covers" that are not even ethnic to Iran. Although she spots this misrepresentation problem in the West, she is quick to see this problem in her own self as she tried to acquaint herself with Western culture. The older Pari admits to having herself designed book covers with incorrect European cultural symbols (figures 11a and 11b).

In addition to the wrong and misleading English subtitle, which explicitly references *Persepolis*, the difference between the Swiss and American

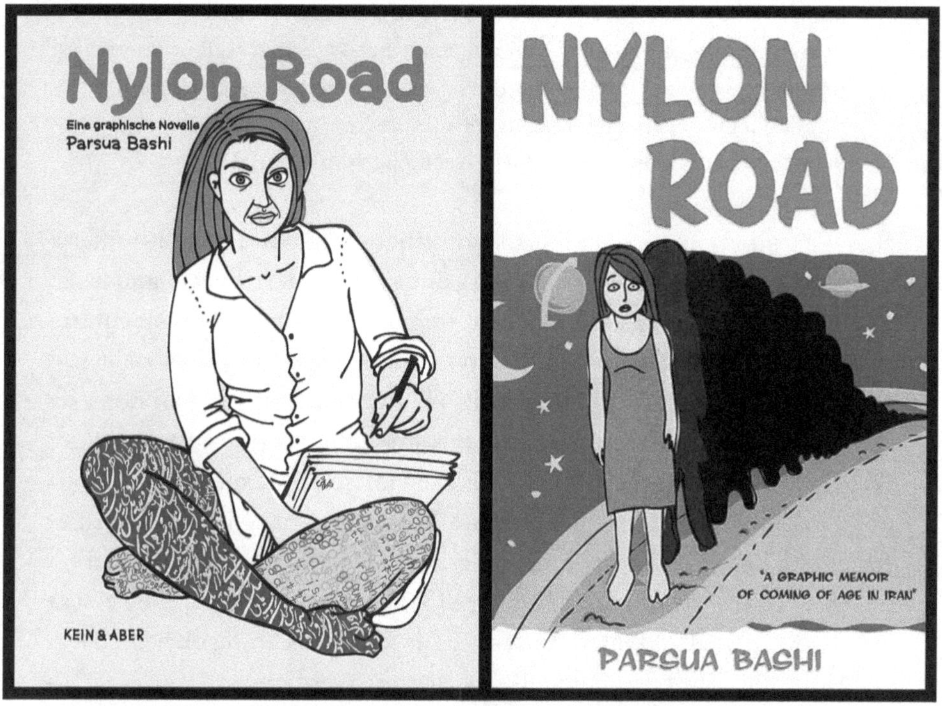

11. Comparison of two cover designs of *Nylon Road* for two different editions: German and English. Left: The original cover designed by Bashi herself for the Swiss edition. Right: The American edition, with the subtitle "A Graphic Memoir of Coming of Age in Iran," which is absent from the original cover, and is quite misleading, according to the author. © 2006 Kein & Aber AG, Zurich-Berlin. Reprinted with permission of both publishers and the artists. *Nylon Road: A Graphic Memoir of Coming of Age in Iran* © 2009 by Parsua Bashi. Reprinted by permission of St. Martin's Griffin, an imprint of St. Martin's Press. All rights reserved.

publishers' taste for the cover is astonishing. Gérard Genette claims that "the paratext is what enables a text to become book" (1997, 1):

> More than a boundary or a sealed border, the paratext is, rather, a *threshold*, or . . . a "vestibule" that offers the world at large the possibility of either stepping inside or turning back. . . . This fringe, always the conveyor of a commentary that is authorial or more or less legitimated by the author, constitutes a zone between text and off-text, a zone not only of transition

> but also of *transaction*: a privileged place of a pragmatics and a strategy, of an influence on the public, an influence that—whether well or poorly understood and achieved—is at the service of a better reception for the text and a more pertinent reading of it (more pertinent, of course, in the eyes of the author and his allies). (1–2; emphasis in original)

It is with an eye on the significant contribution of paratext that I offer a comparative study of the *Nylon Road*'s different facades, images, and texts.

The Swiss cover has only delicate, implicit allusions to Persian culture and history: the graceful calligraphy *siyah mashgh*[2] on Pari's right leg, the author's Farsi signature on Pari's manuscript, and the paronomasia between *Nylon Road* and the ancient Silk Road, connecting East and West. The Latin letters on Pari's left leg, however, fail to create meaningful word combinations, or at least a work of art. This is her challenge when engaging with a new language. Nonetheless, the Latin letters are inscribed on and may form part of her body, her self. The Latin letters and the Persian words are crossed and interlaced as she sits to write, leaning on her left leg, the Latin side. The book, after all, is written in German.

The body inscriptions have intertextual references to Shirin Neshat's play with Muslim female body inscriptions. The author is also in the act of self-representation, or self-portraiture, with her Farsi name signed on the paper, and a curious stare that positions her in the place of both the subject and the object of study. Craig Owens highlights the shifting role of portraiture in contemporary art practices: "the subject poses as an object *in order to become a subject*" (1992, 215; emphasis in original). Bashi is portrayed as the author of a text about herself. Her raised eyebrow and curved bodily gesture connote inquisition before an artistic creation.

This empowering transgression from the role of a Muslim Iranian woman is evident in the Swiss cover through implicit references or winks.

2. *Siyah mashgh* literally translates to "blackening exercise" and is a style of Persian calligraphy in which the artists practice technique by covering a whole page with the black ink of their calligraphic words. *Siyah mashgh*, which was originally homework for pupils of calligraphy, has become an art form in itself. The beauty of the calligraphed words is appreciated in a pictorial sense, even devoid of their cohesive meaning.

The American choice, on the other hand, complies with an Orientalist reading of the phenomenon "Iranian woman." It displays a harrowing blood-red title, hanging in capital letters over Pari's head. It depicts Pari in an awestruck, uncomfortable, standing pose. She might even be hovering without firm ground, without a shadow, on an alien planet. She appears ghostly, ominous, and alien, followed by a train of darkening shadows. That is what "coming of age in Iran" probably signifies: a woman crushed by a murky past tinted with black and bright red. This image was chosen and cropped from the opening chapter, in which Pari meets a younger self for the first time. It depicts the shock of encounter with her happy child self. Cut from the context and twisted with a subtitle and the title font, the panel stands in mimetic repetition of a dictated text.

Religion and Politics

Although in words Pari fights a fair battle, in the recounting of her life story, we encounter no fair Muslims. All Iranian Muslims in the narrative are given revolting facial features. The female librarian looks like a man in chador. The judge's clerk picks his nose and throws its contents around as Pari pleads for a child's custody. All the clergy members are angry and unjust. No Iranian Muslim is endowed with a single admirable quality. In words, though, Pari distinguishes between the oppressive government and religion:

> After years of living outside of my country, in this peaceful Europe, I had almost forgotten how frustrated I used to be—just like other Iranians—because of our fundamentalist government. We were all so poisoned by rage that we falsely projected everything on religion. (Bashi 2009, 56)

The argument about religion occurs after a dreadful encounter with an unnamed young Iranian science student in Switzerland. The latter could be described as a pseudo-intellectual who carries chauvinistically racist beliefs about Arabs. She boasts about a millennia-old civilization and blames all that went wrong with Iran on the young government's Islam. Pari wants to distance herself from avid Persian, pre-Islamic nationalists, but her younger selves remind her of the science student. Replying to the avid student, Pari asks herself:

> Is it really possible for a 2,500-year-old civilization to change from white to black simply by being oppressed for 27 years by the acts of a government? . . .
>
> The great Persian paradise of hers might even have existed—how do I know?—but for 1,400 of those 2,500 years, Islam was the religion of these people. Islam merged with the Iranian culture and mentality to the extent that they now might be inseparable. (56–57)

The slightly younger Pari not only shares the young scientist's views, she goes even farther: "If those grasshopper eating Arabs had left us alone I wouldn't have had to live my entire life under these mullahs!" (55). Hatred brings with it generalization. The self-identified intellectual youth of Iran are quick to mix Arabs, Islam, and the Iranian government, relating them all to a backwardness they want to escape by adopting a Western lifestyle. Under cross-examination, chauvinism leaks through the intellectual air. It is in this spirit that *Persepolis*'s heroic journalist who published comics against the Islamic government shows dogmatic qualities against his own wife in quotidian atmospheres. The problem cannot all be transferred to the Islamic governance. For Bashi, that is a misconception:

> No, they [Islamic government] don't believe in Islamic law as much as we think. It's simply for political purposes. Imagine: if they got rid of the hijab and alcohol laws, they'd look just like a dictatorial regime, or like any other atheist, secular, totalitarian regime in the world. . . . And then under the cover of this sacred mission, they get exclusive hold of the national wealth. They love it when everyone calls them a strict religious regime. (58)

The double-sided blade of generalization cuts both ways: it helps the propaganda machine in the West to gain favor for invasion and suppression of peaceful dissensus (figure 12). It also gives the extremists in the Iranian government an excuse to point to an external enemy and in turn curb civic liberties. "If we too blame every wrong thing on Islam, we are

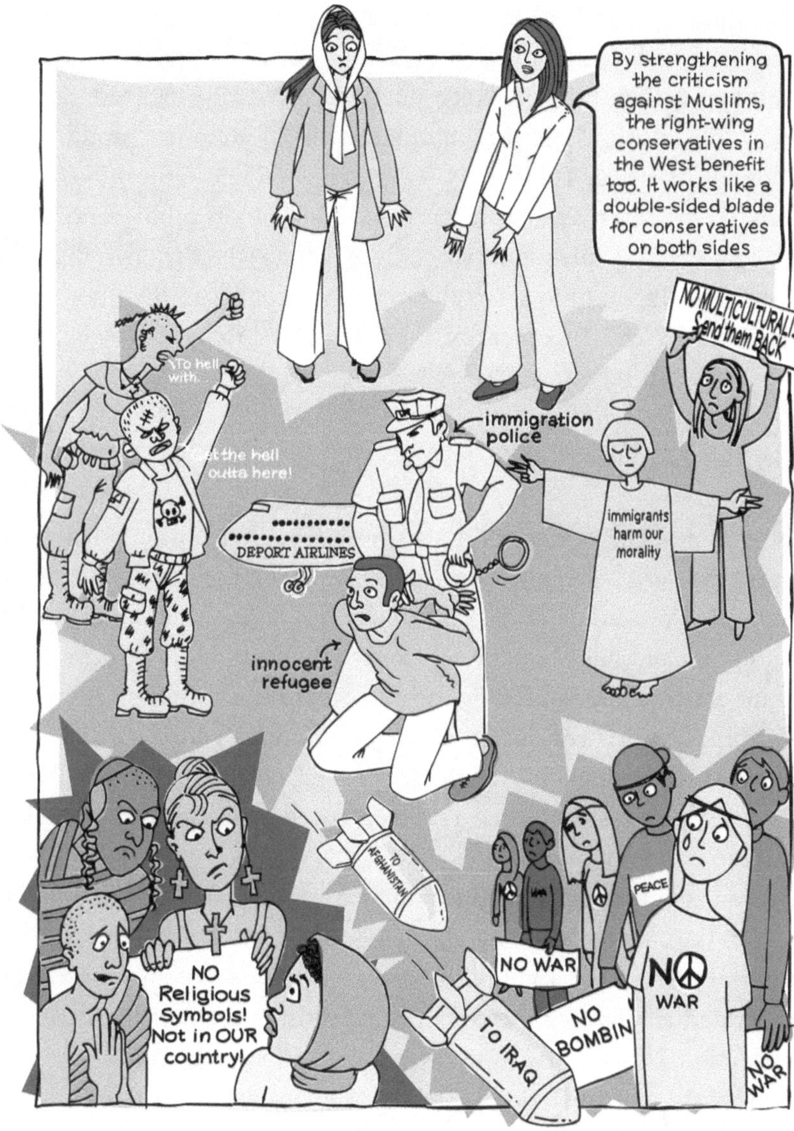

12. Common Western attitudes toward Muslims, wars, and refugees. From *Nylon Road* by Parsua Bashi. © 2006 Kein & Aber AG, Zurich-Berlin. *Nylon Road: A Graphic Memoir of Coming of Age in Iran* © 2009 by Parsua Bashi. Reprinted by permission of St. Martin's Griffin, an imprint of St. Martin's Press. P. 59.

helping the propaganda which is based on those false clichés. The stronger the anti-Islam criticism the better for Iranian and other undemocratic systems. It makes their mission look even more sacred" (58–59).

Such observations are rare in other works of literature produced by the Iranian diaspora. The strictly self-judgmental and ethical look at all the mistakes the Iranian culture has passed down to its immigrants needs much courage for expression, especially at a time when Iranian diaspora writers are trying hard to assert their sense of identity in their newfound homes in the West. This identity, they claim, is strictly non-Arab, non-Islamic, and non-religious.

Autocritique in *Nylon Road*

Bashi is one of the few memoirists who explicitly mentions that Iran's sole problems are not the women's dress code and the ban on the public consumption of alcohol. While the hijab and the prohibition on alcohol consumption and sale are nuisances for the upper and middle classes, the most urgent challenges faced by the majority of the nation lie elsewhere. Bashi comes to this conclusion at the end of one of her lengthiest and most fierce self-dialogues: "Yes the Iranians' problems are not alcohol or scarves. My people's problems are the oil-based economy and the lack of education, freedom, and democracy" (2009, 61). However, the beautiful discussion is cut short by the introduction of another chapter. While in *Persepolis* the chapters are dialogically relevant, there is a rift between the theoretical discussions and life stories in *Nylon Road*. None of the selves is elaborated enough for the reader to establish a relationship based on identification. Chapters two and seven are only four pages each.

One of the most memorable narratives in *Nylon Road* is the tale of the thirteen-year-old Pari, who flirted with what she calls a branch of "Leninist Marxism" as a teenager. The teenage self ambushes the current-day Pari as the latter is peacefully people watching from a café terrace on a sunny day in Zurich. The young and old Western women she is observing appear to follow the same fashion: tight, short pants, a short tank top revealing the belly button and breasts, and a ponytail. All of a sudden the communist teenager Pari appears, the one who became involved with political groups that were finally freed after the demise of Shah. These leftist ex-prisoners joined ranks against the new Islamic Republic and soon became a threat to the new government with their booming public support and their armed activities, including political assassinations. Like the Shah's regime, the new government banned radical leftist groups and imprisoned their activists. Many faced summary execution during the crisis of the war with Iraq. For young Pari, joining the communist party is explained as a rational decision: "To me, as the daughter of an old leftist, choosing a radical communist party seemed reasonable" (Bashi 2009, 103). However, the haphazard nature of the choice is explicated in a panel in which the thirteen-year-old is plucking flower petals in order to choose her affiliation. The petals are inscribed with separate tags of "Fidelists, Marxists, Maoists, Socialists, Trotskyists, Reds, Leninists." She enthusiastically plucks out "Marxist Leninist."

She recounts the years of her early adolescence, spent chanting slogans of her party in the streets; engaging in fiery arguments with members of other groups, such as the Islamic Socialists, Mujahideen and the Islamic Republicans; participating in group discussions of the books "specified by their party's reading list"; partaking in fierce physical training and self-criticism; and preaching to immediate family members (figure 13). She obviously fails to carry out her commitments at such a tender age. Outside novels, she does not understand any of her party's choice books, including works on history, materialism, and revolutionary theory.

For the older Pari, "communist activities were a teenage fashion just like any other," to which the partisan answers: "The bourgeois class doesn't pay any price for following their class-based selfish desires. We paid a big price for being faithful to our ideology, for the people's sake. That is not a fashion" (Bashi 2009, 109). The older Pari corrects herself, saying that she is not "talking about true fighters" but about "teenagers" (111). Trying to prove her point, Bashi looks at three classes of people: the petit-bourgeois consumers of the latest fashion, self-sacrificing religious people, and teenage activists (figure 14). For Bashi, during adolescence fashion cults and political groups are comparable because they both need young consumers of their ideologies (figure 15). She concludes that: "No matter what cult you are involved in, anything that is dictated from above is garbage. The

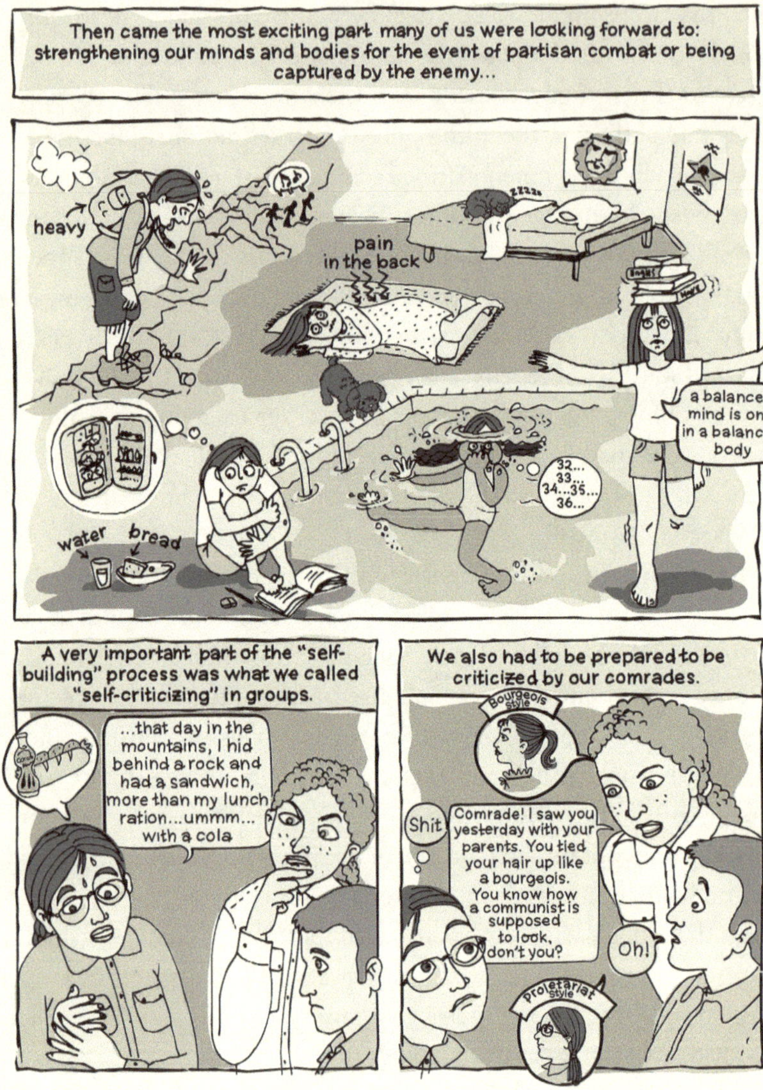

13. Pari training to become a young, leftist guerrilla fighter. From *Nylon Road* by Parsua Bashi. © 2006 Kein & Aber AG, Zurich-Berlin. *Nylon Road: A Graphic Memoir of Coming of Age in Iran* © 2009 by Parsua Bashi. Reprinted by permission of St. Martin's Griffin, an imprint of St. Martin's Press. All rights reserved. P. 106.

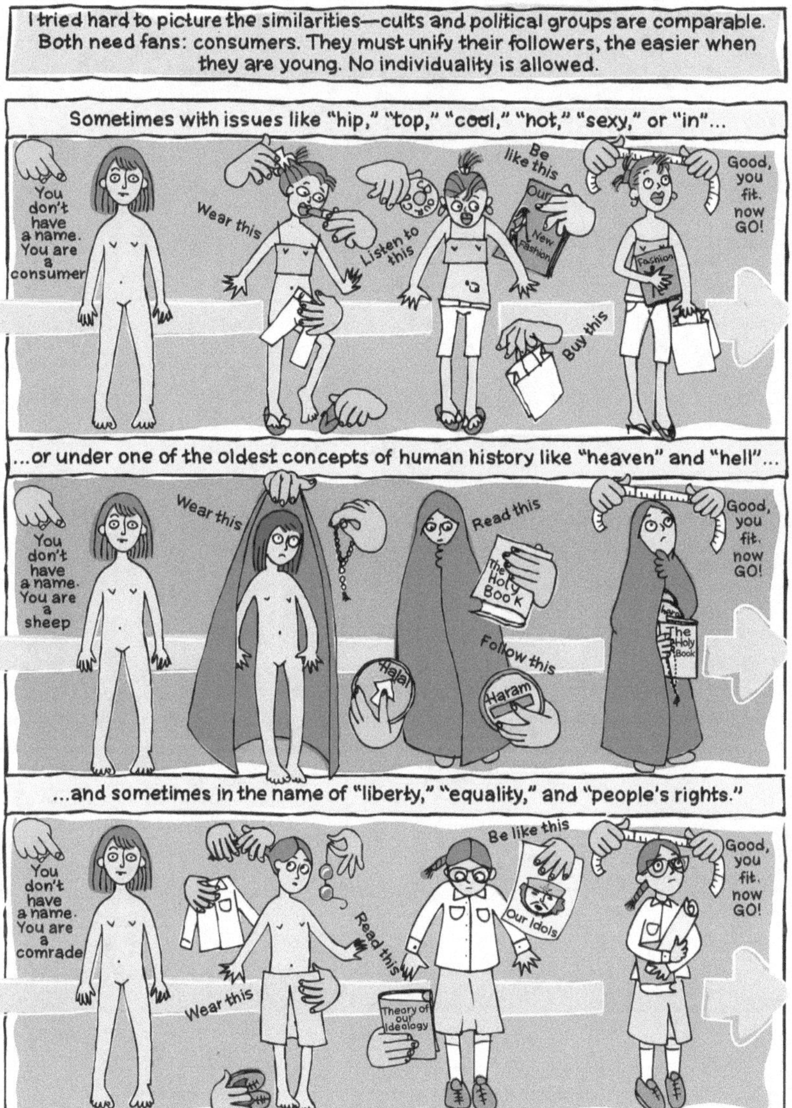

14. Comparing the cults of fashion, religion, and politics. From *Nylon Road* by Parsua Bashi. © 2006 Kein & Aber AG, Zurich-Berlin. *Nylon Road: A Graphic Memoir of Coming of Age in Iran* © 2009 by Parsua Bashi. Reprinted by permission of St. Martin's Griffin, an imprint of St. Martin's Press. P. 110.

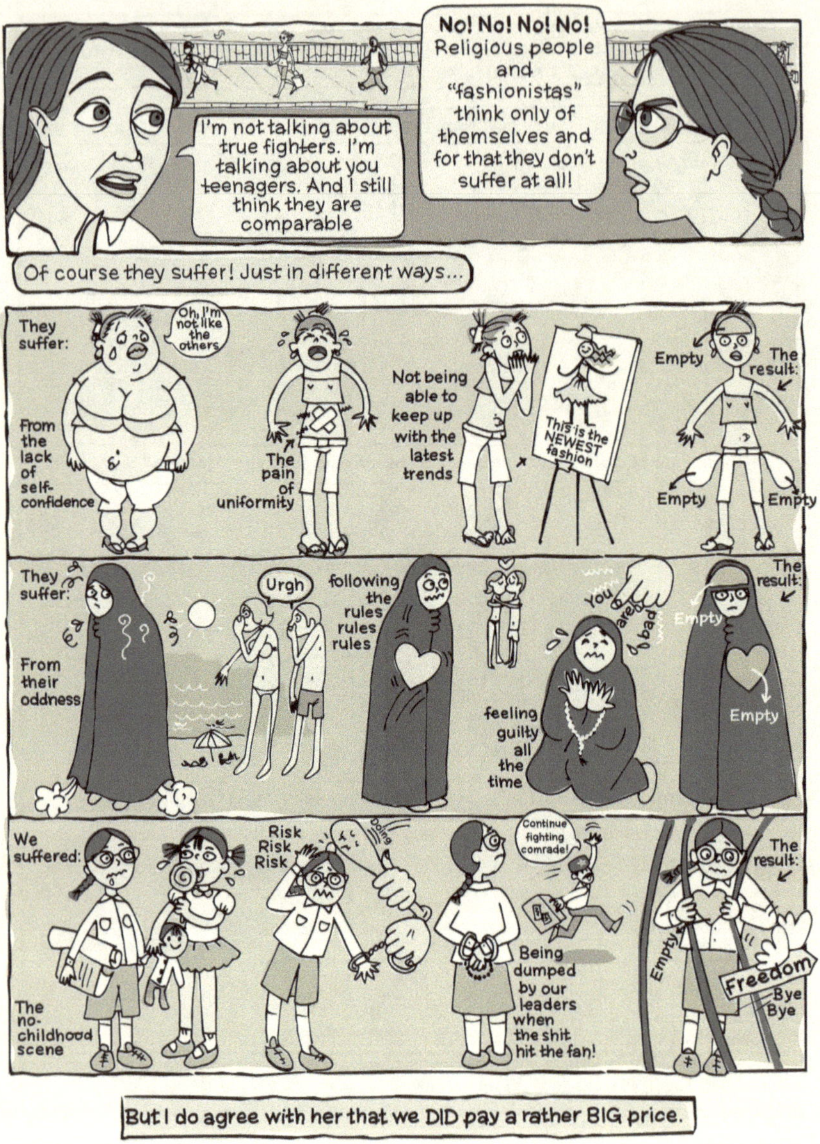

15. Similar outcomes for teenagers who follow cults. From *Nylon Road* by Parsua Bashi. © 2006 Kein & Aber AG, Zurich-Berlin. *Nylon Road: A Graphic Memoir of Coming of Age in Iran* © 2009 by Parsua Bashi. Reprinted by permission of St. Martin's Griffin, an imprint of St. Martin's Press. All rights reserved. P. 111.

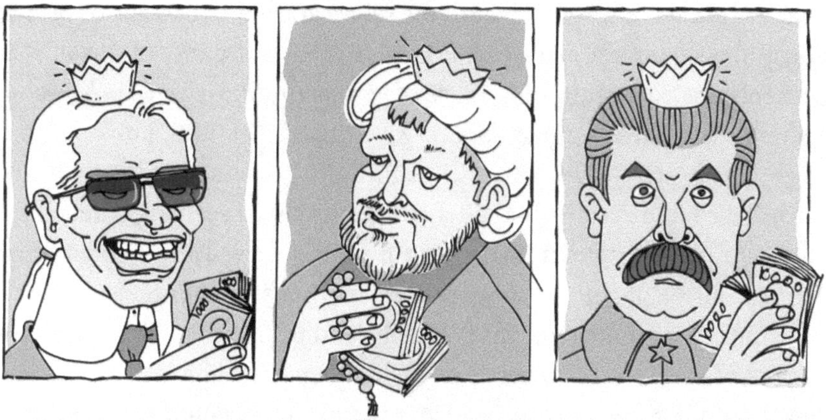

16. Cults of fashion, religion, and politics produce similarly wealthy leaders. From *Nylon Road* by Parsua Bashi. © 2006 Kein & Aber AG, Zurich-Berlin. *Nylon Road: A Graphic Memoir of Coming of Age in Iran* © 2009 by Parsua Bashi. Reprinted by permission of St. Martin's Griffin, an imprint of St. Martin's Press. All rights reserved. P. 112.

existence of the cult depends on the number of its followers. And do you know why? It's all about power and wealth" (112).

The inclusion of these two page-long panels is strategic. Although Bashi advocates agency as opposed to cult assimilation, the bottom of the second panel illuminates an internal lacuna in the argument, a moment of antinomy. It is only the activist child who is depicted as intelligent, the only one who has not lost her brain. Of the three representatives, the activist is the one most like Pari. It is the one she identifies with. Pari herself argues that the activist is brainwashed but refuses to void her mind. It can be argued that the teenage activist has been brainwashed into risking her life for a cause in which even the leaders of the movement do not believe (figure 16). The religious and the fashionista teens end up losing their brains, but the activist only loses her heart and possibly her freedom.

Diasporic Visual Self-Presentation

The importance of self-portrait cannot be stressed enough with regard to a book concerned with the position of self in diaspora, with characters that are almost entirely the author's selves at different stages of psychosocial development. Just as in *Persepolis*, the first panel of *Nylon Road* presents a self-portrait. In the case of *Persepolis*, Marji gazes boldly at the viewer with a direct, unapologetic gaze (figure 17). Pari, however, looks slightly upward (figure 18). Although both cartoon avatars are shown with their hands crossed in a defiant gesture, Pari seems less rebellious, more at ease in her situation. Appearing without a veil as a young woman, Pari exhibits a posture that references her almost comfortable status as a new immigrant outside Iran. While little Marji is veiled, she looks more recalcitrant and gazes directly at the audience while being cut off from her classmates. She stands out from the group. *Nylon Road* has several intertextual references to *Persepolis*. It even shows the protagonist reading *Persepolis* as an adult. However, from the start it appears that the book is not about the dilemmas of growing up in Iran. The entire book could be described as a self-portrait in which chronology plays the least important part. In *The Poetics of Literary Self-Portrait*, Michel Beaujour clarifies: "The operational formula for the [literary] self-portrait therefore is: 'I won't tell you what I've done, but I shall tell you *who I am*'" (1991, 3).

Nylon Road opens with a full-length image of a strong modern woman who has a barely noticeable smile, standing with arms crossed. The severity of the defiant crossed arms is in contrast to the coyness of the contrapposto stance. There is a tension between the laxity of the stance and the rigidity of the crossed arms, reflected in the eyes that slightly escape the direct gaze in order to look above and beyond. The same tension is carried out throughout the book as the author shifts her weight from one leg to another, from one perspective to another, and from one self to another. The protagonist's outfit is also significant. Except in one scene (depicted on the cover page of the American edition), she does not change her clothes throughout the book. This is strange for an author who is a self-proclaimed fashion designer and has written chapters on the link between fashion and politics, especially for Iranian women. She wears a simple white shirt and grayish blue pants, with walking shoes. Her outfit could be called gender-unspecific, middle-class, casual-modern. She wears no jewelry. In a personal email interview, Bashi explains the choice:

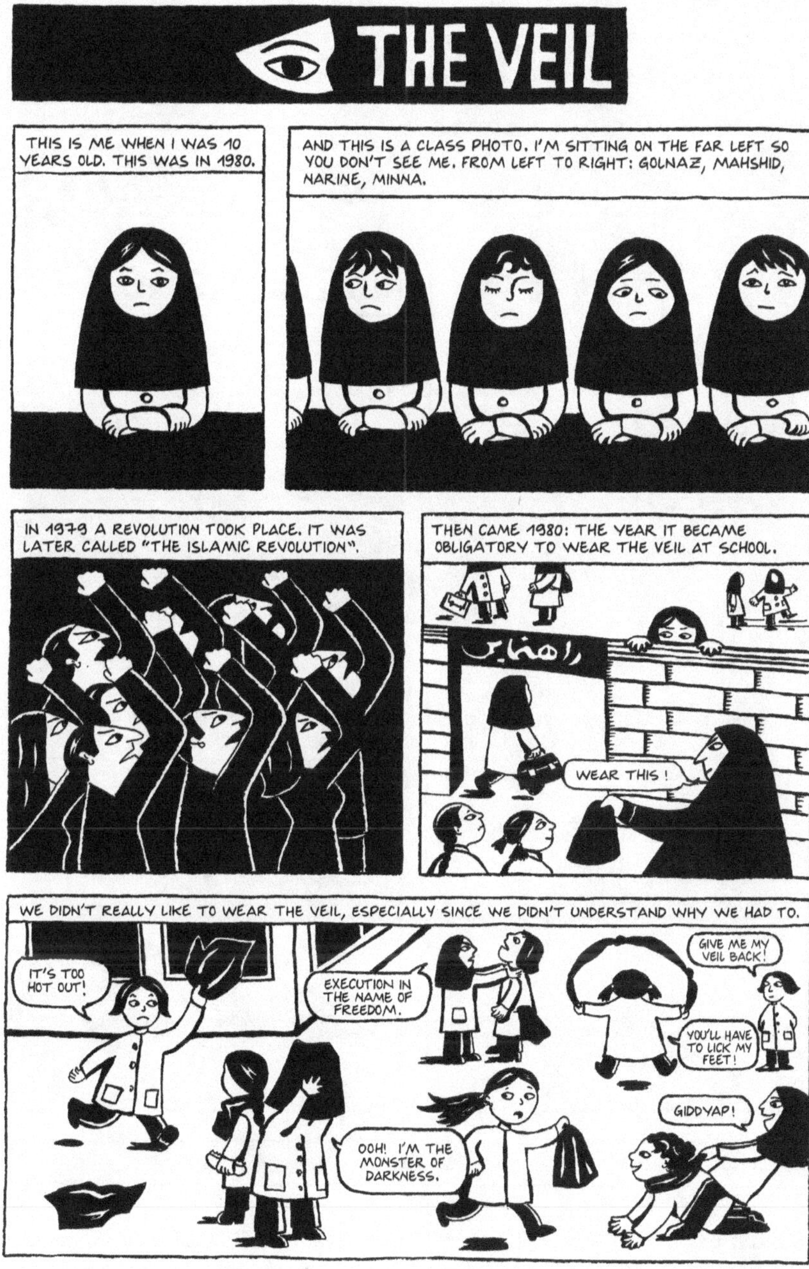

17. First panel from *Persepolis: The Story of a Childhood* by Marjane Satrapi, translation copyright © 2003 by L'Association, Paris, France. Used by permission of Pantheon Books, an imprint of the Knopf Doubleday Publishing Group, a division of Penguin Random House LLC. P. 3.

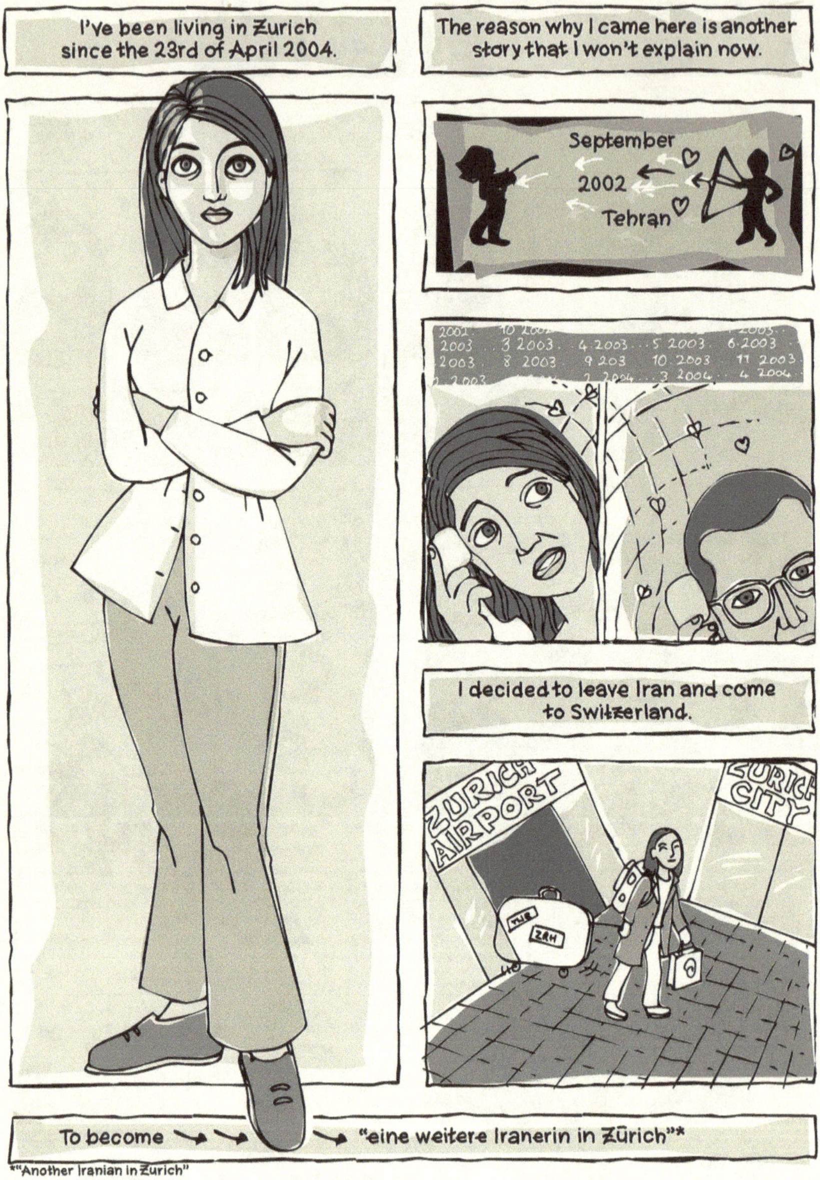

18. First panel from *Nylon Road* by Parsua Bashi. © 2006 Kein & Aber AG, Zurich-Berlin. *Nylon Road: A Graphic Memoir of Coming of Age in Iran* © 2009 by Parsua Bashi. Reprinted by permission of St. Martin's Griffin, an imprint of St. Martin's Press. All rights reserved. P. 1.

> As Iranian women, we are supposed to change our appearance according to circumstances. I have always fought with this mental and physical masquerading. In the streets, we are dressed according to the legal code, in order to fit among our fashionable co-workers we are supposed to follow artistic dress codes. Even in the circle of relatives, we are not supposed to exceed the norm: dressing down and wearing less make up will not do. We are supposed to fit-in and assimilate to the shifting settings. The same is true about our behaviour. I have paid a hefty price by escaping from these masks to appease this or that cult. . . . I have tried to be myself. (Parsua Bashi, email interview with author, December 2014)

Striving toward an uncomplicated dress code as the struggle toward a homogenous self fails nonetheless. The Iranian woman's body and its attire is the haunted territory of contested ideologies regarding gender, class, political affiliation, religious beliefs, and identity. Bashi tries but is unable to escape their grasp. The continual self-argumentations are only a hint at the impossibility of unifying the self, free of all ideological markups. The fluidity of the concept of self is reflected in the dichromatic water wash of the coloring style as well. The water color wash is soft and flowy. Bashi claims that she has adopted the two-colored tonality to facilitate an economical printing process—an unnecessary precaution, she adds.[3] Shades of ocher and gray fill the delicate outlines of the figures in *Nylon Road*. In contrast, *Persepolis*'s inking style is in blunt black and white with limited shading, marked by an absence of color or delicate lines; it is "simplified to amplify." Many of the clashing past selves never reconcile with the present Pari, and the book ends abruptly in the middle of her ponderings regarding a conclusion.

Nylon Road Conclusions

In *Nylon Road* the overpowering, self-effacing ethics leaves less room for aesthetic *repartage* in the visual memoir. Ethics as primarily a technology for self-correction is expounded through prolonged dialogues between

3. Email interview with the author, December 2015.

the present and past Pari. This relationship with the self does fill a gap in the Iranian memoir corpus. It gives the space and time to an Other perspective for voicing a dissensual argument—the very stuff of ushering in democracy through literature. Using the comic form, she animates lively discussions of controversial topics ranging from religion, politics, and jurisprudence to censorship in Iran and the West. However, the systematic autocritique prevents her from stepping outside self-argumentation to tell an intimate life story.

It is deeply ironic that the English paratext tries to sell the book by playing with the common stereotype of Islamic brutality against women, which Bashi argues against throughout the book. She differentiates between religion and the government's political manipulation of Islam and heeds the perils of generalization and demonization in Western media. *Nylon Road* presents a "persistent dredging operation" vital for works written by the new brigade of Iranian diasporic authors. It keeps reminding the critics and authors that they may not be free from what they criticize (Spivak 1999, 1). *Nylon Road* is self-therapeutic, in the words of the author, and perhaps that is why it is much less known and read than the other graphic narratives in this selection. It embodies a comprehensive critique of a generation of Iranian diasporic self-renditions without being a complete autobiography, memoir, or full-length manifesto.

Part Two

Diasporic Iranian Visual Literature Manifested in the Art of Shirin Neshat

Photo-Poetry and Poetic Film

The second part of this book moves on from the medium of graphic novels produced by women of the Iranian diaspora to Shirin Neshat's photography and film. Her art speaks the ancient language of visual icons, signs, enchanted gazes, and inhabitable realms of phantasmescapes and dreams. Although unabashedly mediated, her photographic point-blank subjects depict the face and body of the Other, with its incorrigible difference dangerously close-up. Neshat's art reaches a poetic minimalism that functions through allusions, elision, and collage. To explain this, I put her feature film *Women without Men* in dialogue with Shahrnush Parsipur's eponymous novel and Forough Farrokhzad's short documentary film *The House Is Black*. This way I delimit the confluence of politics with ethics and aesthetic play in Neshat's abstract art.

The age of terror has been brought to the domestic space of the Western world through images. Images of violence and distant traumas abound in the popular imagination, but not all incite a sense of curiosity, attention, and response-ability. Neshat's images can bring the poetry of radical alterity to intimate proximities in order to foster an ethical bond with her subjects. What is it in their aesthetics that makes this possible? To answer this question I first survey the way photographic images, in contrast to other media, represent the trauma of the Other. I explore how the medium relays affect, awakens a response, and possibly reproduces the hegemonic discourse. In a quick review, I grapple with concepts such as photography's clutch on truth, the ethics of representation of alterity, photography's inherent violence, and the politics of space as well as skin.

I want to test the power of Neshat's images to create a shared community of humanity, even a small one. After the brief familiarization with the nature of photographs, or what Susan Sontag calls "memory freeze frames" (2003, 22), I take a closer look at Neshat's early photographic oeuvre, which depicts Muslim women, guns, and veils with a unique aesthetic poetry. I look specifically at one of her untitled photos that superimposes poetry onto the hand of a woman in order to consider the extent to which the complex net of signification of another nation can be transferred via the medium of photo-poetry. For this face-to-face encounter with the armed yet alluring Muslim woman, I consult Emmanuel Levinas. His ethics stares into the naked face of the Other, a face that shivers with excessive exposure and vulnerability. This gaze into the vulnerable, naked face of the Other urges violence, according to him, while also beckoning ethical responsibility.

Moving from graphic novels to photography and film, I wonder whether photographs still hold a degree of authenticity that aids them in bringing humans closer to one another. Because commercial images have had a certain clutch on truth, audiences have lost faith in finding truth in images. Images of violence have been dubbed intolerable so audiences avert their gaze, or have been ignored as advertisements. For an image that depicts the trauma of an Other to receive its due attention, a fresh approach to the concept of distant traumas is required.

What regime of representation can be used to show the misery of Others in which we might be complicit, even through our silence or lack of imagination? I believe that the cause for the failure of imagination is not public apathy; it is rather the way that the artists have chosen to represent trauma. For images of atrocities to hold the world's imagination, they have to use regimes of aesthetic representation in order to awaken a deep-seated curiosity regarding alterity. With reality shows, round-the-clock news coverage of decontextualized war footage, and the advertisement industry competing to sell their version of truth, images have started to lose their ability to shock and awe or to inspire curiosity, attention, and imagination. Even gory footage of civilian casualties is treated with either skepticism or an averted gaze ("The world is full of misery so I don't need to know more"). Aesthetics, on the other hand, as a reconfiguration of common space, can do more than de/familiarize us with those who suffer. Images by Shirin Neshat, for example, bring the radical Other—the armed Muslim Woman—to point-blank immediacy, demanding an engagement through the faculty of imagination, beckoning an encounter, a response-ability. Her art is not documentary, but intimate and metaphoric. This engagement of the imagination by the artist may be more useful for the world than the media's bombardment with images of violence. With media desensitization, can the cult of the image be the catalyst of an aesthetic *repartage*?

Creating a Virtual Community of Humanity by Disseminating Images that Incite Curiosity and Attention

We are living in an era of the hegemony of images. Ocularcentrism, or the domination of sight, prevails over our private and public sense of identity. Visual communication has been called a democratic means of connecting world spectators who are divided by language, geography, and social class. Images seem to need no translation or even literacy. The terrors and traumas of distant Others reach us through images. Sharon Sliwinski argues that images of atrocities regarded by world spectators during the past two hundred years have created a shared understanding of human rights violations in the world. Humanity is connected through the dispersion of such images: "Humanity is not simply given but rather exists only as a precarious, virtual community brought into being, in part, through our grappling with world events at a distance—in camera" (2011, 144).

Sliwinski revisits several historical sites where the attention, recognition, imagination of world spectators have advanced the formation of a virtual community. She points to the first great human rights intervention—that of the Congo Reform Association in reaction to the abuses of Belgium's King Leopold II. This first alignment of witnesses around the world was instigated by what Sliwinski recognizes as images of violence viewed from afar.

Critical distance is necessary for ethical imagination. It is the nature of trauma to disrupt vision. Cathy Caruth calls the failure of vision in grasping trauma "the ceaseless betrayal of bodily sight" (1996, 50). Our psychological defense mechanisms prevent access to the moment of unbearable pain. Photographs of atrocities as "memory freeze frames" (Sontag 2003) can bypass those defense mechanisms and create a novel engagement with terror. The safe distance of an image and the absence or presence of violence contained in the frame allow for the working of the faculty of judgment.

The fascination with gazing at violent, excessive imagery of ecstatic bodies in pain or pleasure is a recurring motif in the visual arts and literature. For Sontag, "It seems that the appetite for pictures showing bodies in pain is as keen, almost, as the desire for ones that show bodies naked. For many centuries, in Christian art, depictions of hell offered both of these elemental satisfactions" (2003, 41). Violence performed to the imagination through representation of the unrepresentable has been a long-standing subject of inquiry for philosophers. It is the distance from this violence that allows the intellect to grapple with it and overcome it. Aesthetic photography provides this safe distance of contemplation.

A Greek rhetorician, Pseudo-Longinus, has been credited with the first conceptualization of the sublime in literature. He looks at writing as the gateway to great conceptions that lead to transcendental pleasure. While for him the ecstasy of the sublime leads to a loss of reason, Kant categorizes the sublime as a "twofold mode of representing an object" (2007, 78). In the Kantian sublime, in order for the "negative pleasure" to arise, the engagement with the sublime should be performed from a safe distance; otherwise aesthetic judgment cannot crystalize. This double process of attaining rational pleasure through a painful tear in the imagination is envisioned thus:

> The feeling of the sublime is a pleasure that only arises indirectly, being brought about by the feeling of a momentary check to the vital forces followed at once by a discharge all the more powerful, and so it is an emotion that seems to be no play, but a serious matter in the exercise of the imagination. . . . Since the mind is not simply attracted by the object, but is also alternately repelled thereby, the delight in the sublime does not

> so much involve positive pleasure as admiration or respect, but it merits the name of a negative pleasure. (75–76)

Standing against the sublime, violence is done to the imagination as it reaches its limits. The subject gasps. There is an initial feeling of terror in the idea's utter unrepresentability to the faculty of imagination. It is the mind that recognizes this supersensible fissure. Imagination flutters and fails to perceive the magnitude of horror. Some critics have taken up this failure of imagination as a complete failure of the human ability to represent trauma. Many believe that in the face of absolute terror, language completely halts, imagination withers, and the tongue stutters. For me the failure to narrate a cohesive tale can provoke the onrush of powerful feelings and a reaching out through other creative means. Kant considers "imagination itself as an instrument of reason"—one that refines thought (2007, 99). The sublime points toward the power of the mind to hatch and grow toward a higher purposiveness.

However, to consider the sublime an arrest of imagination in front of the unrepresentable does not do justice to the creative judgment of the spectator. For Jacques Rancière the unrepresentable is a function of terror. Everything is representable, he insists, yet the regimes of making present define the contours of the politics of aesthetics. Speaking against the utter unrepresentability of the Holocaust, he claims:

> It is because everything is representable, and that nothing separates fictional representation from the presentation of reality, that the problem of presenting the genocide arises. This problem is not to know whether or not one can or must represent, but to know what one wants to represent and what mode of representation is appropriate to this end. (Rancière and Corcoran 2015, 196)

The silence and stutter that accompany an encounter with the Lacanian Real can give way to "a discharge all the more powerful" of "vital forces" (Kant 2007, seg. 23). The "ceaseless betrayal of bodily sight" (Caruth 1996) in the face of terror can be doted on from afar through aesthetically playful images that engage the faculty of imagination and reason, and thus bypass defense mechanisms against distant dilemmas.

Images of atrocities have stopped engaging the cultural imagination of Western audiences. Presented with raw footage of violence, the generic response is to express incredulousness or to look the other way. According to Rancière, this aversion is due to the lack of an appropriate aesthetic regime for representing atrocities. Analyzing a collage by Martha Rosler, "Bringing the War Home," in which a dead Vietnamese child is superimposed over a comfortable middle-class house, Rancière analyzes the elitist method of displaying Others' sufferings. Rosler gives the viewer the question and the answer on the same page. She chooses a regime of representation in which the engaged artist dictates: This is how you are supposed to feel, guilty of living in a luxurious house while children are being killed. Such a view of world spectators as an ignorant mass waiting for the wisdom of the artist to translate world events is against Rancière's belief in the equality of intelligence. If the artist tries to raise curiosity as opposed to trying to enforce guilt, the artwork might engage the spectator's imagination more actively.

This is one of the pitfalls of committed art; it presupposes that audiences are ignorant and that emancipatory ideals should be dictated to them. Artists believe that by forcing audiences to view violent, gory images, they can force them to understand the sordid state of the world. However, presenting intolerable images is not the way to awaken public empathy. On the other hand, aesthetics and its playful regimes of representation can help.

In a chapter named "The Intolerable Image" Rancière contends that depictions of raw violence are either decontextualized, clouded by the voice of experts, or devoid of the voices of victims, and thus rarely awaken real engagement in the audience:

> The stock reaction to [intolerable] images is to close one's eyes or to avert the gaze. Presenting an image of a traumatic incident does not guarantee or necessitate the "understanding" on the part of the viewer of the historico-political context of the world affairs that have led to such injustices. They do not even imply the viewer's sense of implication in the atrocities committed in the photo since in order for that to happen, the viewer must already feel guilty about standing there, in front of an image of trauma, and doing nothing about it. (2009b, 85)

For the Kantian faculty of judgment to function, the attention and curiosity of the viewer must be incited through an aesthetic regime of representation, one that is fluid, poetical, and playful. It is not that there is no engaged art. Art can be engaged without being fascistic. A dictatorial art is based on an elitist binary: I, the intellectual, will school the ignorant masses about the shame of capitalism. An aesthetic regime of representation does not dictate an affect but incites "curiosity and attention" in the audience:

> I speak here of curiosity and . . . attention. These are in fact affects that blur the false obviousness of strategic schemata; they are dispositions of the body and the mind where the eye does not know in advance what it sees and thought does not know what it should make of it. Their tension also points towards a different politics of the sensible—a politics based on the variation of distance, the resistance of the visible and the uncertainty of effect. Images change our gaze and the landscape of the possible if they are not anticipated by their meaning and do not anticipate their effects. (Rancière 2009b, 104–5)

This curiosity and attention, this negotiation of proximity and distance, are absent in the media's widespread dissemination of images of atrocities. Meaning is spoon-fed to the spectators by the omniscient voice of the expert or the embedded journalist. But spectators are not clean slates. Without an active engagement of the faculty of imagination, the possibility for the creation of a shared community of humanity diminishes. What Rancière is battling here is visual domination that dictates the message of the image. Images of violence disseminated in the news without a historical context or voices of the victims or witnesses are prone to the averted-gaze phenomenon. This defense mechanism is rather recent and rose with the spike in the appeal of images.

Only recently has humanity been able to visually witness distant crimes. In ancient times oral narratives of the elders, as well as epic poetry, were reminders of crimes against humanity. Those who survived a genocide and witnessed a conquering army burning the libraries and building bridges of the defeated army's skulls would tell of the plight of their people to others via tall tales. To this day epic poetry that is memorized and narrated feistily in the tea houses in Iran is a remnant of the classical communication and survival techniques.

The *Shahnameh*, or "Book of Kings," composed in AD 1010 by the wise Ferdowsi, is the oral history of Persia in epic verse. It visually, through miniature drawings, as well as verbally envisages wars, conquests, and the love lives of Iranian nobles from antiquity to the Arab invasion in the seventh century. The polymath's approximately 100,000-line poem revived the Persian language and invigorated a sense of Persian nationalism during those turbulent years. The *Shahnameh* has been compared with the Odyssey because its ancient songs capture the spirit of a nation.

The Book of Kings is the name of one of Neshat's photographic installations that appeared in the aftermath of the 2009 popular revolt. In the installation she visits Iranians' faces point-blank and inks their bodies with scenes of the people's historical resistance against conquering armies. Neshat superimposes the historical struggle of the people of Iran over the bodies of modern Iranian subjects who are currently battling against the oppressive regime (figure 19). She does not equate the two but hears echoes from the forgotten battles of what this resilient nation has endured in current-day Iran. In the photomontage, tenth-century epic poetry

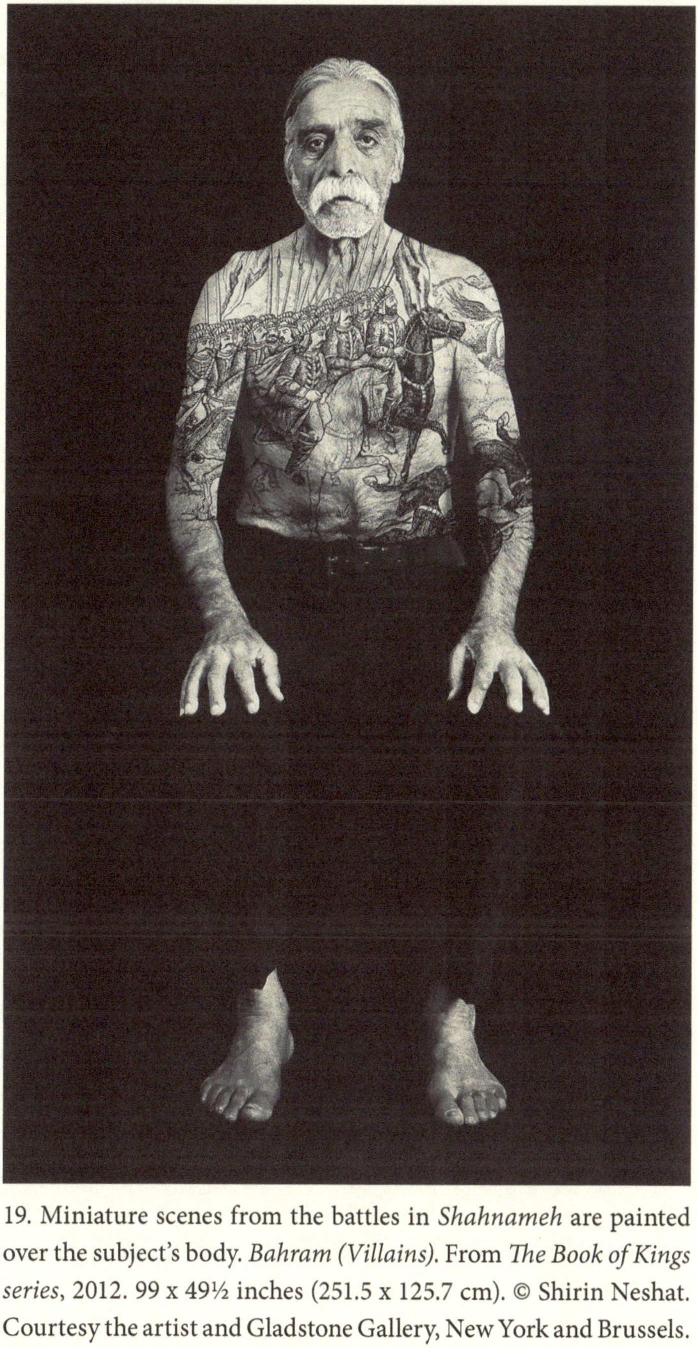

19. Miniature scenes from the battles in *Shahnameh* are painted over the subject's body. *Bahram (Villains)*. From *The Book of Kings series*, 2012. 99 x 49½ inches (251.5 x 125.7 cm). © Shirin Neshat. Courtesy the artist and Gladstone Gallery, New York and Brussels.

enchants twenty-first century subjects in an aesthetically playful manner. The subject could be read at once as political, aesthetic, and ethical. Neshat, as usual, asks questions without answering them, leaving space for viewers' imagination, identification, and curiosity.[1] For those who are strictly interested in the question of politics, the truth in images is of prime importance. What truth does the photography of Neshat convey?

Although epic poetry has not lost its purchase in the Iranian tradition, modernity brought a different spectacle to the attention of the world. For Sontag, being a spectator of catastrophes taking place in another country is "a quintessential modern experience, the cumulative offering by more than a century and a half's worth of those professional, specialized tourists known as journalists" (2003, 18). With images, the wound is felt immediately, viscerally. But how true can this distant pain be?

Truth in Images

Whether shocking or not, images are relatively unbound by complexities of language in translation. The modern spectator sitting comfortably before a screen is bombarded by images. Equipped with a remote control, a mouse, or a bag of popcorn, the spectator is anything but a clean slate, a quiet consumer. The images are diverse: advertisements, entertainment, news, bodies in pain or in pleasure. Although the advertisement industry has become more sophisticated at creating and rearranging desire, the human mind is not a tabula rasa to be imprinted by ads. The complex ability of the human being to connect, empathize, and imagine differently can soar above the Hollywood brouhaha by using the faculties of

1. Reading the poems about national defense, courage, and honesty closely and relating them to current-day events of the country is another feat that an intrepid researcher can accomplish. It does not fit the scope of this research, however.

imagination and reason. The usually safe spectator goes through this "quintessential modern experience" of peering into distant dilemmas with different eyes, voyeuristic, incredulous, skeptical, truth-seeking.

The messy entanglement of photography with journalistic truth has urged a retreat from aesthetically pleasing photography: if it is truthful it should not be beautiful. The "shady commerce between art and truth" (Sontag 1977, 4) has penalized the aesthetically pleasing in favor of what is perceived to be the raw, rugged, naked truth. But what are these truths for which we dismiss images of atrocities?

> Truths are illusions about which one has forgotten their origins; metaphors which are worn out and without sensuous power; coins which have lost their pictures and now matter only as metal, no longer as coins.
>
> We still do not know where the urge for truth comes from; for as yet we have heard only of the obligation imposed by society that it should exist. (Nietzsche 1968, 46–7)

This quote by Nietzsche points to human beings' metaphorical understanding of truth. It is always salutary to remember that truth can be truth claims, limited by frames and circumstances. The quest for truth in images is ubiquitous. I do not deny the urgency of presenting atrocities, but I call on aesthetics not to shy away from fulfilling this responsibility in an ethical manner, one that does not compromise the intelligence of the viewer or try to sell guilt.

Photographs dutifully witness and function as evidence. This might be because, as Sontag contends, "Photographed images do not seem to be statements about the world so much as pieces of it, miniatures of reality that anyone can make or acquire" (1977, 2). With its claim to truth content and mimetic honesty, photography has become a witness to the traumas of modernity and documentation of the inhumanity of the human animal, lest we forget. Photographs' quality of being traces, pieces of the real, and "radiations of life" makes claims of authenticity. This is the case even though each image is framed in a subjective perspective, cropped and focused, foreclosing the rest of the visible landscape. This intrinsic battle between the objectivity and subjectivity of photography is its existential double bind. "Photographs had the advantage of uniting two contradictory features. Their credentials of objectivity were inbuilt. Yet they always had, necessarily, a point of view" (Sontag 2003, 26).

The truth that an artistic photograph emanates is not a juridical one. It is a truth of the essence of time concentrated in a gaze, an eternal memento mori, an air. Without the superimposition of a master narrative, a meaning, or a message, the selected images in this part of the book speak with the ancient language of visual icons, signs, enchanted gazes, and inhabitable landscapes of imagination.

Ethics in Images: Levinas and the Danger in the Other's Face

Although unabashedly mediated, Neshat's frontal, point-blank images in the *Women of Allah* collection bring the face and body of the Other, with its incorrigible difference, dangerously close up. With Levinas I face radical alterity in Neshat's self/portrait photography. His philosophy of the face is useful in coming into contact with Neshat's Muslim women with guns. Levinas famously accounts for the face of the Other as the nakedness that beckons a deep-seated violence in us. We are stopped by an internal ethical interdiction: "Thou shalt not kill." That first instinct for violence is checked only by an ethical call for peace when we encounter the vulnerable face of the Other:

> The proximity of the other is the face's meaning, and it means from the very start in a way that goes beyond those plastic forms, which forever try to cover the face like a mask of their presence to perception. But always the face shows through

> these forms. Prior to any particular expression which cover over and protect with an immediately adopted face or countenance, there is the nakedness and destitution of the expression as such, that is to say extreme exposure, defencelessness, vulnerability itself. This extreme exposure—prior to any human aim—is like a shot "at point blank range." . . . From the beginning there is a face to face steadfast in its exposure to invisible death, to a mysterious forsakenness. Beyond the visibility of whatever is unveiled, and prior to any knowledge about death, mortality lies in the other. (Levinas 1989, 82–83)

It is useful to gaze back at self/portraits with an understanding of the ethical implications that this extreme exposure entails. The face (or the body) here is a synecdoche of the self and of being. In the Levinas oeuvre, the face is naked, destitute, defenseless, vulnerable, and mortal, exposed to an "invisible death," to "a mysterious forsakenness." Portraiture of radical Others are suitable venues to test the urge for destruction and violence that Levinas bemoans, and the terror that resides in the world. The photograph initially distances us because it is a foreign object, a flat representation of what is assumed to be reality, so even before we grapple with the photograph's content we are confronted by its own strangeness in an uncanny way.[2] On a slightly different angle from Levinas, I believe that when we gaze at the eyes of the Other, it takes but a split second to identify with or disengage from their alterity. The image, with or without its plastic features, emits clues that demarcate our distance from or proximity to the Other: gender, race, age, social class, air, attire. It is the proximity or distance from which we locate our subjectivity that triggers or neutralizes the initial urge for combat.

For Levinas, the urge to harm is hampered by the ethics of responsibility. This responsibility toward alterity is a demand, a

2. Thanks to Tim Blackmore for suggesting this connection.

fact, a bond. "An ethical philosophy of responsibility grounded in the phenomenology of the face" is a central concern for him (1994, 3). He quotes Dostoyevsky as saying: "We are all responsible for all for all men before all, and I more than all the others" (in Levinas 1985, 101). This sense of ethical responsibility for the Other, which is not a reciprocity, is a primary and fundamental structure of subjectivity:

> I speak of responsibility as the essential, primary and fundamental structure of subjectivity. For I describe subjectivity in ethical terms. Ethics, here, does not supplement a preceding existential base; the very node of the subjective is knotted in ethics understood as responsibility. I understand responsibility as responsibility for the Other, thus as responsibility for what is not my deed. (Levinas 1985, 95)

Image and Death

In her last monograph, published in 2003 before her death from cancer, Sontag wrote: "Ever since cameras were invented in 1839, photography has kept company with death" (24). Portraits, specifically, manage to freeze an instant in time, while the source of that radiation ages or dies. Those photographed faces, nonetheless, become sockets of affect and temporality.

Photography is a gift from advances in technology. Walter Benjamin cautiously hails the advent of new technology and the mass accessibility of the arts, claiming that they are freeing humanity from its dependence on ritual function, religion or superstitious cults:

> For the first time in world history, mechanical reproduction emancipates the work of art from its parasitical dependence on ritual. . . . But the instant the criterion of authenticity ceases to be applicable to artistic production, the total function of art is reversed. Instead of being based on ritual, it begins to be based on another practice—politics. (Benjamin 1969, 6)

However, the religious, the magical, even the auratic, did not just melt away with the advent of photography. Benjamin himself attests to this: "For the last time the aura emanates from the early photographs in the fleeting expression of a human face. This is what constitutes their melancholy, incomparable beauty" (1969, 7). So, the face, or the gaze, can be the repertoire of magic, aura, air, or ritual, despite the photographic battle with authenticity. Regarding the portrait of loved ones kept close at hand, Sontag believed: "all such talismanic uses of photographs express a feeling both sentimental and implicitly magical" (2003, 12). Neshat's photographic faces bring together the religious and the magical, the violent and the aesthetic.

Punctum and *Studium* in Neshat's Photography

The evocative, or rather provocative texture of Neshat's art stems from its capacity to present a simple archaic binary and at the same time to shatter it into a million fragments with an aesthetic *punctum*. Standing still in front of her oeuvre, armed with theory, stigmas, or suspicions, the spectator is drawn in by the familiar, minimalistic dialectic of all her favorite universal binaries: man/woman, life/death, black/white, private/public, illusion/reality, beauty/violence. All of a sudden a different plane of cognition, a detail, an anomaly, pierces the visual/audial field, which playfully and teasingly subverts and displaces the hierarchies established by the ancient dichotomy. It shakes the firm ground under the viewer's feet, disarms the critics, and shuttles the viewer from the comfortable familiarity of the known to the uncanny strangeness of nightmares, or daydreams of a collective, affective, unconscious.

I borrow the Greek term *punctum* from Roland Barthes's phenomenological reading of photography in *Camera Lucida*. Like all borrowed tools, it is modified slightly so it fits within my purview. Barthes describes the *punctum* as a "sting, speck, cut, little hole—and also a cast of the dice. A photograph's *punctum* is that accident which pricks me (but also bruises me, is poignant to me)" (2012,

27, emphasis in original). The spectator's position within a specific cultural milieu, her personal investment, and a repository of cultural imagination will aid her in finding a unique, piercing *punctum*. The distinctive function of this detail, which in my reading is on a different plane of the sensible (as found in poetry, aesthetics, self/portrait, and music), is that it carries the spectator and the art beyond: "The *punctum*, then, is a kind of subtle *beyond*—as if the image launched desire beyond what it permits us to see: not only toward 'the rest' of the nakedness, not only toward the fantasy of a praxis, but toward the absolute excellence of a being, body and soul together" (Barthes 2012, 59, emphasis in original).

In Barthes's lexicon, the *studium*—the subject matter—can be jarring in many images, but it cannot necessarily wound the affective unconscious.

> The *studium* is that very wide field of unconcerned desire, of various interest, of inconsequential taste: *I like / I don't like*. The *studium* is of the order of *liking*, not of *loving*; it mobilizes a half desire, a demi-volition; it *is* the same sort of vague, slippery, irresponsible interest one takes in the people, the entertainments, the books, the clothes one finds "all right." (27)

The *studium* is deliberate, culturally specific, coded. It pleases or displeases without "pricking." The spectator glances through loud images of violence quickly, averting the gaze here, moving on. But piercing images linger with the viewer long after the eyes are shut. Their imprint burns on the affective unconscious a negative that—just like an encounter with the Real—demands re-vision. This encounter with the uncanny asks questions, beckoning a reply. Neshat's art does not spit back a regurgitated answer to the viewer. After all, it is my eyes that re-view the vibrating superimposed planes of reality. "I refuse to inherit anything from another eye than my own" (Barthes 2012, 51).

3

Shirin Neshat's Political(ized) Aesthetics

This chapter brings the visual art of Shirin Neshat under critical attention. Neshat's subjects shuttle between symbols of femininity, violence, eroticism, and poetry in order to parcel out a new humanity for the represented Muslim woman. In the words of Audre Lorde, Neshat "gives name to the nameless" to imagine alterity anew, to change our gaze and envision a different landscape for ethics (Lorde 2007, 36). In a face-to-face encounter and through an excessive exposure to Neshat's mysterious women, a rearrangement of desire occurs that can crush notions of proximity and distance with alterity.

When we are in contact with radical alterity at point blank, Emmanuel Levinas reminds us about an ethical philosophy of responsibility. The distance from which we locate our subjectivity against the Other triggers or neutralizes the initial urge to combat. Aesthetics, politics, and ethics can reverse and readjust problematic hierarchies and partitions that we draw with the one outside the self. Inscribed over Neshat's women's bodies is the material history of Iran in its condensed form. Their photographed bodies become "the inscribed surface of events" (Foucault 1998, 83), glowing with poetry, violence, seduction, enigmas, and religion as well as myths.

In this chapter I look at Neshat's controversial debut photographic collection, *Women of Allah*, and then I move to her feature film *Women without Men* in the following chapter. I argue that through the work of Neshat, the Other is brought to a face-to-face encounter that beckons an ethical response-ability. Inspired by Levinas, I consider Neshat's intimacy with the radical Other through self/portraiture a daring move that "objectifies in order to subjectify" (Barthes 2012). What distances her work from claims of tokenism and kitschiness are the aesthetic regimes with which she superimposes layers of verbal and visual poetry in a way that annuls the possibility of fixing a quick prejudice or meaning over the work. The photographs and poetry instigate curiosity and attention regarding an aesthetic world with which we are unfamiliar. Neshat's subjects violently traffic between Eastern and Western iconography, tradition and modernity, religion and superstition, conformity and revolt. The binaries are strategically and playfully drawn to be shattered.

Shirin Neshat's artistic and actual personas occupy an irreconcilable paradox. On the one hand, as a charismatic cult figure she is one of the few artists who continually challenge, critique, and analyze their own work, impelling themselves to move from one visual medium to another. On the other hand, as a public speaker she resorts to the grand and bland tales of Muslim women's subjugation. Her masterful adoption of aesthetic regimes of representation confuses and plays with easy binaries and dichotomies regarding agency and subjecthood.

When I first attended one of Neshat's popular public speeches on the binaries between Western and Muslim women, I immediately thought of those native informants who "identify a middle-class readership and then pander skillfully to its whims" (Holland and Huggan 1998, viii) and cash in on what I call a first-world compassion industry. Her speech seems contradictory to her artwork. What she says fortifies the very binaries that she dismantles in her artwork. But tagging her as a native informant does not do justice to her multifaceted artwork. Of course, the concept of native informant as delineated by Gayatri Spivak is not an alien one with regard to Iranian diaspora artists in general. There are quite a few Iranian authors who, by holding a distorted mirror up to the narcissistic, paranoid cultural imagination of their target audience, faithfully reproduce the fears and anxieties about generic terrorists that have already been instilled in the popular imagining through coercion and consent.

Native informants can definitely produce "an effective alibi for the perpetuation or reinstallment of ethnocentrically superior attitudes to 'other' cultures, peoples, and places," ab/using "the defamiliarizing capacities of travel writing" (Holland and Huggan 1998, viii). I consider Marina Nemat's

Prisoner of Tehran and Azar Nafisi's *Reading Lolita in Tehran* as such examples in that they use the selfsame rhetoric against Islam as the American propaganda and war machine. Both authors, coming from elite, upper-middle-class families, are alienated from the concerns of their population and uphold a white feminist framework for understanding the situation in Iran. Not a few of such works have proved manna for the warmongers in the government. Politicians take up such rhetoric as proof of the righteousness of their paranoid attitudes against the new Other of the West: the Muslim terrorist, a term that mistakes religion for political dispute.

Spivak does not shy away from implicating herself as the object of her own critique. She dockets a "class apartheid," in which cultures of class and access to discourse are often more important than East/West coordinates (2013b, 27). Spivak borrows the problematic term *native informant* from ethnography to describe a person who is given the space and time to speak on behalf of her ethnic group or nation. This is typically done for the benefit of Western audiences. The term denotes informants from the third-world diaspora who are living in the West. Spivak cautions against making marginality fashionable and against putting the native informant's voice on a pedestal as representative of an ethnic minority. As a plethora of other critics after Spivak have noted, if ethnicity is used as a token or a badge, it runs the risk of essentializing one's ethnic identity and romanticizing national origins.

It was in this spirit of disdain that I first beheld Neshat's now renowned photographs, videographic installations, and feature film. However, the poetics of her visual world transformed my judgment. In the words of Levinas, she brings the Other into a face-to-face encounter in such a way that one enters into an ethical discourse with those who may have been excluded from the domain of the human. This address to an Other is the condition that makes discourse, even language, possible. On the other hand, she puts the realm of the poetic in juxtaposed visibility with the visual. The interstice creates a different dimension for the toppling of fixed hierarchies. As a multifaceted artist Neshat has access to the "hermetically sealed culture" (Dabashi 2003, 936) of Persia and possesses the artistry to bring that sealed culture to visibility in the globalizing market of art.

Born in the small town of Ghazvin, Iran, in 1957, Neshat left the country at the age of seventeen on the advice of her physician father, who had a preference for Western education systems. Even in Iran she attended a Catholic boarding school away from home in Tehran, which led to her lifelong battle with anorexia. Almost six years before the Revolution of 1979, she left Iran for the United States. When she returned decades later, she was shocked at the post-Revolutionary atmospheric change. This homecoming shock was condensed visually for her in the new Islamic dress codes, the war propaganda, and the skewed relationship between the sexes. Not only had she missed out on the blooming of a nation into a body of dissent against the monarch, she also did not witness how an internationally isolated country had to battle against Iraq and the world, using aesthetic means of gaining public support. What wasn't her unique style "wasn't just the revolution," she clarifies. "It was all these years of war with Iraq, . . . years of grief. . . . In a very strange way I was envious of them. . . . In looking at how profound their experience had been, I felt so very much an outsider and so stupidly narcissistic" (Enright and Walsh 2009).

Neshat had escaped the terrorizing as well as enchanting war years. This enchantment came from a sense of belonging to a national community that only a war or national trauma can foster—the sense of belonging to a unique society for which you are willing to give up your life. She did fortunately miss the bombardment by Saddam's planes over cities in Iran. But with that she also missed the war chants and icons that incited the youth to kill or be killed in order to defend the motherland. She missed the women taking up arms in the absence of men to act as guardians of the sacred garden: their homeland. In those violent but formative days the social fabric of the new Iran was being woven. She missed the songs that bound the people together, the resilience and communality that is almost only possible during wartime. Her sudden artistic outpouring after a decade of productive silence expressed an urge to reconnect with the lost culture through her artwork. She meant specifically to make sense of the role of women in defying gender norms by actively participating in the sacred defense of the homeland. After the war against what appeared to be the whole world, the women started their own private war against oppressive laws.

Twenty years after the debut of her *Women of Allah* photographic collection, Neshat is among the best-known speakers at art venues on all matters pertaining to Iran, Islam, and women, and is the recipient of numerous international awards.[1] Her photography, video, and sound installations have been purchased by major art institutions and museums, including the Guggenheim, the Whitney, and the British Museum. Cindy Sherman was the first person to buy her photography from the *Women of Allah* series.

Neshat is one of eight female artists referenced in a critical retrospective of women artists and their influence on contemporary art. Titled *After the Revolution: Women Who Transformed Contemporary Art* and co-edited by Eleanor Heartney, Helaine Posner, Nancy Princenthal, and Sue Scott, this collection surveys the work of women artists at their full artistic potential, women who help inform American contemporary art and its global impact. Neshat rubs shoulders there with Louise Bourgeois, Nancy Spero, Marina Abramović, Cindy Sherman, and Kiki Smith. Some critics believe that Neshat's recipe for success is using the most vicious orientalist discourse against Muslim and Iranian women in her speeches and in the narrative of some of her installations. Strangely it is only through breaking from the didactic-mimetic regimes of narrative and leaping into the uncharted waters of poetico-aesthetics that she morphs into the painter of a new polychromic constellation. Although when talking about her artwork and in some of her visual grammar she adheres to a reductionist binary that equates the veil with oppression and the West with emancipation, the aesthetic language of her artistic work since 1995 sings an unworldly, reworlding song.

1. These awards include the First International Prize at the Venice Biennale (1999), the Grand Prix at the Kwangju Biennale (2000), the Visual Art Award from the Edinburgh International Film Festival (2000), the Infinity Award from the International Center of Photography in New York (2002), the ZeroOne Award from the Universität der Künste Berlin (2003), the Hiroshima Freedom Prize from the Hiroshima City Museum of Art (2005), and the Dorothy and Lillian Gish Prize in New York for beautifying the world and helping humankind (2006). The last award has also been awarded to Arthur Miller (1999) and Chinua Achebe (2006).

Neshat launched her artistic career in 1991 with a collection of photographs titled *Unveiling* as a part of the larger series *Women of Allah*, which took over art venues in 1995. In *Women of Allah* she depicts (mostly) herself clad in her signature black chador, with guns at hand (or held by her feet, placed behind her ear, and so on), and inscribed with scripture in untranslated Persian. Neshat's oeuvre is dynamic and defies easy categorization. It is not limited to photography and film. From Shakespearean ballet choreography of the Tempest in Amsterdam (2014) to depiction of tribal love songs and courtship rituals of elderly people in Laos in her *Games of Desire* collection, her signature is made unique via her attention to the poetics of the mundane and by liberating dichotomies, as well as by a relentless attraction to themes of love accented by a restless, exploring spirit. The color of her palette is tainted with the same spectrum as that of the female modernist poet Forough Farrokhzad (1935–1967). Neshat composes the embodied fundamentals of humanity under strains of a collective nightmare.

A nonexhaustive list of her artwork runs as follows:

Photographic collections:

Unveiling/Women of Allah (1993–1997), *Games of Desire* (2010), *The Book of Kings* (2012)

Videographic installations (short films):

"Turbulent" (1998), "Rapture" (1999), "Soliloquy" (1999), "Fervor" (2000), "Passage" (2001), "Tooba" (2002), "Logic of the Birds" (2002), Mahdokht (2004), Zarin (2005), Munis (2008), Faezeh (2008), Possession (2009)

Directed films:

Women without Men (2009), based on the novel of the same name by Shahrnush Parsipur (1990); *Illusions and Mirrors* (2013), featuring Natalie Portman; *Looking for Oum Kulthum* (2018), about an Iranian artist fascinated with Egypt's legendary female vocalist, Oum-Kulthum, who bloomed internationally in a male-dominated industry.

Finally, Neshat is said to be currently working on an autobiographical film.

Women and War: Sociopolitical Context for Neshat's *Women of Allah*

To help readers grasp Neshat's allusions to armed Muslim women, I have identified two significant streaks in the highly metaphorical collection: the concept of Shiʿite militant women and modern Persian poetry. Forough,[2] the most renowned female Iranian modernist poet, lends her imagery, atmosphere, and words to Neshat's enigmatic work. I study the influence of poetry in general and Forough in particular in the context of Neshat's oeuvre.

Neshat draws a parallel that playfully parcels out a different agency for her veiled figures. The eight years of the Iran-Iraq war acquainted women with guns. In the absence of young men, who had been killed by the millions in the war, women become the guardians of the land and its green memories. Despite presuppositions that Iranian women are absent from the country's historical armed struggles, their support or lack thereof is the secret cause for the success or failure of all Iran's revolutions. Time and again Neshat confesses that she shot the photo collection to acquaint herself with the enigma of the Muslim Iranian woman: on the one hand, she is covered from head to foot; on the other, she takes up arms and defends the land, all the while shuttling between subjecthood and objecthood by a certain poetics.

Women in Iran have been the signposts of the government's ideology. Imposed dress codes both hamper and boost women's bodily visibility in the work force. Despite the forced modernization of the shahs, Iran is a country that cherishes its traditional beliefs. Among them is reverence for modesty, chastity, and decency in women, which have always been playfully subverted. These traditions are not confined to religious beliefs. They are an amalgamation of *Adab* (proper conduct), *Adabiat* (literature, which plays a significant role in the Iranian sense of national identity), culture (or what Edward Said calls systems of friendly inclusion and hegemonic exclusion, which have been tweaked for survival purposes in Iran), myths, oral traditions, and the unofficial knowledge below the hearts and homes

2. Iranians call Forough Farrokhzad by her first name as a sign of endearment.

of people, as discussed à la Michel Foucault in *Persepolis*. The dress codes imposed after the Revolution in many respects facilitated the parade of women into the public space, which they could enter with "decency." They liberated many housebound women to explore the streets outside without being tarnished by tags of immodesty. No longer were women called streetwalkers if they worked in offices or had a bold presence in the shared space of the community. "Properly" clad, they took to arms to defend the country in times of invasion, and they peopled universities and became surgeons, lawyers, and engineers. In post-Revolution Iran more than 60 percent of university students and thus degree holders are female. And with the drastic rise in women's postsecondary education, a new wave of gender-oriented dissent against the government rose.[3]

The Magic of Poetry for Neshat

As an aesthetic rearrangement of the audiovisual field, poetry is prominently featured in Neshat's installation. Even her feature film, analyzed in the next chapter, is imbued with a feminine poetics: "Perhaps this clear and long interaction of poetry with, and within, other art forms explains our implied acknowledgment that poetry exists independently of any one medium and that therefore film, too, can be poetry" (Harrington 1977, 176).

Poetry is part of the photographs in Neshat's collections. Especially prominent are verses by Forough. Not only the poems themselves are embodied in the photographic collections, videographic installations, and feature film, but the aura of the poems has been metaphorically incorporated into the fabric of the artworks. The stylized and visually haunting world that Neshat brings to life tastes, smells, and feels like the world of Forough's poems. In Lorde's vibrant words:

> For women, then, poetry is not a luxury. It is a vital necessity of our existence. It forms the quality of the light within which we predicate our hopes and dreams toward survival and change, first made into language,

3. The BBC claims that the number of women graduates in some subjects is as high as 70 percent (Harrison 2006).

> then into idea, then into more tangible action. Poetry is the way we help give name to the nameless so it can be thought. (2007, 36)

Forough was a pioneering female poet in Iran's long tradition of versification. She gave name to the nameless, as Lorde suggests. She gave name to feminine erotics, and above that, to humanity's embodied solitude with its simple pleasures and deep tears. Forough's poetry was her own way of survival, a new birth that is compared to procreation, vegetation, and growth.

Over the course of her twenty-year career, Neshat has visited other classical poets as well. Some of her photo and film collections feature prominent ancient Persian poetry books. These include the *Book of Kings* by Ferdowsi and the *Logic of the Birds*. The latter is a multimedia performance that borrows its title from the magnum opus of the thirteenth-century Persian poet Attar. In this long poem, a large number of birds embark on a self-discovery voyage to find the mythical simorgh (phoenix), the everlasting bird of fire that rises from its own ashes. At the end of the journey, only thirty birds remain: in Persian, "Si Morgh." These thirty birds are the simorgh themselves (a pun on the word for thirty birds, which is the same word as *phoenix* in Farsi); they just needed the trial of the dangerous journey to discover themselves as the object of their discovery quest. Playing on the Persian pun, the poet connotes that the prize of your quest is within you; if you discover yourself, you discover eternity. The voyage of self-discovery, which opens forking gates within as much as it looms without, inspires Neshat on her own artistic odyssey. Her *Logic of Birds* is accompanied with singing and Sufi dancing and performance by the renowned vocalist Sussan Deyhim in front of three screens showing dreamlike films. However, what gives Neshat's work an uncanny poetics is her bond with Forough's unabashedly feminine universe.

Poetry of Forough; Poetics of the Feminine

Forough affected the accent, color, and atmosphere of the artistic productions of both Neshat and Shahrnush Parsipur. In Iran poetry is not just a literary form reserved for the elite or the avant-garde. It is arguably the most constitutive part of an Iranian sense of identity. Poetry is a way of life, a survival instinct that makes it possible to bear life's fair share of hardship and yet dream of transcendental beauty. In the Rancièrean terms, it is a reconfiguration of the space of the possible and the sensible. The young and the old, the educated and the illiterate, people across the social divide, each has a reservoir of memorized verse used on a regular basis to make sense of the situation at hand. In the words of cultural critic Hamid Dabashi:

> Iranians take poetry quite seriously, a habit that tends to lend a certain poetic diction to our historical recollections, the way we remember ourselves. If jazz is the cadence of American culture, . . . then Persian poetry is the pulse of Iranian culture, the rhyme and rhythm of its collective memory. It is said that what Muslims do is not memorize the Qur'an but Qur'anify their memory. If that is what Muslims do, then that must be what Iranians do too with their poetry, when they remember their past as the poetic resonance of their present—in fact, of their presence in history. (Dabashi 2007, 13)

Poetry creates a shared community of aesthetics in Iran. It is as important as the bread on the table, and the lover by the side. For example, in the playful quatrains of Persian polymaths, politician and astronomer Omar Khayyam (eleventh–twelfth century AD) wrote:

> A Book of Verses underneath the Bough,
> A Jug of Wine, a Loaf of Bread—and Thou
> Beside me singing in the Wilderness—
> O, Wilderness were Paradise enow! (Khayyam 1999, i)

Even with the onset of the Islamic Republic, Persian poetry, which is overflowing with carnal and spiritual desires; with wine, dance, lovers, and music; and with its nonconformism to religion and politics, still found its way into official children's schoolbooks, universities, and the publishing houses. Verse has the flexibility to playfully escape censors. This is language distilled into a creature that cannot be tamed or pinned down into a single meaning. It cannot be defined. As Oscar Wilde reflected, "to define is to limit" (2008, 251). In Iran, even politicians use poetry in their speeches to indicate their ties to the culture. Iran's minister of foreign affairs for sixteen years Ali-Akbar Velayati, who is also the counselor to Iran's leader, was the subject of hearty laughs and public ridicule as he misquoted a line of Hafez verse—almost a graver blasphemy than stuttering on a verse of the Qur'an.

Rumi, Hafez, Attar, Sa'di, Ferdowsi: thousands of master poets have not only provided Iranians with a sense of belonging to a community of aesthetics, they have also passed down visual metaphors cherished or challenged by younger poets of the contemporary generation. Forough is an heir to this visual poetic tradition. A fatal accident at the age of thirty-two ended her fifteen-year career in poetry composition, theater performance, translation, and film direction.

Forough's persona has had a revolutionary impact on a generation of artists, especially women after her. Neshat's visual art and Parsipur's novels contain distinctive motives that have a Foroughean accent. Abbas Kiarostami, the internationally renowned Iranian filmmaker, quotes one of her poems in its entirety—"The Wind Will Carry Us Away"—in an eponymous film. Forough's short documentary film, "The House Is Black," debuted Iran's now globally recognized New Wave cinema. Not only has Neshat's aesthetics been inspired by that of Forough, but her poetry itself is an integral, and arguably the most central, part of Neshat's photography and installations and her feature film. In an interview with *Border Crossings* magazine, Neshat rejects Kafka's and Rumi's influence in favor of that of Forough:

> —BORDER CROSSINGS: There is something positively Kafkaesque about "The Last Word" [one of Neshat's videographic installations]. The way the woman is treated by the interrogator seems to come entirely out of Kafka.
>
> —SHIRIN NESHAT: Well one of the major influences I had, and continue to have to this day, was the poet Forough Farrokhzad, who died when I was only 10 years old. . . .
>
> At that time [of Forough, before the revolution], we were a very progressive society and were quickly becoming

> Westernized, but there were still religious and social taboos about women speaking openly about sexual issues, about the body's temptation and about love. She was immediately considered a whore, but nevertheless she became a ground-breaking writer. She is one of the figures I became very close to—not just me, but a whole generation of younger artists and writers as well.
>
> —BC: Would you gravitate towards [Forough] Farrokhzad more than Rumi because she's a woman and a contemporary poet?
>
> —SN: Absolutely, as opposed to Shoja [Neshat's partner], who is well read in the classics. My tendency was for more contemporary, darker, sadder and more melancholic writing. (Enright and Walsh 2009)

The *Women of Allah* collection (1993–1997) is dedicated to Neshat's familiarization with the role of women in the eight years of Saddam Hussein's war against Iran. Recently declassified US Central Intelligence Agency (CIA) files confirm that the CIA aided Saddam in chemical weapon attacks against Iran and Iraqi Kurds. Armed with Forough's prognostic poetry, Neshat's arduous subjects morph into guardians of the invaded garden, the endangered homeland. No longer the mute, immobile victims imagined in the Western unconscious, these Muslim women have a different story to tell. Though they are Muslim, they have a certain eroticism in their camouflaged bodies; their gaze speaks louder than their closed or covered lips. The words are inscribed on their bodies as poetry, as tradition. Forough, whose poetry is widely used by Neshat, is the first female Persian poet to have sung of intimate, visceral, female experiences after a millennium of male-dominated poetic tradition. There were many female poets before Forough, but none had her distinct, confident voice.

During the turbulent heydays of the Revolution and the war, when disparate social strata were unified under the symbols of Shi'ism, a revived ideal of womanhood appeared. These strong revolutionary figures were called Zeynab-like women. Neshat had the strong sight to capture them in her debut collection.

Warrior Shi'ite Women: the Zeynabs

The Women of Allah are the postrevolutionary Zeynabs. In order to understand the rise of powerful veiled women in Iran—and to a lesser extent in the Islamic world generally—it is vital to be aware of the link between women and war in Islam. In the Iranian Shi'ite tradition, the most iconic Muslim woman are Zeynab the Great and her mother Fatima. The tragedy at Karbala not only is the nexus for the growth of Shi'ism, it is a trauma passed down and narrated by a woman. Every year during the Ashura mourning season, street dramas of the event are recreated and the tales retold. Zeynab is the woman who kept the trauma alive for the Shi'ites, and she can help us understand the women at arms in Neshat's work.

After the assassination of Zeynab's father, Imam Ali—the fourth caliph of Islam—as he led the morning prayer in a mosque, Yazid, the son of the second caliph, claimed the throne of the world's largest and wealthiest empire in the seventh century AD. Ali was the son-in-law of the Prophet Muhammad, a scribe for the illiterate Prophet as he narrated the revelations, and a poet and scholar whose books, such as the *Sea of Wisdom*, are still revered today. Shi'ites believe that he was stripped of official service after the death of the Prophet due to Ali's justice-seeking qualities, which incited vengeance in the wealthy empire.

Hasan, Hussein, and Zeynab, the children of the martyred Ali, and the beloved grandchildren of Prophet Muhammad, did not pledge allegiance to Yazid, who was known to be a corrupt and tyrannical leader. To join forces with other insurgents and rise against the usurpation of power by Yazid, the three children of Ali and their supporters were invited by the town of Kufa in Iraq to form an alliance. Zeynab left (probably divorced) her husband to join her brother's marching caravan of political rebels. However, as the caravan reached the midway point and was stranded in a desert, the Kufis betrayed their oath to Hussein and instead gave their allegiance to Yazid. They ambushed Hussein in Karbala, set siege on the families for a few days, cut off their water supply, and violently killed, looted, and burned the starving caravan, women and children included.

Zeynab was a survivor and a witness of the tragedy at Karbala. She took a proactive role in narrating the injustice that befell the house of Muhammad. She risked her life to save and nurse their ailing brother Hasan, through whom the bloodline of Muhammad's children survives for the Shi'ite believers. When brought to the foot of Yazid to plead for her life, she stood strong to eloquently and vehemently reprimand him, delivering a fiery speech in front of a large audience of men. Yazid unbound and freed her after the speech, fearing more protests to his weak rule. She died six months later from sorrow because she had witnessed the assassination of both of her parents, her brothers, their children, and her own children. At the age of seven, she had seen the murder of her mother, Fatima, as her pregnant body was crushed behind a door that she tried to hold locked. Later Zeynab had lived through the ordeal of her father's assassination during his short caliphate. As a great scholar and the first Muslim man, Ali had grown up in the house of Muhammad. After the Prophet's death, he was refused power for twenty-five years.

The Shi'ite religion of dissenters would not have been created had it not been for Karbala, and Karbala would not have survived had it not been for the power of Zeynab's march of dissent, her taking up arms, and finally her witness testimony. Describing women's agency in the paradox of postrevolutionary Iran, Farzaneh Milani writes:

> Women fully veiled but carrying guns on their shoulders, or in conventionally male arenas, contrast sharply with any traditional or simple definition of womanhood. A woman bearing arms is not quite the secluded and segregated other/wife. Herein lies the paradoxical nature of this neo-traditionalism regarding women: veiled but not excluded from a traditionally male domain; silent and obedient yet outspoken and articulate like Hazrat Zeynab in Kufa where upon the martyrdom of her brother in 680 A.D., she showed amazing courage, resiliency, and eloquence in defending and pursuing his cause. (1991, 5)

And such are the women of Neshat's photo collection: paradoxical, neotraditional, veiled, but not excluded from public service. Neshat composed the collection upon her return from Iran, after decades of living in the diaspora. She stands in awe of these women, incapable of understanding what propelled them to kill or be killed during the war with Iraq, unable to translate their beauty, their *adabiat*, their poetry, their tradition, except through portraits. She stands in a Levinasian face-to-face encounter that urges violence, but stops at point blank for the imperative of acknowledging the nakedness and vulnerability of the Other's mystery. Those clothes, that gaze, those arms bespeak of centuries-old battles against injustice fought by women, who are remembered through their stories, their poems, their bodies. It is this genuine curiosity and withholding of quick-fix answers that emancipates the work from mere propaganda about angry Muslim terrorists. Neshat says: "From the beginning I made a decision that this work was not going to be about me or my opinions on the subject. I put myself in a place of asking questions but never answering them. The main question and curiosity, however, was being a woman in Islam" (Rondeau 1999).

The militant Shi'ite aspect is only one hue in the kaleidoscope of Neshat's art. She is unique in that she effects a redistribution of the space that the visual provides her and rearranges its aesthetic elements in her poetics. Facing her art, the eye does not know in advance what it beholds, and the mind does not know how to judge it. Grappling with the controversial topic of Muslim women, violence, and poetics, she effects an ec-stasis by stepping into the position of the object: objectifying to subjectify. After *Women of Allah* she moved into short and long films, in which she draws a personal reading of universal symbols of gardens, orchards, and trees in relation to the female body and the life circle. But what unites her magical signature is a poetic flare that she inherited from Iran's gem: Forough.

Case Study: "Standing in Awe"

Here, as the Persian poet Sohrab Sepehri demands, I "wash my eyes, to regard anew" an untitled photograph in the *Women of Allah* collection, published in 1996. The charm of this specific photograph—which, for ease of communication, I have dubbed "Standing in Awe"—is manifold. A close reading and seeing of this image illuminates many of Neshat's most enigmatic motifs. In "Standing in Awe" Neshat's art reaches a poignant, poetic minimalism that functions through allusions, elision, and collage. The shot is emblematic of her visual grammar. Nonetheless, the veil, the gun, and the seductive gaze are completely absent from it. The visual field is covered by a hand, which in turn has been covered by Persian and Arabic calligraphy. The fingertips are gently touching voluptuous lips. The magic of this image is in an explosion of the affective sensorium that the lull of the quiet image cannot hide. The partially covered lips speak with poetry and symbols.

Each plane of imagery forks into many possible fluid, interpretive dimensions, including:

1. Forough's poetry, especially the "garden poem," colors the whole oeuvre of Neshat. Forough reclaims a feminist epistemic space for a different aesthetic rebirth through the garden enclosure imagery.
2. Neshat sacrileges poetry and the body by inscribing the hand with Islamic calligraphy. It is ironic that Neshat chooses religious calligraphy because the words of holy texts are not to be touched, save with pure bodies.
3. The hand displays several kinds of symbolism:
   3.1. The *Khamse* (literally, the number five) sign of the hand is used in traditional religious performances of Shiʿite mourning in Ashura as a banner under which the mourners march.
   3.2. Number five (as in the five fingers) has significance for Shiʿites, who believe in the holy family of five: the Prophet and his immediate family, who were all murdered soon after Muhammad's death.
   3.3. The name of Imam Hussein's half-brother is written at the centre of Neshat's hand. یا قمر بنی هاشم *Ya Ghamare Bani Hashem* translates to "Oh, Moon of Bani Hashem tribe." It literally alludes to Hazrat Abufazel. He lost his hands in the battle of Karbala trying to bring water to the thirsty children of the besieged camp. As he was carrying the water flask by his mouth, he was shot and killed by an arrow.

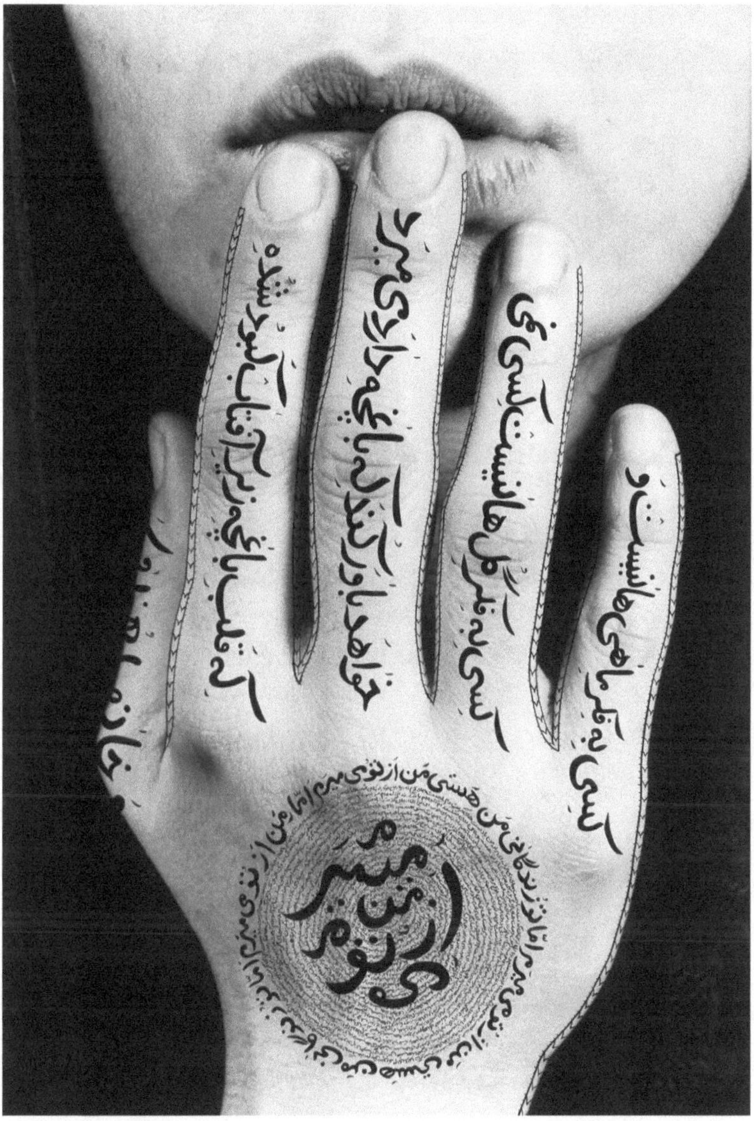

20. "Standing in Awe"; an enigma. *Untitled* (*Women of Allah*), 1996, ink on RC print 47 7/8 x 33 1/4 in. (121.6 x 84.5 cm), photograph taken by Larry Barns © Shirin Neshat. Courtesy the artist and Gladstone Gallery, New York and Brussels.

3.4. Inscribed hands are a pre-Islamic sign from deities such as the Babylonian goddess Ishtar. The patron of war, sex, fertility, and love, she is a predecessor of the Greek Venus. Ishtar, with her inscribed hands, was the most renowned goddess of the entire Middle Eastern and North African region.

4. The gesture of touching the lip with the hand or covering the mouth is a gesture of reverence or awe that appears even in Achaemenid reliefs. Other possible universal interpretations of touching or covering the lip with the hand include an invitation to silence, the preservation of a secret, a sensual touch, or revelation of a lie.

Space Politics: Embodied Geographies in the Symbolic Garden

The interstitial space of the garden in Forough and in the classical Persian tradition figures prominently as the safety of home, *heim*, the archetypal Eden or Elysium. In the Lacanian lexicon, this precarious garden can represent the forever-lost security of the imaginary womb. The garden in front of complex Persian houses transits the highly *harem*ed (guarded as sacred) interior space of the house to the *namahram* (not sanctified) outsiders. Structured between the inside and the outside world, the walled garden creates a liminal, Bhabhaesqe productive and regenerative space for the flourishing of the poet's metaphors, as in:

> I will plant my hands in the garden
> They will sprout I know, I know, I know,
> and swallows will lay eggs
> in the inky grooves of my fingertips
> (Forough Farrokhzad, "Rebirth")[4]

The ink-stained fingerprints synecdochically refer to the lonely poet whose profession demands visceral acquaintance with ink. This ink—or, by extension, this poetry—is to revive the stifled air of the country, to

4. Translations of Forough are mine unless mentioned otherwise.

engender a new birth. After all, the intellectuals, whose vocation is ink-stained, finally incited the Revolution. The nation and the garden are connected via a plethora of motives. It is the artist who heralds a new age of generation, vegetation, and flight.

Inspired by the poetry of Forough, both Parsipur and Neshat trace the garden to the body of the woman, to the homeland, and to a sense of security and fruition. What distinguishes the Foroughian small, enclosed garden (*bagh-che*) from classical Persian poetry gardens (*bagh*, *bostan*, *golestan*) is that Forough's small garden stands in exigent danger of neglect, invasion, rape, political turmoil, and military coup. The *locus amoenus*, or the idyllic garden, can transform into a perilous *locus terribilis*. In the same way, in *Women without Men* Neshat shows the destruction of the garden as the country falls to its knees with the CIA-backed coup.

Forough's geopolitically situated poetry is budding with an embodied feminine sensuality through which she reaches out to the public and the abstract. Whether she is singing about her male lover (almost absent from female speakers in classical Persian poetry), or lamenting the scars thereof ("and my scars are all of love"), her feet are firmly rooted in space and time. The poem "Standing on This Soil" illustrates this embodied defiance:

> I've never longed to turn into a twinkling star in the mirage of heavens
> or like the spirit of saints, enter the silent circle of angels
> I've never been estranged from this soil
> never affiliated with the stars
> I have stood firmly on this ground
> so that my body, like a green offshoot
> sucks in the sun, the wind, and the water to survive.
> Fertile with desire, bursting with pain
> I have stood on this soil
> so that the stars worship me
> so that the winds caress me.
>
> (Forough Farrokhzad, "Rebirth")

The revolt against the transcendental, given the context of mysticism prevalent in Persian poetry, is awe-striking. This physical occupation and reclaiming of solid space is a feminist *repartage* of the politics of allocation of visibility for women. Forough is the woman who dares to say no to the mirage of transcendence and the polite prison of silence.

Mapping the connection of "rhetorical space" to gender hierarchies, Roxanne Mountford asks: "While we are accustomed to the trope 'women's place,' we might ask ourselves why it is that gender hierarchies are so persistently associated with geography" (2001, 53). It is true that gender hierarchies are associated with geography and its allocation of space. But space's power and sanctity are not only the carriers of meaning, according to Mountford; space also conveys authority and power, particularly in the context of gender hierarchies. Space does not have power on its own. The power is endowed on it symbolically by the inhabitants, who represent and are a continuation of that space to the extent that the space becomes a metonymy of the identities of its inhabitants, as do nation-states.

Continuing this trajectory of thought, Valerie Palmer-Mehta designates the woman-space of Neshat's garden as "a site of rebellion" that "functions as a feminist epistemic space: a productive, working site where new meanings are forged and emancipatory visions are produced" (2015, 78). Quickly surveying the significance of world gardens, she turns to Persian gardens and finds Parsipur's and Neshat's gardens unlike those of other poets in the past. My reading of Neshat differs from hers in our understanding of the significance of Forough. In all that Neshat touches, I trace the fingerprints and voice of Forough. Palmer-Mehta, however, has to pierce two walls to access Forough. First she has to read the translated verse, and then she has to enter the intertextual milieu through which Parsipur, Neshat, and a plethora of other female and male authors are linked. Her article refers to Forough through the critique proposed by Farzaneh Milani: "Love clearly exists" in Neshat's garden, Palmer-Mehta writes. "However, it is not the kind of romantic love Milani (1992) identifies in Farrokhzad's poetry. Rather, the garden gives rise to a love, as the title infers, between women (without men)" (Palmer-Mehta 2015, 93).

Without discrediting Palmer-Mehta's brilliant recognition of Neshat's garden as a "feminist epistemic space," I am suspicious of her reductive reading of Forough's garden as a romantic space only. Forough is very pertinent to Parsipur and Neshat's worldviews and frames of mind with regard to a generative female space. The slight confusion in Palmer-Mehta's article may be due to the fact that she has read the poetry of Forough through a double veil—that of a translated poem accessed through the critique proposed by Milani. Palmer-Mehta does not even give the latter's stance due justice. Her reading of Milani is limited, if not flawed: "Milani (1992), for example, argues that pre-Revolutionary poetess Forough creates a utopian garden where a man and woman are equal and share responsibility for their 'needs and deeds'" (Palmer-Mehta 2015, 85). But Forough's poetry, letters, and film have affected several generations of both female and male intellectual voices and senses of identity. Forough has raged against an abstract expression of a utopic love in interviews, mocking the classical ideal lover "Majnoon" as a psychopath. Her poetry is spatially rooted in the political soil of Iran at a specific junction in its history. Maybe this groundedness is a political embodiment of space that contributes to Forough's appeal for the Iranian diaspora specifically.

Body, Woman, Map

In "Notes Toward a Politics of Location" Adrienne Rich rages against the image of the faceless, raceless, sexless, nationless, laborer called woman. For her, the question of the woman is tied deeply to the politics of her location—a map, a space, a body:

> As a woman I have a country, as a woman I cannot divest myself from that country merely by condemning its government or by saying three times "As a woman my country is the whole world" [quoted from Virginia Woolf]. Tribal loyalties aside, and even if now nation-states are just pretexts used by multinational conglomerates to serve their interests, I need to understand how a place on the map is also a place in history within which as a woman, a Jew, a lesbian, I am created and try to create. Begin, though, not with a continent or a country or a house, but with the geography closest in—the body. (2003, 30)

Rich stresses that the body becomes a vessel of meaning and can access power only when geographically situated. Abstractions regarding women's bodies can be deadly. Abstractions of the corporeal can sever it from its roots in the land, history, and social culture.

Many critics, such as Frances E. Mascia-Lees and Patricia Sharpe, argue that the physical body is a cultural site for the expression of a social body. Scholarship about the body is especially prevalent in Western canons. Michel Foucault, for example, theorizes that the body is a nexus for power struggle on a personal and national level. In "Nietzsche, Genealogy, History" he argues that:

> The body is the inscribed surface of events (traced by language and dissolved by ideas), the locus of dissociated Self (adopting the illusion of a substantial unity), and a volume in perpetual disintegration. Genealogy as an analysis of descent, is thus situated within the articulation of the body and history. Its task is to expose a body totally imprinted by history and the process of history's destruction of the body. (1998, 83)

Here the body replaces the mind as the identifier of the subject. In Foucault's work even the abstract concept of history is as an inscription on the body. The question of social change shifts from a focus on ideology to a focus on body inscription. For Foucault, bodies are discursive practices. They are disciplined, overwritten, controlled, and censured. The job of the genealogist is to expose "a body totally imprinted by history."

Reclaiming the body through a feminist resharing of the common space started almost two hundred years ago in Iran with another poet, Tahereh Qurratulayn, in the mid-nineteenth century.[5] Women's occupation of visibility, voice, and authority has been a political struggle the world over. Due to millennia-old traditions of oral storytelling and poetry by women, the Iranian feminist movement was carried over to the field of aesthetics before it gained flesh in the political arena. Forough is the

5. Tahereh was a religious scholar and the leader of a new sect. During a first act of public unveiling, she heralded the new religion of Babism in Iran. Her charismatic character affected many scholars after her. Refer to Milani's *Veils and Words* (1992) for a feminist reading of Tahereh.

culmination of the centuries-old battle for expression of female intimate desires, whether political or private, be they about pleasure or sorrow.

Forough Reclaiming the Corporeal

In Forough's poetry, the woman's space as that of a green offshoot or a tree references not only the connection between the woman's body and the natural cycle of regeneration, but the connection between the woman and the soil. The motherland, trees, nature, and gardens are loaded signifiers that weave the body of woman into the social fabric, into the texture of what is common in society: politics, economy, and social struggle. Jacques Rancière's most important lesson could be that the occupation of a certain space of the visible or audible is the joint task of aesthetics and politics, a task that is undermined by the current universalism of policing.[6] In Rancière's *Aesthetics and Its Discontents* (2009a), the term *political* signifies that which can partition the space of the sensible, reducing the right to visibility, audibility, and perceptual occupancy of certain marginalized themes and groups. Art is also concerned with regimes of visibility, audibility, and occupancy of time and space.

Although the message of the photograph might be policed by being forced into a reductionist slogan, the politico-aesthetic play has the potential to explode the reductionist interpretation into a versatile creative canvas. "Traditionally, in order to deny the political quality of a category—workers, women and so on—all that was required was to assert that they belonged to a 'domestic' space that was separated from public life" (Rancière and Corcoran 2015, 38). They could not put forth an argument or discourse because it was commonly believed that their occupation bound them to what was domestic or private, "and the political aspect of these categories always consists in re-qualifying these spaces, in getting

6. Politics and policing are different. Politics, as having a share in the common fabric of society, has its own aesthetics. Policing, however, is about limiting those rights to visibility and audibility.

them to be seen as the places of a community; it involves these categories making themselves seen or heard as speaking subjects (if only in the form of litigation)" (38).

Forough births that forbidden space for the flourishing of her desires as a woman, not just in the private realm of sexual satisfaction, but in open air, under full light, and with unapologetic visibility:

> I am not talking about trembling whispers in the dark,
> I am talking about the full day, and open windows, and fresh air,
> And a furnace in which useless objects burn
> And a soil fertile with a different crop
> And birth, and maturity, and pride.
> (Forough Farrokhzad, "Conquest of the Garden")

This space of revolt is the Other of hegemonic patriarchal traditions. She creates that space of dissensus in the private realm of the garden, in her poetry, in a space that originally was associated with unthinking laborers, or with private pastimes. The aesthetic and rhetorical space created in Forough's poetry has a strong purchase for Iranian diaspora authors and artists today.[7]

In "Rebirth," Forough ties the woman "to the tree, to water, to fire"—the imagery elements of paradise, life, and love in Persian poetry, respectively. She grasps millennia-old male-dominated, classical, and disciplined Persian poetry to ponder her own ephemeral body, pleasures, nostalgia, and the pain that was a continued thread in her short life.

Forough's short life was haunted by her unorthodox private affairs. After becoming enamored and having an affair with a married filmmaker in the 1960s and because she composed poetry about embodied feminine

7. There are many causes for the appeal of Forough in the diaspora that are outside the scope of this research. These include Forough's poetic sense of alienation, abandonment, melancholy, and nostalgia for a lost homeland. All these sentiments are strongly experienced by members of the diaspora who cannot return and yet cannot stop thinking about return to the homeland. Refer to Farzaneh Milani's scholarship on Forough in Diaspora.

sensuality, Forough was shamed and shunned by her father, by the public, and by the avant-garde. It took another generation for readers to stop judging the biographical in order to appreciate the intricacies of her poetics. She was the first woman to revolutionize Persian verse, standing side by side with pioneers such as Nima Yushij, Ahmad Shamlou, Mehdi Akhavan-Sales, and Sohrab Sepehri.

Returning to Neshat, the *unheimlich* garden in Neshat's oeuvre has distinct Foroughean shades. In the feature film, for example, Neshat's gardens look primeval at first encounter. Then the psychology of its inhabitants affects its bloom. It is a space outside and a space within the women. It whirls, births paper flowers, and falls according to the climate of the country, or the thoughts of its shelter seekers. The garden, which like a dreamwork has superimposed metaphors and concepts, vegetates in exigent times. It is the nature of this gasping realization of standing at the cusp of impending doom that the photograph captures with so much aesthetics. Citing Forough, Neshat has written over the photograph subject's fingers:

> No one cares about the flowers,
> no one worries about the fish,
> No one wants to believe that the garden is dying,
> that the garden's heart has swollen under the sun,
> that the garden's mind is slowly being drained of green memories,
> that the garden's senses are an abstract thing, rotting in the garden's
> isolation
>
> (Forough Farrokhzad, "Let Us Believe in the Beginning of the Cold Season")

Forough's poem "My Heart Is Burning for the Garden"—دلم برای باغچه میسوزد—composed in Iran after the 1953 coup, heralds an age of political suppression for free thinkers. It encapsulates the barrenness of intellectuals' creative energies during the reign of consumerism and terror in the aftermath of the joint CIA-MI5 overthrow of Iran's first democratically elected premier, Mohammad Mossadegh. The incident paved the way for national discontent with the monarchy that led to the Revolution of 1979.

A fatal car crash at the age of thirty-two kept Forough from witnessing the efforts of Iranians who gave their lives for rebuilding the garden. The atmosphere of the garden poem is tinged with a sense of Samuel Beckett's "Waiting for Godot." The poem references the degeneration of the fertile garden under the scorching sun and the uncaring glances of house-dwellers who have lost their hope in its rebirth.

Forough outlines the reactions of several characters to the putrefaction of the Edenic home, or homeland, in their courtyard. She starts with the patriarch, the father, who claims to have no more responsibilities toward the garden because he has retired. He buries his head in historical accounts or the *Book of Kings*. Evading the responsibility to take charge of the present moment, many in Iran still contend with a nostalgic reverence for Iran's golden past.

The mother "is a spread prayer mat." She sees decadence as the outcome of a sin and "imagines that the garden has been corrupted by the unbelief (*kofr*) of a vegetable" (fourth stanza). "She is awaiting the saviour [the twelfth Shi'ite Imam, who is said to be alive and to be coming to save the world] and the prospect of the bounty it will bring." Her attitude, a mix of superstition and religion, makes her fail to see the reality of the trouble and to resort to magic or superstition to cleanse or cure the garden and the country. The religious class eventually gain the sway of power in Iran.

The next stanza describes the brother, who acts as a synecdoche for the intellectual class. He "is addicted to philosophy" and "counts the number of dead fish in the little pond" in a scientific approach to the current disaster. His identity is constructed around this "air of hopelessness" with the political situation, but then he "mocks and laughs at the misery of the garden" with an objective air. Forough's critique of the intellectual class is the most severe. In this poem the intellectual ones do not understand the country. They turn humans into numbers and believe that "annihilation is the only cure for the garden" (fifth stanza). Only in the final stanza does the incongruous nature of the political struggle make itself visible in the space of the private garden:

All through the day
I can hear the tremor of explosions

our neighbours have germinated the gardens with grenades
their ponds are secret wells for gun powder
school kids fill their backpacks with tiny bombs
our yard is hazy.
I am fearful of a Time that has lost its heart
I am afraid of the futility of all these idle hands
and the estrangement of all these faces.

Here in the final stanza the poet envisions the impending battle, a revolution that could have been avoided if the hands were not so idle, the faces not so estranged. Had the intellectuals not segregated themselves from the people and the patriarchs not evaded their responsibilities, the garden may have flourished again.

Words from this poem are inscribed on the hand in Neshat's photograph. For Iranians who enjoy an oral poetry culture, even the title of this poem brings to mind images of the loss of the precious homeland and the responsibility of the people who have failed it. It is written, however, not in the words of politicians, but in the familiar dialect of embodied femininity, fertility, and love. This is an elegy for the allegorical garden, an image to which Neshat returns in "Tooba"[8] and *Women without Men*. In the latter, the garden blooms with the coming to life of Zari, and starts to fall apart with her descent into sickness, which is accompanied by the raiding of the garden by the military. The psychological state of the women in the garden affect its bloom. In "Tooba," like the virgin of Guadalupe, a woman finds solace in a tree and appears to be one with it, at least until the enclosed garden is invaded by a group of angry, bearded men.

Calligraphy, Body-Writing, Magic

Alluding to the Islamic *tazhib* tradition by adorning her images with arabesque and Qur'anesque pagination, Neshat sanctifies the female body and consecrates her poetry. The poetic play in Neshat, however, creates a

8. Also spelled *Tuba* and *Touba*.

protean image that dodges one fixed meaning. The claustrophobic body-writing could also be closely associated with magic: the Other of religion.

The collection *Women of Allah*, created over a span of four years (1993–1997), observes a minimalistic economy with a shared visual grammar: the black and white silver gelatin prints have been overwritten with black or red ink by Neshat herself. They depict black chadors, captivating gazes, rifles, and poetry by modern female Iranian poets. To display the poetry, Neshat opts for a peculiar calligraphy that sits at the interstice between the sacred and the profane; poetry written as Qur'an, or a calligraphy reminiscent of talismanic body-writing or black-magic scripts. Aside from the font, there are *tazhib*-like adornments commonly known as arabesque, which are based on "rhythmic linear patterns of scrolling and interlacing foliage and tendrils" (Fleming and Honour 1977, 40) that can be repeated many times.

These decorations in Neshat's photos are reminiscent of the art of Qur'anic miniature pagination that includes geometric shapes. The curious touches of Arabic accents also reinforce the possibility of Qur'anic sacrilege. As a descendant of Abrahamic religions, Islam looks up to the moment when the prophet Abraham broke all the idols resembling humans, animals, or a combination thereof to retrieve the Ka'ba as a place to worship a single divine, faceless, god. In Islam, God is *Sobhan*, clear and pure from all that a mortal, limited imagination can envisage. In some Islamic art, realistic representations of humans and animals are forbidden as idolatry. In Shi'ite Iran, however, these Sunni orthodox bans on portraiture are much relaxed. Even the prophet's face has been painted in ancient miniatures. Portraiture of Imam Ali and his son Hussein commonly adorn the Iranian cityscape in mourning ceremonies. By adopting an Islamic calligraphy reserved for the Holy Scripture, Neshat elevates the poetry to the level of the divine and sanctifies the female body through its intimacy with the sacred text.

It is ironic that the sacred Islamic texts are written on the skin in Neshat's work because Qur'anic words are sacred and should not be touched, unless by the pure. The skin-deep closeness with poetry pierces the aloofness of transcendental words. On the other hand, the claustrophobic font, which disregards stanza formation or punctuation—so vital

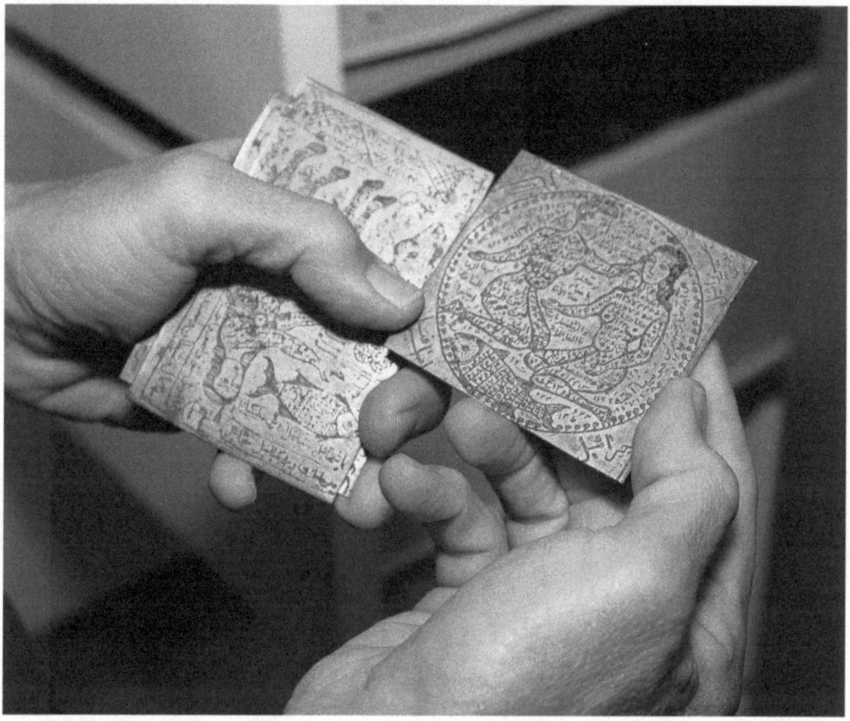

21. Neshat displays magic charms during interview. Body inscriptions convey supernatural powers. © Sarah Trigg. Used with permission.

to the visual effect of poetry—opts for unnecessary Arabic accents on a Persian poem. A tradition that closely resembles this form of body-writing is related to magic, an offshoot and a double of religion. The font is not the traditional poised calligraphy of Persia, which in and of itself is a form of visual art. The font is in the style of black-magic scriptures written over female bodies by semiliterate cup readers or jinn catchers. As a proud owner of several such talisman-depicting chants written over the body, Neshat displays them in an interview (figure 21).

> This is where I got my ideas in terms of writing calligraphy on the bodies. These are charms. When you make a wish. Every one means something. I'm not even sure what the meaning of the symbols are. As you know in Islamic cultures, it was taboo to replicate images, for example,

> of the prophets, but it was allowed to draw outlines of bodies and just fill it in with words.[9] So here, I think, is a very sexual piece of a man and a woman. He's touching her and then there's a fish below, which has to be about fertility. This could be a charm for someone who wants to get pregnant. Some of the writing is in Arabic and some of it is in Farsi, but I haven't been able to make out what it means. (Trigg 2014)

Although Neshat is fascinated by the enigma of the magical plates, she confesses her own ignorance regarding their precise symbolism. Aesthetic intuition and cultural perceptibility lead her toward a selection of *punctums* that are to some extent unintended yet are loaded with signifiers. That moment of undecidability between the photograph's leaning toward magic or religion, agency or suppression, marks the aesthetic play. It helps the viewer to ask questions, to shatter ready-made stigmas, and to explore Neshat's world anew. Her artistic intuition leads her in search of symbols that are only partially visible in the horizon of her own consciousness. "I put myself in a place of asking questions but never answering them" (Rondeau 1999).

But there is much that is incurably unresolved in the photographic collection, leading many critics to tag Neshat as a native informant. The fake veil is made from the wrong choice of fabric, it is not ironed, and she is dressed in a manner that tells of her lack of acquaintance with the heavy cloth. She admits to her generalized knowledge about her subject and her lack of certainty about many aspects of her artwork, including and especially the body-writing. "I was . . . struck by the tradition of tattoo in the Middle Eastern and Indian cultures. Later, when I was composing my images that dealt with the body of a Muslim woman, inscription on her skin seemed appropriate" (Bertucci 1997, 86). Here, her fascination is with the generic orient: as general as Middle Eastern and Indian cultures. Iftikhar Dadi compares her inscription technique to that of henna and

9. In the "Islamic Discourse" use of charms and talismans are forbidden, but the practice is widespread.

tattoos that are "practiced in the generic orient, such as 'Indian cultures,' which are not necessarily Muslim" (143).[10]

Delving into the philosophy of images, this chapter started by questioning "the shady commerce between art and truth." There is a mistrust in representation of beauty. In general, truthful images are supposed to lack in beauty, another binary that Neshat shatters. The history of a country and its women's struggles toward its freedom are condensed in her photographic collections. Skillfully, methodically, and poetically, she superimposes many layers of culturally untranslatable symbols into a simple image. To delve into her abstract yet grounded art requires familiarity with Persian poetry, conceptual art, and the history of a land and a people at war.

After almost two decades of grappling with deeply conceptual icons—mostly accessible to museum goers—Neshat stepped out of the gallery to face a larger audience through the cinematic medium. But as with other nomadic artists who shuttle between media, she carries her signature style of simplified yet amplified tropes into the theater. Her body-writings morph into poetic voice-overs. Of prime importance to her are images of a lost or invaded garden, an endangered *heim*, a homeland under attack. Here in the new medium, narrative steps forth: Muslim women's bodily history and space politics are narrated through a story line as opposed to photographic "memory freeze frames" (Sontag 2003, 22). As Neshat transits from photography to film, narrative and characterization become paramount. Speaking in terms of the distance between film and photography, Neshat asserts:

> In the art world you are very free, but you end up making something that few people see. In the film world anybody can view your film for

10. In the Philippines as well, the sacred ink of tattoos is used to drive evil spirits from the body in a religious ceremony. The power and magic of the inscribed words are so strong that they possess the whole being of the devotee. See a documentary film and photo exhibits by Cedric Arnold called *Yantra: The Sacred Ink* to view an elaborate ritual around religious tattooing in the Philippines, in which the person being tattooed is freed from evil, haunting spirits.

> the small price of a ticket, but you are not as free. There is also a big difference between film producers and art dealers. Producers are extremely involved. Everything has to go through them, while an art dealer basically leaves you alone and remains uninvolved in the production. (Heartney 2009)

Neshat moved from the solitary studio of an artist to a large crew working on a visual narrative that reaches more viewers. In the new cinematic medium, the trace of her visual signatures, poetic imagery, and aesthetic accents can still be discerned. The next chapter will closely regard Neshat's feature film, which took six years to complete and brought home the Silver Lion award for best director at the 2009 Venice Film Festival.

4

Neshat Moving on to Movies

Shirin Neshat's poetic feature film, *Women without Men* (2009), based on Shahrnush Parsipur's eponymous novel (1990), raises questions regarding the ethics of representing radical alterity. The film exposes to the witnessing eye the camouflaged, corporeal, imprinted skin of Iranian women at the crossroads of history, politics, and democratic outburst more than half a century ago. Woman, nation, and freedom are intertwined in a magical, feminine garden.

The worldviews of both Neshat and Parsipur are colored by the courage, poetic vision, and cinematography of Forough Farrokhzad. Forough's documentary film "The House Is Black" (1963) lighted the path for Iran's cinematic new wave and was an inspiration for Neshat. In "The House Is Black" Forough visits a leper colony in a forgotten corner of the country, where the literally and metaphorically effaced and ostracized lepers live in absolute destitution. What brings an ethical, humanizing touch to this otherwise pathological and sociopolitical work is the excess of dignity, life, and beauty that abounds in the camera's loving eye toward radical alterity. Forough's lens is a human one, focusing on the joys of life, children's play, a limping dance. Forough's voiceovers have a melancholic tone as she recites her own poems over the heart-wrenching scenes of tormented individuals. Jarring noises such as those of a wheelbarrow, or the monotonous footsteps of a blind man pacing along a mudbrick wall, stand in sharp contrast to the dirge-like poetry. This cinematic juxtaposition reminds the audience of the chasm between the beauty of the poetic voice and the utter devastation of the subjects. At the end, it is this aesthetic repartitioning that gives the lepers visibility, audibility, and a sense of belonging to the world community.

This house in which the rejects of the society have been incarcerated is comparable with Neshat's garden, which houses four women who themselves have rejected social norms and found shelter in a utopic, Elysian orchard. The women manifest arboresque fertility and resilience, drawing attention to the politics of the body, skin, and space. To better explore these theoretical streaks, I individually visit two of the most enigmatic characters—Munis and Zarin.

Characterization and storytelling are the objet trouvé of Neshat's cinematic journey. Regarding the significance of characterization in cinema, Neshat claims:

> In the end, I learned that the fundamental difference between cinema and art is the question of character development. In all my past work, such as the videos *Rapture* [1999] and *Passage* [2001], I had treated people sculpturally, devoid of any character or identity. They were simply iconic figures. But with this film, I had to learn how to build characters, how to enter their inner worlds, their mindsets. This was an entirely new experience for me. (Heartney 2009)

Especially in focus regarding characterization is Munis. She is the narrator of the film, who rises from the dead to find freedom in suicide or "disclosure in effacement." I will compare her to Gayatri Spivak's Bhubaneswari in *Can the Subaltern Speak*?

Women without Men the novel, written in the style of magical realism, contrapuntally looks at the questions of gender and feminine intergenerational and interclass bonding while keeping political concepts such as democracy and dictatorship at arm's length. In her cinematic adaptation, Neshat brings out and highlights the political through the bodily. Regarding the political backbone of the film, Neshat says that she composed the film as a reminder to "Westerners" about their roles in the interrupted democracy of Iran:

> Selfishly, I found it very timely to revisit history and remind Westerners that the American and British governments were directly responsible for overthrowing a democratic system in Iran. The CIA organized the

> coup in 1953, which in turn paved the road for the Islamic Revolution in 1979. As far as I know, this is the only film made so far that tries to depict this monumental political moment. (Heartney 2009)

To help convey the complexity of Neshat's cinematic creation, I quickly glance at the novel that inspired it. Looking at the novel does not solve the mystery of the film, but it does unravel Neshat's preference in highlighting, lowlighting, and erasing certain characters and events.

Parsipur's Novel

The novel *Women without Men* was first published during the presidency of the moderate Mohammad Khatami, who wished to relax publishing restrictions on intellectuals. The book sold out in less than two weeks, but it was soon banned in Iran. Despite the air of change that Khatami ushered in, he was not omnipotent in the cultural arena. Power is not centralized in Iran. Different hardline factions reacted strongly to a rising wave of what they understood to be a "Western frame of feminism."[1] The traditionalists prohibited publication due to the allegedly light handling of issues pertinent to female virginity, infidelity, and so on.

Having once been imprisoned by the Shah's notorious secret police, SAVAK, because of fears that her short stories were left-leaning,[2] Parsipur was incarcerated again after the publication of *Women without Men*. Before the Revolution Parsipur had belonged to prolific intellectual circles that pushed the boundaries of the state and the people's sense of

1. For a comprehensive study of the disruptive nature of Western feminism in Iran in the past two hundred years, see Nima Naghibi's *Rethinking Global Sisterhood: Western Feminism and Iran*. Naghibi outlines the way in which the idea of global sisterhood created an Other of Eastern sisters in order to justify Western women's own feminist advantage, leading the way to a postrevolutionary backlash against and mistrust of the feminist efforts of Iranian women themselves.

2. In her prison memoir, *Kissing the Sword*, Parsipur claims that she is not a communist and that she can, with difficulty, call herself a Social Democrat.

normativity. She was a contemporary and acquaintance of Forough, but their friendship was cut short by Forough's tragic death. Parsipur studied Chinese philosophy at the Sorbonne, and her publications, such as *Touba and the Meaning of Night* (which inspired an installation with the same name by Neshat), address the concepts of Sufism, femininity under Islam, women in rebellion, and Iranian tradition and modernity. *Women without Men* was later reprinted in the United States and Europe and translated into several languages.

Women without Men was originally penned as a collection of several short stories about five different women. More than halfway through the volume, Parsipur decided to connect the stories of the female characters and turn the collection into a novella. Neshat became infatuated with the portraits of the five women in this novel and spent more than six years producing short films, or videographic installations, on each of them separately.[3] The *locus amoenus* in the novel, this Karadj garden, is bursting with fertility, with growth and sprouting of a different kind, and yet it stands in danger of doom. The garden or orchard can signify a feminine sensus communus that moves along with the currents of social freedom and democracy. With the rise of the Western-backed dictatorship during the 1953 coup, the garden begins to fall. Woman, nation, and freedom are intertwined in this magical dwelling place.

Parsipur's vision is acute and metaphoric with regard to the physical sex organs, even the nature of the hymen. Her book displays a tongue-in-cheek sarcasm that is absent from the more politicized feature film. The physical merges with the magical in this Edenic womb. Zarrinkolah (Zarin), the prostitute, marries the gardener without the conventional clerical blessing. She turns into a translucent body of light when pregnant. They give birth to a lotus flower,[4] which they plant on the bank of the fro-

3. These include *Mahdokht* (2004), *Zarin* (2005), *Munis* (2008), and *Faezeh* (2008). She received a copy of the novel by the cultural theorist Hamid Dabashi.

4. "*Gole Niloufar*" has been mistranslated as "morning glory" in the English edition. The original word in Persian, *niloufar*, refers to a flower that has foliage and is planted in a pond, thus referencing the lotus flower. Given Parsipur's facility with Eastern mythologies and mysticism, lotus seems a more likely translation.

zen river. The germination thaws the ice of the orchard. The two friends Faezeh and Munis walk through the gates, having been raped on the way to the garden. It is the female social life there that heals them.

The new owner, Fakrolleqa (Fakhri), has just reached menopause when she decides to buy the Karadj garden. Shortly before this, she has inadvertently killed her husband by punching him in the loins and causing him to roll down the stairs. In the novel she has been unfaithful to her disdainful, distant, and mocking husband for eight years. She goes to the garden in order to cultivate intellectual friends, find her poetic voice, and eventually climb her way to the parliament—an aspiration she fails to realize. She is unable to compose poetry and leaves the garden to the girls so she can live a fuller life outside the garden with a newfound companion. Women's creative capacities and metamorphoses from sterile to proactive happens through a union in this symbolic garden. Here I turn my lens toward Neshat's adaptation of these ancient motives, through Forough and Parsipur.

The Human-Tree: Mahdokht

"Mahdokht" is a three-channel video and audio installation in color, filmed in Morocco in 2004. The enigmatic character of Mahdokht has been omitted from the feature film due to a directorial decision of Neshat, who has called her "the most magical" character of them all. In Parsipur's novel, Mahdokht embodies the obsessive compulsive spirit of a purist in search of absolute harmony. She has an aversion to sexual or physical intimacy, while at the same time she is obsessed with procreation. This leads her to imagine and become a human tree, planted in the Karadj garden. Fed by the breast milk of Zarrinkolah and the morning dew collected by the Kind Gardner, Mahdokht-Tree becomes the nexus of rebirth as she explodes into a thousand seeds scattered in the wind. In the words of Rebecca R. Hart: "Mahdokht explores issues of fertility and the links between women, fecundity, and the earth" (Babaie et al. 2013, 120). Hart argues that it is her olive skin complexion that leads her to wonder about the origins of a green pallor. But nonetheless she has a desire to become a tree. "My virginity is like a tree. . . . Perhaps that is why I am green [olive skinned]. . . . I am not an acorn, but a tree. I should plant myself" (Parsipur 1998, 8).

In her ode to Mahdokht, whose portrait is the first one introduced in the book and who has been omitted from the film for the sake of narrative flow, Neshat depicts a slender, dark-haired woman past her prime of youth who has phobic tendencies but dreams of caring for hundreds of children. These children run through the woods of the mystical garden toward her, wearing her woolen clothes. She knits yellow clothes interminably for them. The film pays a quick homage to this scene by depicting a knitting woman in the brothel, using the same vibrant yellow thread.

Women and Trees: An Arboresque Resilience

Exploring the mythological symbolism of trees in the novels of Parsipur, the visual poetry of Neshat, and the groundbreaking verse of Forough is revealing. It joins the three women to a long tradition of dissent through space politics. In the novel, the women's embodied sexuality is closely associated with the political turmoil in the country, and with blooms in the cycles of a tree's life. Woman and the tree are linked to such an extent that the milk of a lactating woman (Zarin) is given to a human tree (Mahdokht). Virginity, prostitution, struggle for political seats, pregnancy, rape, and menopause have close links to the psychological contours of the characters that eventually adorn the enchanted garden.

The gateway to the garden is a stream that feeds its lush green trees through a hole in the mud wall. In the poetry of Forough the garden is of utmost significance as a space for women's liberation and emancipation. Forough alludes to "planting her ink stained hands in the garden" so that they will grow and writes that "sparrows will lay eggs in her inky fingertips." This poem links the working of intellectuals (through the metonymy of ink-stained fingers) to future growth and freedom (hatched eggs, flight). Neshat, in turn, has taken all these verbal allusions to trees, the garden, sexuality, and growth and turned them into a new visual poetry. She has also intuitively accentuated the political unrest of a nation at the bursting moment for political democracy in the ruined garden called Iran in 1953.

There is a corpus of scholarship based primarily on the significance of Persian and world gardens in literature and the visual arts. Haim Bresheeth, for instance, writes:

> The oldest texts of Babylon, and some of its architecture, deal with the garden—a secret, private and sacred space, devoted to love and to the deity, symbolising the Garden of Eden which the ancients placed at the source of four different major rivers, variably, in Iran, Asia Minor or Iraq. Babylonian, Assyrian, Persian and Egyptian art, as well as Indian and Chinese, are all focused on the garden and its beauty, so it is little surprise that the Bible also uses the garden as a simile of the female body and the act of love. This sexualised space will of course also appear in Western art. The Renaissance was clearly influenced by the gardens of Islamic Andalus, an implant of the sensuality of the East at the heart of Christian Western Europe. (2010, 756)

In a videographic installation called Tooba,[5] Neshat returns to the haunting analogy of woman and tree. Parsipur, too, has a novel titled *Touba and the Meaning of Night* (2009). In Neshat's work, a gracefully aged woman is standing tall inside a tree, embraced by it. It is as if she is part of the tree and vice versa. The enclosed space is invaded by angry, judgmental men. Neshat comments:

> In the Qur'an,[6] the myth of Tooba is explained as the "sacred tree," the "promised tree," which in popular Iranian culture is also identified as a feminine tree. But interestingly enough one finds this symbol exists in other religions such as in Christianity where the Virgin Mary is portrayed inside a tree and I believe it is called the Virgin of Guadalupe. Furthermore, the garden itself is a universal concept—man's attempt to re-create a fragment of paradise on earth, a place where one can truly

5. Tooba, also spelled Touba or Tuba, is derived from an Arabic word that means pure, sanctioned, and clean. It is a tree, referred to several times in the Qur'an, that has roots on earth and fruits in heavens.

6. Abraham: 24–26.

> escape the banality of the material world and transcend into the spiritual realm. (Neshat 2005, 7)

Trees and gardens are among the most ancient archetypes of humanity signifying life, sustenance, fertility, sexuality, growth, abundance, and knowledge. Civilization is based on the cultivation of trees. In the Abrahamic cosmogony it was the (sexually charged) forbidden fruit of a tree that expelled the first humans from the Garden of Eden. The universal myth of the world tree with its branches in the skies and roots deep into the earth connects the three worlds: heaven, earth, and the underworld. A tree is both a feminine symbol, bearing sustenance, and a masculine phallic one, a union.

For the old master Lao-tzu whose philosophy Parsipur studied at the Sorbonne, a tree is the enigmatic sign for resilience through flexibility:

> When life begins, we are tender and weak; when life ends we are stiff and rigid. All things, including the grass and trees, are soft and pliable in life; dry and brittle in death. Stiffness is thus a companion of death; flexibility a companion of life. An army that cannot yield will be defeated. A tree that cannot bend will crack in the wind. Thus by Nature's own degree, the hard and strong are defeated while the soft and supple prevail. (2001, 89)

Not just resilience, but asexual flourishing is possible by the arboresque. This metamorphosis from flesh to seeds ensures the intellectual longevity of the woman without the need for physical procreation. After all, seeds of knowledge have been a metaphor for the proximity of trees to a different sort of rebirth: through the words written on paper produced by the tree. Daphne, in ancient Greek mythology, turns into a tree to avoid the loving embrace of Apollo under the spell of Eros. Pierced by the lead arrow of the god of love, she harbors a loathing of Apollo, who unfortunately has been hit by a golden arrow of *amour.* While she is in his arms, her skin cracks into bark and her hair turns into flowing branches of laurel. Apollo vows to give the tree eternal youth: ever green branches. In this light, Daphne gains eternity and her leaves are worn by kings and queens, an eternity without the need for carnal union. The tree here is an asexual signifier for regeneration. Daphne becomes immortal not through a displeasing coitus, but through a metamorphosis to a different medium.

So far the connection between arabesque resilience and longevity, and women's political struggle for a partage of the sensible has been established. The garden of Forough's poem reappears in the novels of her acquaintance Parsipur and in the works of the next generation artist, Neshat. Another lasting impact of Forough on the artistic creations of Neshat is Forough's short documentary film.

Forough's "The House Is Black": A Precursor to Neshat's *Women without Men*

It is not only Forough's poetic imagery that enriches Neshat's art; Neshat also quotes directly from Forough's short film "The House Is Black." These quotes appear in melancholic poetic voice-overs, and Neshat shows comfort in handling paradoxes such as freedom in death and beauty even without skin, and pays painterly attention to frame composition and sequencing, displaying a poetic outlook on the mundane. In an interview with *Border Crossings*, Neshat agrees that Forough's images have left a lasting impact on her work:

> [Forough] is a really heroic figure for me and, in fact, I have an obsession with the only film she ever made, a short 20-minute-long film called "The House is Black." . . . She was revolutionary and extremely subversive in the way she spoke out. She is one of the figures I became very close to—not just me, but a whole generation of younger artists and writers as well. (Enright and Walsh 2009)

Hailed as the touchstone of Iran's cinematic new wave, "The House Is Black" has been dubbed as "the greatest of all Iranian films" by critic Jonathan Rosenbaum. The documentary takes a tender, poetic, and humanizing look at the people affected by leprosy in the northwestern province of Azerbaijan in Iran. Rosenbaum brings to sharp relief the paradoxical demonization of Iran in the West against the universalization of its ethical cinema:

> More than any other Iranian film that comes to mind, it highlights the paradoxical and crucial fact that while Iranians continue to be among the most demonized people on the planet, Iranian cinema is becoming almost universally recognized as the most ethical, as well as the most humanist. (Rosenbaum 2010, 260)

"The House Is Black" is the only film directed by Forough. At twenty-seven years of age, she worked on the film with a crew of three for twelve days in the Baba Baghi leprosy colony. The original 21.23-minute black and white film won the top documentary award at Oberhausen Film Festival in 1963.[7] Like the human unconscious, Forough's "The House" is filled with the *refusé* of social normativity, the abject, the Other. Ejected to the outskirts of the town of Tabriz, this house is black and is shunned by society due to deep fears of leprosy contamination, human touch, and interpersonal bonding. Forough is not bound by fears of abjection. She looks fears in the eye, identifies with the rejects, and laments the condition of humankind, imprisoned by its own stigmas.

In a society censured by the royalist Shah against any opposition to his divine rule, speaking of the ills of class divisions and the shortcomings of the medical system needed much poetic maneuvering. The producer Golestan (Forough's paramour), fearing the censors, claimed that film has no sociopolitical critique to offer and is made solely with the humanitarian intention of aiding the lepers. His voice-over in the film is surgical, objective, and matter-of-fact. His presentation is in stark contrast to

7. A different version with additional scenes was screened in the United States recently. The original producer of the documentary, Ebrahim Golestan of the Golestan Film House, rejected the longer version and questioned the accuracy of its subtitles. A still better version—with French subtitles, taken mainly from the print shown in Oberhausen, and authorized by producer Golestan—was issued on DVD along with "A Fire" as part of the then-biannual French magazine *Cinéma* (#07, printemps 2004), edited by Bernard Eisenschitz and published by Editions Léo Scheer.

Forough's affectionate, melancholic, intimate voice-overs. The short essay-film benefits from fast montages and jarring yet musical ambient sounds, and the images are superimposed with passages from the Torah and the Qur'an. Rosenbaum describes the tone of Forough's voice-over recitation as a "dirgelike tone, halfway between multi-denominational prayer and blues lament" (2010, 260). The magic of Forough's lens is in the sensitivity with which she depicts the subjects: not as victims, but as humans with aspirations, joys, and wounds. Abbas Kiarostami's film *ABC Africa* is said to be a kindred spirit to Forough's "The House." His 2001 work depicts the small joys of children of Uganda's AIDS victims, focusing on human agency in trauma instead of victimization.

Forough's black screen opens with a disclaimer: "There is no shortage of ugliness in the world. By closing our eyes and averting our gaze, we work to intensify that ugliness. But mankind is resourceful." Made at the request of the Leprosy Aid Association, the film creates an analogy between our modern conditions and that of the lepers, who are incarcerated due to ostracization, poverty, and genetics. They are bound by physical walls while the people outside those walls are bound by mental ones. In an interview with Farajollah Saba, Forough outlines how at first she was troubled by encountering the lepers, but then how she befriended them, gaining their confidence:

> The colony was full of people who had all the qualities and emotions of a human being except for the face. I saw a woman whose entire face was one hole, through which she spoke. It is terrible. But I had to gain their trust. They hadn't been treated well before. Anyone who had approached them in the past had only seen their defect. But I swear to god, I would eat from their food and touch their wounds. I would touch their toes, devoured by leprosy. It was so that the lepers trusted in me. As I left them, they prayed for my wellbeing. Now after one year, some of them still write me letters asking me to pass their requests to the ministry of health. (Heydari 1998, 189)

If the face is the condition of discourse for Emmanuel Levinas, what happens to the effaced subjects of Forough's film? The charm of Forough is her ability to identify with the effaced, creating a faceless relationship with those who are allegedly outside the possibility of discourse. Such bilateral human relations are the basis of her radical humanism. In an interview, Forough claims:

> Ugliness is not a material concept, in my opinion. I saw the lepers as humans who are only sick, just like any other person who catches a disease. Nonetheless, when you see a leper mother breastfeeding her babe in a close embrace, absorbed in the child's countenance, you are faced with complete beauty. Only at first glance, a leper might appear appalling. But with a humane bond, you are in relation with a number of human beings where there is affection, where there is love. (Heydari 1998, 190)

It is these moments of radiant beauty in a dark house that have a lingering effect in the memory. In the film, a leprosy-affected woman brushes her long black mane and smiles after putting on makeup. A destitute, barefoot, limping man dances to his own song under the sun—a joyous, sonorous dance. At the end it is the lepers who finally shut the gates onto the audience's gaze, as if we are not worthy of their company—as if we are not yet ready for the human encounter. Without denying the severity of the condition, Forough manages to enter the gate, to see a human face-to-facedness, or better yet, to extend an ethical, loving embrace to the effaced, the Othered.

Neshat's Feature Film *Women without Men*

Women without Men is not a documentary. The foundation of the film, however, circles around the effect of the fall of Iranian democracy on the lives of four women with different social status, class, age, and aspirations who have taken refuge in an enchanted, symbolic, Elysium-like garden. Historian Dominick LaCapra contends that documentary truth claims may shine better through the medium of fiction, which relays affect more easily:

> Narratives in fiction may also involve truth claims on a structural or general level by providing insight into phenomena such as slavery, or

> the Holocaust, by offering a reading of a process or period, or by giving at least a plausible "feel" for experience and emotion which may be difficult to arrive at through restrictive documentary methods. (2001, 13)

This magical-realistic movie, which sits at the juncture where the force of history blasts through the psychology of the female characters, delivers "plausible 'feel' for experience" of a nation experiencing unrest. Just like Forough's House, the garden envaginates the *refusé* of social normativity: a prostitute, a raped girl, a middle-aged independent woman artist, and a political activist. Neshat politicizes Parsipur's novel—or rather, brings out the political that is already latent in its fabric. She explains in an interview:

> I politicized the book more when I turned it into a film. The perspectives on the *coup d'état* of 1953 were not detailed in this book. So from the beginning it was interesting for me to consider the efforts of these women to achieve democracy, freedom and independence at the same time that Iran as a country was searching for democracy and freedom. I tried to make a film that when it reaches its audience they can make a relationship between these woman and Iranian society, which are both pursuing the same goal. Women pursuing freedom and Iranian society pursuing democracy. (Dabashi 2009)

Neshat's garden is a mirror for the aspirations of a nation, of women, of democratic emancipation cut short by dictatorial coups. While Forough's "The House Is Black" starts with the concrete house and moves to the metaphoric country, so viewers see in the lepers the same inhibition of movement that is latent in the mental predisposition of people outside, Neshat starts with a symbolic, Edenic garden and transforms it into the backdrop of the feminine psyche. She draws a lifeline between the garden, the women, and the turbulent, occupied homeland. The garden is a generative space that changes with the mindset of its inhabitants. It thrives as Zarin's health improves and starts to fall as Iran's democratically elected prime minster is ousted by the CIA and MI5.

The garden is an erotic, camouflaged female space, a political space, a space of generation and growth, as well as decay and fall. But what makes this house and orchard comparable with Forough's house is their respective ease with ambiguities and paradoxes. There are several scenes of radical Otherness in Forough's film, such as one in which a doctor shaves a leper's skin, but she manages to bring out radical humanity, aesthetic beauty, play, and joy in a documentary about a leprosy colony. Neshat, too, uses an aesthetic regime of representation in which paradoxes are the norm. Munis's fall from the roof becomes flight, and her death marks the moment of her freedom. The prostitute, Zarin, becomes prophetic, connected to the garden, the implanter of paper flowers that impregnate a barren land. The language and imagery are multifaceted, metaphoric, and layered with interpretation. In the new foreword to Parsipur's novel, Neshat pinpoints the enigmas with which she grappled:

> *Women without Men* has a powerful and paradoxical arc that traverses various notions of opposites: magic/realism, nature/culture, local/universal, men/women, mystical/political. Shahrnush situates the city of Tehran as a point of entry to all sorts of cultural, sociopolitical, and historical realities, while the orchard functions purely on a metaphoric level. (Parsipur 1998, viii)

Iranian cinema is replete with images that bespeak alterity, poetry, and transcendence. Persian mysticism, or *Erfan*, is a lifestyle, and not a religion or etiquette. The ability to read metaphors in the concrete real and to see the real as illusive has historico-political roots. For Hamid Dabashi, this camouflage of the real, the material, the bodily, in favor of the unseen and metaphoric is a function of resistance to power politics:

> In its colonial context, the Islamic body has been denied its corporeal materiality, mutated into a politics of power or aesthetics of resistance to power, in a hermetically sealed culture that has given birth to . . . a globally celebrated pararealism in Iranian cinema. (2003, 936)

Whether flight from reality toward the realm of metaphors was instigated by a fear of life or resistance to oppression, this para-realism has become a staple in Iranian cinema and visual poetry. Magical realism is no longer even relevant. All reality is already magical, symbolic, incorrigible. But

Neshat brings the intercultural, insider secrets of this "hermetically sealed culture" to the global market:

> Shirin Neshat is singularly responsible for having successfully punctured that hermetically sealed culture, defeated its inflated self-absorption, and dared it to "step outside" from the self-suffocating air of its own environment, out into the open air of a public space globalized beyond a particular politics of power or a marked aesthetics of resistance to that power, where the categorical differences between private realities and public truth can be settled in completely different terms. (Dabashi 2003, 936)

Neshat uses different terms to bring to the global movie market what was ostensibly a coveted, Persian way of speaking, acting, and looking. She represents the political Other in an aesthetic and ethical manner.

Scene and Character Analysis

The trill of a muezzin opens Neshat's feature film, as Munis is dying by suicide. On the surface, it appears that Neshat is resorting to the FOX News strategy of superimposing *Allah-u-Akbar* over death. But as the mistress of paradoxes, Neshat builds binaries and stereotypes only to break them with the help of the audience. As the most politically invested character, Munis ties the personal narrative of the women to the political upheavals of the nation at a democratically significant pivot point. Munis's fall is visualized as a free flight, her death as a rebirth in the garden. Images of flight, fluidity of movement, and rebirth in the garden make intertextual connections with Forough's verse: "I will plant my hands in the garden / They will grow, I know, I know" ("Rebirth") and "Remember the flight / the bird is only mortal" ("Let Us Believe").

The human flight, plantation in the garden, and the phrase *Allah-u-Akbar* are in themselves allusions to the incomprehensible, the magical, the divine. *Allah-u-Akbar* literally translates "God is greater." It highlights the limits of human perception and points to the beyond. The mysterious unraveling of the narrative is also beyond comprehension. Between the cadences of the call, the murmur of a distant demonstration is heard. The poetic voice-over with Forough's signature tone stops the circular echoes and the distant hum: "And now, there was silence / silence / and nothing more." In an interview with Eleanor Heartney, Neshat gives a reading of this first scene: "The film begins with Munis's flight from the roof, which could be interpreted as a suicide but also as a leap toward freedom, since the shot is exaggerated. She is also now the narrator, who is telling us a story while flying and observing the world below" (2009).

Moving across several different media in her career as an artist, Neshat has expressed her desire and constant challenge to tell a story in the cinematic medium. With the original novel composed as separate short stories that connect halfway through the book, the narrative sequence for the story becomes paramount. The black of the first scene gives way to the white, pyramid-like Tehran roofs, in accord with Neshat's renowned, minimalist black and white style. The blue of the sky is in stark contrast to the white roofs and the dark figure of Munis. The whirling white clouds create the visual link to the next scene: the whirling translucent water stream (reflecting the clouds), through which the Karadj garden is irrigated. An airy, fluid quality is established from the beginning: the flow of the black veil in the wind, the whirling of the clouds, the flight of Munis. They are in contrast to the granite ground and the mud wall of the garden. Harsh realities are traversed and surpassed in the magical realism of the tale. However, physical reality does not stop the fluid motion. The wall gives way to the stream, and the fall toward the granite ground does not mute Munis's voice.

Munis

In the now classical text *Can the Subaltern Speak?* (2010), Spivak contends that masculine imperialist rescue missions obstruct the alternative histories that subaltern woman might write with their bodies. One of these alternative histories is suicide as an act of self-negating agency. Speaking in terms of sati, the practice of widow burning, Spivak points to it as a theologically illegitimate practice performed to prevent the woman from receiving a material inheritance. However, Spivak rejects criminalizing sati and turning it into the object of a rescue mission by colonial armies. In tandem with that, the rescuing of Muslim women from the claws of Muslim men has become a rallying cry for the globalizing economies today.

Spivak warns that ideology attaches to any young woman's suicide, and the task of the critic is to unlearn these ideologically colored judgments. As an example, she points to the suicide of Bhubaneswari Bhaduri in 1926. Bhaduri had failed to carry out an assassination against the British colonizers. In order not to reveal the whereabouts of her comrades, she committed suicide. But she waited until her menstrual cycle to stress the fact that the suicide was not due to an act of dishonor such as illegitimate pregnancy. This was a "figure who intended to be retrieved, who wrote with her body. It is as if she attempted to 'speak' across death. . . . She spoke, but women did not, do not, hear her" (Spivak 2010, 22).

Munis's death is also an attempt to speak across death with her body. Her traditional and abusive brother Amir Khan hides the suicide of his sister, fearing dishonor to the family name. With the help of Faezeh, he stealthily buries her in the garden. Faezeh—who is in love with Amir Khan—has become his co-conspirator in Munis's murky burial in order to win his affection. She resorts to witchcraft and philters to stop his engagement to an infamous girl. As she is blowing enchanted words and burying a talisman in Amir's garden, she hears Munis beckoning from the ground. The magic of the love charm intertwines with the magic of Munis's character and with the magical realism of the movie. Munis is resurrected from a Foroughean garden of rebirth. These details are highlighted more in the novel. Neshat claims to have politicized the character of Munis. In an interview, she confesses a personal identification with her: "Just as Parsipur constructed the characters according to her own personality, I've done the same. Munis and I share a passion for political activism, a belief in social justice" (Heartney 2009).

In the author's note at the end of the novel, Parsipur too confesses that Munis is the character that closely resembles her own persona, mixed with that of her cousin (1998, 121).[8] Hers is the voice of the narrator. As a political brainchild of Neshat, Munis is the character who deviates boldly

8. The cousin was a simple and righteous young woman and a victim of an unhappy arranged marriage. She later divorced her husband and lived a pious life as a dervish (Parsipur 1998).

from the novel. She is the one who attends the communist party's underground meetings and stands in vigorous demonstrations against the military alongside men.

Munis of the novel is not as powerful as Munis of the film. Listening to the news on radio is the most politically charged activity in which Munis of the novel partakes. She is eventually raped by a driver and his aide as she makes her way to the garden with her friend Faezeh. Her first suicide attempt follows her conversation with Faezeh about the nature of hymen.[9] Feeling betrayed and misinformed, she decides to jump off the roof. She doesn't die, however. After the suicide attempt, she roams Tehran's streets, buys and read books about sexuality, and eventually returns home after a month of wandering. This time her brother Amir stabs her, thinking she has run away from home as a fallen woman. This murder attempt gains the approval of Faezeh, who is madly in love with Amir. Neshat claims: "With Faezeh, I share the desire for a normal, traditional life" (Heartney 2009). Faezeh, who yearns for the traditional pleasures of marriage and religious prudence, witnesses the withering of her dreams when she and Munis are raped. Munis returns once again from the dead and, after scolding her friend, confesses that she now has the power to read people's thoughts. She takes Faezeh to the Karadj garden.

However in the film, Munis belongs to the world of politics more than to the domestic arena. She refrains from entering the garden and remains the knowing voice-over of the narrative. Through her we learn of the forgotten fighters for ideals of freedom and democracy—ideals that were trashed by the needs of the globalized market.

Zarin

If the garden is interpreted as Iran, a feminine space, and the body of the woman, then on a symbolic level Zarin embodies Iran's essence and its spirit of freedom. She is the hope for its salvation as she makes the desert bloom, planting her paper flowers in the barren land (a Foroughean

9. She has been restricted from climbing trees since childhood, for fear that she will break her hymen "curtain," but Faezeh informs her that the hymen is not a film, but an orifice.

image). The garden flourishes with her health, and her health improves with the rise of Iran's anticolonial government. The film's most aesthetically pleasing scenes and enigmatic imagery include Zarin. As Jacques Rancière reminds us, aesthetics and politics intertwine.

Played gracefully by Hungarian actress Orsolya Tóth, Zarin is the saintly prostitute who escapes the brothel for the holy shrine upon encountering a faceless man. Hysterically scrubbing her naked, anorexic body red and blue in a magnificent *hamam*, she is ready for ablution, the ritual cleansing of the body that signifies purification of the soul. The shame in the skin is a metonymy for a sense of guilt or filth in the self, the ideological makeup of the mind, the political frame of the nation. Neshat declares that she shares Zarin's bodily aversions: "[What I share] with Zarin, the character that I perhaps feel closest to, it is the problem of the female body and feelings of shame. As a Muslim woman, I have grown up with a complex about my body, always feeling inadequate" (Heartney 2009).

As Zarin lights candles in the shrine, she inadvertently becomes the object of prayer of a congregation of men who sit upright after touching the ground with their foreheads. We as the audience cannot see their faces, but Zarin can. This is a powerful image that transforms the stigmatized sex worker into a holy *qebla* toward which the believers kneel. Ironically, she may recognize many of their faces as those of her costumers. After her purification frenzy, she has now become an essence of purity, the worshipped sanctuary.

Finally entering the Karadj garden like the stream through the hole in the wall, Zarin finds shelter. She is later discovered by Fakhri and the gardener as she floats, Ophelia-like, in the pond, baptized, born again. Zarin soaks in the algae-green water in an image that is closely linked with Forough's poem "Summer's Green Waters":

> Lonelier than a leaf I gently row
> through the summer's green waters
> with my load of bygone joys,
> moving towards autumn's grave shores,
> toward the land of death
>
> (Wolpé 2010, 36)

She is the first inhabitant of the garden, guarded by the gardener (who marries her in the novel). For the entire film she is voiceless and does not enter into dialogue with any other character. Hers is the realm not of words, but of images: the imaginary, phantoms, and sensations. Maybe that expressive silence and intense presence is what immortalizes her act in this movie. In the novel she does not die, but is wrapped in a lotus flower she gave birth to and disappears into the sky. The last words of the book read:

> "Zarrinkolah" [Zarin], her husband called to her, "we must go on a journey."
>
> Zarrinkolah cleaned the house and packed a bundle of clothing for the journey.
>
> "But we don't need clothes where we're going," her husband said. "Leave your bundle behind." She obeyed, and took her husband by the hand.
>
> They embraced the [lotus flower]. The flower wrapped its foliage around them and they all rose to the sky in a puff of smoke. (Parsipur 1998, 113)

But in the more political movie, as the military takes over the intellectual, the private, and the activists' quarters, Zarin starts to hover above the garden rootlessly. She is feverish and finally dies simultaneously with the death of a boy-soldier, superimposed over the climax of Fakhri's party song. If the garden is symbolic of Iran, Zarin is the spirit of hope for its salvation. The precarious soul of freedom is finally trampled under military boots with the help of foreign friends and domestic intellectuals.

Faezeh

Devout and traditional, Faezeh closes the film as she walks away from the garden toward the town. The garden has been left to ruins by the military and by the detached and collaborator intellectuals.[10] Zarin has died, and

10. Forough, too, in "My Heart Is Burning for the Garden" laments the indifference and the objective gaze of intellectuals in the death of the garden.

Munis is torn in the political struggle. Faezeh's resolute walk, without her veil, toward the capital is a return of the repressed. The traditional, marriage-seeking woman shuns her previous beliefs in order to march toward the cause of the trouble. Spivak contends that the agency of the third-world woman[11] has been forgotten in the battle between subject-constitution and object-formation. Faezeh is that woman caught between tradition and modernization, but her aporetic voice is not lost in the movie:

> Between patriarchy and imperialism, subject-constitution and object-formation, the figure of the woman disappears, not into a pristine nothingness, but into a violent shuttling which is the displaced figuration of the "third-world woman" caught between tradition and modernization, culturalism and development, . . . a violent aporia between subject and object status. (Spivak 2010, 61)

In the space of the movie, the aporia of the repressed third-world woman reappears. Having shuttled violently between the rule of the patriarchy and the boot of the military, Faezeh—the weakest and the most grounded of all the women—stands tall and marches forth toward the epicenter of political unrest.

Neshat Film Conclusions

Neshat's cinematic pallet is colored by several transnational influences. The most prominent of Neshat and Parsipur's muses is Forough, Iran's beloved avant-garde poet, filmmaker, theater actress, and translator. More than half of Neshat's artistic career has been devoted to translating Parsipur's novel characters into cinematic personages and a feature film. The most intimate motif prevalent in the three women's texts is the possibilities that space politics allocates to female characters, and their embodied resilience, resistance, and revolt.

11. I use words such as *Third-World* and *West* strategically with full knowledge of the problematic binaries they create. I use them to facilitate communication, not to validate the dichotomy.

In Forough, Parsipur, and Neshat, the body, or rather the skin—this disturbed surface of modernity—is peeled, bruised, chopped, pierced, and scrubbed bare. The largest organ of the human body, the skin, is the interstice between the inside of the human being with the world outside. With the tension put forth by poverty, moral stigmatization, and armed struggle, the symbolic skin fails to mediate between self and the other.

Throughout a grueling ritual in the film, Zarin scrubs off what she perceives to be the source of her impurity, her skin. Jean-François Lyotard calls the skin a "Moebian-Labyrinthine skin, single-sided patchwork of all the organs (inorganic and disorganized) which the libido can traverse" (2015, 4). From the faceless men of Neshat to the effaced lepers of Forough, skin-deep fears and bodily aversion lie at the junction between us. Body enhancement, adornment, and mutilation techniques have been prevalent for more than thirty thousand years. Critics argue that the physical body is a cultural site for the expression of a social body, and scholarship about the body is especially prevalent in Western canons.

Michel Foucault famously theorizes that the body is a nexus for power struggle on a personal and national level. He calls the body "the inscribed surface of events" (1998, 83). Genealogy, or "an analysis of descent, is thus situated within the articulation of the body and history. Its task is to expose a body totally imprinted by history and the process of history's destruction of the body" (148). In his work even the abstract concept of history is as an inscription on the body. The question of social change shifts from a focus on ideology to a focus on bodily inscription and embodied ideology. For Foucault bodies are discursive practices. They are "disciplined, overwritten, controlled, and censured" (148). However, as Spivak criticizes, the godfathers of modern philosophy, Kant and Foucault included, do not directly consider the effects of the colonization of the past and the globalization of the present on the bodies of third-world women.

Although recent scholars from the Middle East and India, such as Sara Ahmed, Farzaneh Milani, and Hamid Dabashi, have tried to write an alternative history for the women of the global South, the works of visual artists, entangled with a long tradition of poetry and prose, accomplish much more in a single stroke or visual shot. Neshat, inspired by Forough and Parsipur, illuminates our eyes with bodies imprinted by the history of Iranian women and their forgotten struggles for emancipation. In displaying their erotic as well as grotesque realities, the bodies as material and discursive practices point all toward the violent shuttling that Iranian women, and by extension humanity, have undergone in the transition between object-formation and subject-constitution (Spivak 2010).

Neshat does not let the exhausted affect of the image of the veiled Other dominate the surface of her enigmatic work. With Neshat, the eye does not know in advance what it sees, and the mind does not know ahead of time how to analyze the artwork. She perhaps achieves a displacement of the exhausted affect of indignation and leads the eye toward curiosity and attention when it is confronted with radical alterity. In an age when a simple icon of a veiled woman carries with it connotations of subjugation, abuse, lack of agency, and victimhood, Neshat's female characters create aesthetically playful, political personalities that cannot be oversimplified into a cliché. The aesthetics, politics, and ethics in Neshat's lens foment a bond with the radical alterity of these women, creating curiosity and attention in the viewer regarding what was previously only a loaded signifier.

Conclusion

This book proposes a fresh practice of reading and regarding literature and art produced by members of the Iranian diaspora in an age of war against terror. In line with Gayatri Spivak, it aims to "uncoercively rearrange desire," or train the imagination to see the complicity of the self in the plight of Others (Spivak 2013a, 375). I read these interstitial works of art and literature through their engagement with the trio of aesthetics, politics, and ethics. The New World Order has uprooted millions of refugees, expelling them from the only real human rights, which according to Hannah Arendt include that of belonging to a political community. For Arendt, the "loss of national rights in all instances entail[s] the loss of human rights," maybe because "the world found nothing sacred in the abstract nakedness of being human" (1949, 31). Arendt was speaking in the aftermath of the World War II and as a refugee herself. Her words resonate in these dark days of silent war that witnesses millions of displaced humans living outside the conditions of humanity and citizenship. In the popular imagination, the image of the radical Other shuttles between violent terrorists and destitute refugees on flimsy boats. Aesthetics can intervene in this bipolar representation of the radical Other by giving a human face to the plight of the Other.

Nietzsche warns about the dangers of fighting a "monster": "Whoever fights monsters should see to it that in the process he does not become a monster. And if you gaze long enough into an abyss, the abyss will gaze back into you" (Nietzsche 2009, 146). Through an ethical engagement with alterity, a new bonding, engagement, and imaginative embrace are made possible, and the privileged are no longer exempt from the trauma in the putative third world. It is the pain of the Other that lets us step outside our comfort zone (a state of *ex-statis*) and extend an imaginary arm. This is what Spivak calls ethics: an embrace, an act of love. The face of the Other, brought forth through the artists and authors in this collection, can perhaps act as a metonymy of that outstretched arm that creates a virtual community of humanity. While the military, funded by taxpayers, ravishes the world, tearing the shared fabric of humanity, it is the task of artists to bring its fissures to touch. The danger to the civilized world, as framed by Arendt, does not come from without. When people are forced into desperate situations through wars, famines, sanctions, regime change, and military coups, the menace will come from within. "The danger is that a global, universally interrelated civilization may produce barbarians from its own midst by forcing millions of people into conditions which, despite all appearances, are the conditions of savages" (1949, 34).

The graphic novels, photography and poetry collections, and feature films discussed in this book occupy the fertile interstice between the visual and verbal domains, where, just as in gutters, there is space to dismantle fixed hierarchies of a policed mentality. The domains of politics and aesthetics are interlocked in such works as *Persepolis*, *Nylon Road*, *Women of Allah*, and *Women without Men*. Space politics, or the occupation of a place, constitutes the basic unit of human existence and a cornerstone whence all rights emerge. "The fundamental deprivation of human rights takes place first and above all in depriving a person of a place in the world which makes his opinions significant and his actions effective" (Arendt 1949, 29). Jacques Rancière teaches that aesthetics also concerns itself with ideas of occupation of the space of the visible, and a re-partage of what has previously been off limits. Aesthetics cannot be severed from its political texture, studied in isolation, or put on a pedestal independently. This luxury of looking at decontextualized beauty in literature and the arts is a ploy of mental policing, prevalent in the ivory towers of academia. Detached aesthetics has purposefully given up on its response-ability of belonging and connecting to a world community. Artists such as Shirin Neshat have confessed that they do not have that luxury to produce works of art in vacuum after having experienced life as a member of the Middle Eastern and Iranian diaspora.

The ethical is the third knot in my Borromean circle. It adds a humanitarian bond to the study of aesthetics and politics. Ethics brings the question of the treatment of the Other to the forefront. It has been compared to an embrace, a relationship, or an act of love. Emmanuel Levinas and in turn Judith Butler and Susan Sontag look at the face of the Other, or its visual reproduction, as the surface whence ethics springs forth as a responsibility with regard to the vulnerable, naked Other. The proximity of alterity can change precepts, from violence to ethical bonds. The face of alterity has been brought to an intimate proximity through the works of graphic novelists and their personal avatars, such as Marji and Pari in *Persepolis* and *Nylon Road*, respectively. The face can be synecdochically read in hands, feet, lips, or eyes in Neshat's photographic collection, as an "inscribed surface of events" (Foucault 1998, 83).

There are serious dangers associated with externalizing an enemy or seeing the cause of current-day misery in a detached Other. Evil does not possess a single leader who will kill all who bring justice to the country. Such is the tall tale sold to the military. As Foucault explains, power moves in circular fashion, from the bottom up, in society. It is only the people of a society who can renounce their leader. As in the case of the latest regime changes by the world's superpowers, elimination of a tyrant will not usher in democracy. Democracy cannot be exported. Democracy is an awakening of people who come to acknowledge a sense of belonging to a community of politics, in which the subjects are willing to rule and to be ruled, to speak and to listen, alternatively. When that empowerment is stolen from citizens, rulers resort to violence to control the crowd. This is not feasible without the help of a certain class of society that benefits from the actions of such a ruling elite. To eliminate the simplified notion of evil, more force from below is required, much more than a US invasion and decapitation.

Once a military body is convinced that there is an Other outside the self, outside its nation, its ideology, who is completely independent of "us" and is the source of all that is wrong in the world, then the brutal, generic crushing of such a distant enemy needs no explanation. In the cognitive process of pesticization, the enemy is turned psychologically into a pest ready to be crushed. Democracy is not a given that can be shipped with missiles; it is achieved only when the people come to awareness of their share in the common allocation of politics in a country. Any other interruption in the democratic process by an outside force, such as the CIA coup of 1953 and the current interference of world superpowers in the Middle East, will only backfire and stall the process.[1]

Art intervenes here. As a reallocation of space to the forbidden, aesthetics shatters the deadly binary between self and the Other. It is useful to gaze at the faces brought forth by Iranian graphic novelists or the self/portraits and characters of Neshat with an understanding of the ethical implications that this bilateral relationship invokes. The comic technology used in *Persepolis* and *Nylon Road* aids in shuttling the face of the Other to intimate enclosures. Face (or the body) here is a synecdoche of the self and of being. The decision to move closer to or farther from the Other is weighed against an ethical responsibility. This responsibility toward alterity is a demand, a fact, a bond. As Levinas writes, "An ethical philosophy of responsibility grounded in the phenomenology of the face" marks our relationship to others (1994, 3).

Training and rearranging human perception through an ethical aesthetics can change worldviews and perhaps the world. In this book I started by delving into the roots of Othering as it contributes to democracy and terror. Many diasporic memoirs and works of visual art are received with the axiom or the self-explanatory mind-set that the West is ripe with democracy while the Middle East is brewing with terror. Pandering to the whims of the imaginative audience, many ex-patriate authors, such as Azar Nafisi and Marina Nemat, reproduce the troubled mentality in exchange for tokens that can range from immigration papers to international podiums, academic seats, and public recognition. These native informants ride the tide of public curiosity about Islamic cultures, of the demand to pierce the veil. The perpetuators of the war, on the other hand, claim to bring "infinite justice" (Rancière 2009a, 111)[2] to the axis

1. The reinforcement of ISIS by arming Syrian rebels with Western weapons is an example of such a backlash.

2. Iran, Iraq, and North Korea were dubbed the "Axis of Evil" by George W. Bush in his State of Union Address in 2002, as governments that aided terrorism or possessed or sought weapons of mass destruction. Even the military operation in Afghanistan was to

of evil produced by the imagination of the superpowers. Infinite justice here becomes a displacement of terrorism, as human-rightist imperialism feeds fundamentalism. The philanthropic discourse of aiding the third world and saving the Muslim woman becomes our present-day alibi for yet another civilizing mission.

The trouble overseas, with its wars, famine, and exile, is presented to us with difficult-to-view images. Our sight fails to grasp the magnitude of suffering without an aesthetic, political, and ethical bond. What is the cause of what Cathy Caruth calls the "ceaseless betrayal of bodily sight" (1996, 50)? How can we see and see again the trauma of the Other, outside the set visual clichés of war escapes and destitute individuals? Aesthetic photographs, images, and graphic narratives can bypass the defense mechanism against viewing distant traumas, and in so doing can create a novel engagement with terror. The safe distance of an image and the absence or presence of violence contained in a frame allow for the working of the faculty of judgment. After all, "nothing separates fictional representation from the presentation of reality" (Rancière 2009a, 123). What brings success to authors of the diaspora who engage with the distant Other, the religiously different, and the racially dissimilar is the narration or representation of an embodied existence with art, play, and imagination.

The bodies and portraits in the graphic narratives, photography, and films in this study are "the inscribed surface of events (traced by language and dissolved by ideas), the locus of dissociated Self (adopting the illusion of a substantial unity), and a volume in perpetual disintegration" (Foucault 1998, 83). The embodiment and occupation of space empowers the precarious women in these chapters. The space of the garden in Neshat's *Women without Men* creates a *locus amoenus* that bursts with fertility and creates a community for fallen women. This woman-space stands in conjunction with the nation and its striving toward freedom. In her *Women of Allah*, the sanctified, visible skin of the Muslim woman becomes the telltale heart of ancient rhymes with new messages. The occupation of

---

be dubbed "Operation Infinite Justice," but due to opposition it was switched to "Operation Enduring Freedom."

space and embodiment within a labyrinth of skin are material traces over which abstract struggles take place regarding agency, visibility, and individuality. Within the articulation of the body, history, politics, and aesthetics, the exposed face of the Other looms, making a demand, waiting for a response. Literature and the arts allow the mind to revel in an aporia, to struggle with antinomies and find tolerance for paradoxes. To offer change in lethal desires for domination and destruction, academia can deal very well with the aporia of the religiously, traditionally Othered.

Not much intellectual activity is expected from the media or the movie industry, but academia as well, quite contrary to its claims to challenge the reason of the state, successfully manages to either profess neutrality[3] or, in most cases, to reproduce the sanctioned government stance. Resistance to such domination would entail recognition of the complicity of the self in the globalization of capitalism, its liberation missions, and its aesthetic-political engagement in world affairs. However, in the post-political biopolitics of today even the educated can become reminiscent of apathetic, Nietzschean "last men" who have no great passions and no binding commitments (Nietzsche 1940, 6). Tired of life, taking no risks, they seek only comfort and security while expressing tolerance toward one another:

> Taking a little poison now and then: that makes for pleasant dreams. And much poison at the end, for a pleasant death. They have their little pleasures for the day, and their little pleasures for the night, but they have a regard for health. "We have discovered happiness," say the Last Men, and they blink. (Nietzsche 1940, 6)

My subject position as a woman of Islamic background oscillating between the Middle East and North America has created a critical distance from and an intimacy with disparate psychological geographies that facilitate the questioning of the concept-metaphors of freedom of thought

3. In a memoir that takes his remark as its title, Howard Zinn claims that "you can't be neutral on a moving train." Neutrality, indifference, or silence in the face of atrocities is comparable to and contributes to the fascist shift. For a discussion of this shift, please refer to the introduction.

and expression, and my ability to critique, deconstruct, and doubt, which I can do more here in Canada than at home. The corrupt government within Iran and the fierce reality of global sanctions without have put the onus on citizens to lift their voices and challenge the system. Such dissensus, such voicing of citizen's needs, imprints the freshly woven and rewoven fabric of the political.

Having spent nine years of nonsequential residence in Canada, I have rarely encountered departments of humanities dissenting against corporatized universities that boast of their outstanding schools of law, business, and dentistry.[4] What I have mainly encountered has been brilliant retracing of the history of thought within the European and recently American tradition, quite unparalleled in breadth and abstraction, but one that does not loudly and clearly threaten the government's stance. Many of the courses offered and much of the research undertaken reiterate the authorities' stance and do not connect the ivory pinnacles of theory to the material existence of humanity, right here, right now. Adrienne Rich remarks that "theory—the seeing of patterns— . . . can be a dew that rises from the earth and collects in the rain cloud and returns to earth over and over. But if it doesn't smell of the earth, it isn't good for the earth" (Rich 2003, 31).

An optimistic reading of the situation would call this a hoarding of data perhaps, and a certain elitism of liberal humanists that avoids embracing the Other or even looking at its human condition eye-to-eye. Some believe that it is our zeitgeist, that the consumer culture has turned even education and cultivation of the mind into a commodity created for quick liquidation:

> Again, while it is a great blessing that a man no longer has to be rich in order to enjoy the masterpieces of the past, . . . this ease of access . . . can become a curse. We are all of us tempted to read more books, look at more pictures, listen to more music than we can possibly absorb, and the result of such gluttony is not a cultured mind but a consuming one; what

4. The Québec student uprising and the Occupy movement are among the few flares of hope against this anesthetization of the universities with regard to political affairs.

> it reads, looks at, listens to is immediately forgotten, leaving no more traces behind than yesterday's newspaper. (Auden 1984, 476)

However, this approach to the disciplines, these cement, impenetrable walls that have been built to secure the domain of influence of each faculty—to partition the visible, sayable, thinkable, grievable—at once systematic and repetitious, establish categories of verifiable truth that are quick to dismiss research done outside the security of the domain. With interdisciplinary practice in vogue, the hardening of these divisions becomes most palpable in cross-hatched departments. Looking at the history of ideas and theories is a legitimate undertaking, and I intend not to disavow that, but to point to the lack of autocritique that would tease the easy binary of outside and inside, self and Other, aesthetics and politics—while heeding at every step the risk of falling into essentialism, oversimplified reification, or nativist utopianism.

The recognition of a single evil one (for example, Hitler, Stalin, or Saddam) purges the self and locates the cause of misery outside the self. Those leaders are of course to blame, but so also are the powerful people who watched quietly, from a distance. Politically disengaged yet educated youth learn about humanitarian catastrophes in the world, such as genocides, illegal occupations, coups d'état, and human rights abuses without recognizing their ongoing contribution to them currently and historically. Such desensitized education, which supports ignorance and privileges security instead of opening the possibility of an encounter with the dangers of that which is distant, inhibits ethical relations between the self and the Other. The paranoid relationship with the so-called enemy is based on a narcissistic self-preservative securitarianism that will not benefit the imprisoned self, which is cut off from the lifeline of an ethical relation with the Other. Although the aim of such unethical regimes is to protect a fragile, vulnerable self (nation, civilization, or religion), the isolated metonymy of the self implodes and disintegrates inwardly. The mission to salvage the self becomes the cause for its annihilation.

The unethical, securitarian approach backed by the world's strongest iron fists will crush the self along with the Other, using the transcendental signifiers of democracy and terrorism as alibis, unless a relationship is established that, while not selfing the Other, does not expunge the Other entirely. This is where the aesthetic break intervenes. Artists can challenge the status quo not by succumbing to an engaged literature, but by using aesthetic means to bring the traumas of distant Others closer. In an era of compassion fatigue, media desensitization, and parochialism, the contributions of intellectuals, artists, and philanthropists to the perpetuation and reinforcement of hegemonic discourse—or, on the contrary, of challenges to that discourse—are undeniable.

Only through an ethical balance with regard to representing radical alterity can rusty hierarchies of subjugation be subverted, displaced, and turned on their decapitated heads. As Sharon Sliwinski reminds us, "humanity is not simply given but rather exists only as a precarious, virtual community brought into being, in part, through our grappling with world events at a distance" (2011, 144). The dynamic interlocking of aesthetics and politics enables a throbbing and shifting of boundaries that were previously codified and untouchable. When wars are fought over images, the diasporic visual literature produced about a distant land's march toward freedom may be able to change our gaze and help us to imagine a new landscape of what is possible. If it is not anticipated by a quick-fix interpretation, and if it leaves space for the play of the imagination, aesthetics can reshape the sense of belonging to a world community via its entanglement with politics and ethics.

Works Cited

Index

Works Cited

Arendt, Hannah. 1949. "Human Rights, What Are They?" *Modern Review* 3 (1): 29–36.

Auden, Wystan Hugh. 1984. *Secondary Worlds*. London: Faber and Faber.

Babaie, Sussan, Rebecca R. Hart, Shirin Neshat, and Nancy Princenthal. 2013. *Shirin Neshat*. Detroit: Detroit Institute of Arts.

Barthes, Roland. 2012. *Camera Lucida: Reflections on Photography*. New York: Noonday.

Bashi, Parsua. 2009. *Nylon Road: A Graphic Memoir of Coming of Age in Iran*. New York: St. Martin's Griffin.

Baudrillard, Jean. 2002. *The Spirit of Terrorism and Requiem for the Twin Towers*. London: Verso.

Beaujour, Michel. 1991. *The Poetics of Literary Self-Portrait*. New York: New York Univ. Press.

Benjamin, Walter. 1969. "The Work of Art in the Age of Mechanical Reproduction." In *Illuminations*, edited by Hannah Arendt. New York: Schocken.

Bertucci, Lina. 1997. "Shirin Neshat: Eastern Values." *Flash Art* 197 (November/December): 84–87.

Blackmore, Tim. 2012. "Eyeless in America; Hollywood and Indiewood's Iraq War on Film." *Bulletin of Science, Technology & Society* 32 (4): 294–316.

Bloom, Harold. 2007. *A Map of Misreading*. New York: Oxford Univ. Press.

Bresheeth, Haim. 2010. "Shirin Neshat's *Women without Men*." *Third Text* 24 (6): 754–58.

Butler, Judith. 2004. *Precarious Life: The Powers of Mourning and Violence*. London: Verso.

Caruth, Cathy. 1996. *Unclaimed Experience: Trauma, Narrative, and History*. Baltimore: John Hopkins Univ. Press.

Chute, Hillary. 2008. "The Texture of Retracing in Marjane Satrapi's *Persepolis. Women's Studies Quarterly* 36 (1/2): 92–110. www.jstor.org/stable/27649737?seq=1#page_scan_tab_contents.

Dabashi, Hamid. 2003. "It Was in China, One Moonless Night." *Social Research* 70 (3): 935–80.

———. 2007. *Iran: A People Interrupted.* New York: New Press.

———. 2009. "Interview with Shirin Neshat." *MrZine*, October 2009.

Dadi, Iftikhar. 2008. "Shirin Neshat's photographs as postcolonial allegories." *Signs: Journal of Women in Culture and Society* 34 (1): 125–50.

Davison, Andrew, and Himadeep Muppidi, eds. 2017. *The World Is My Home: A Hamid Dabashi Reader.* London: Routledge.

Derrida, Jacques. 2005. *Rogues: Two Essays on Reason.* Translated by Pascale-Anne Brault and Michael Naas. Palo Alto, CA: Stanford Univ. Press.

Enright, Robert, and Meeka Walsh. 2009. "Every Frame a Photograph: Shirin Neshat in Conversation." *Border Crossings* 28 (1): 16–24. http://bordercrossingsmag.com/article/every-frame-a-photograph-shirin-neshat-in-conversation.

Farah, Randa. 2002. "'To Veil or Not to Veil Is Not the Question': Palestinian Refugee Women's Voices on Other Matters." *Development* 45 (1): 93–98. https://link.springer.com/article/10.1057/palgrave.development.1110325.

Fleming, John, and Hugh Honour. 1977. *Dictionary of the Decorative Arts.* New York: Harper & Row.

Foucault, Michel. 1998. "Nietzsche, Genealogy, History." *Nietzsche: Critical Assessments.* London: Routledge.

———. 2008. *The Birth of Biopolitics: Lectures at the Collège de France, 1978–1979.* New York: Palgrave Macmillan.

———. 2011. *The Courage of Truth: The Government of Self and Others II: Lectures at the Collège de France 1983–1984.* New York: Palgrave Macmillan.

Foucault, Michel, and François Ewald. 2008. *Society Must Be Defended: Lectures at the Collège de France, 1975–1976.* London: Penguin.

Freud, Sigmund. 1953. "The Neuro-Psychoses of Defence." In *The Standard Edition of the Complete Psychological Works of Sigmund Freud*, ed. James Strachey et al. London: Hogarth.

Genette, Gérard. 1997. *Paratexts: Thresholds of Interpretation.* Cambridge, UK: Cambridge Univ. Press.

Harrington, John. 1977. *Film and/as Literature.* Englewood Cliffs, NJ: Prentice-Hall.

Harrison, Frances. 2006. "Women Graduates Challenge Iran," *BBC News*, September 19, 2006. http://news.bbc.co.uk/2/hi/middle_east/5359672.stm.

Hayden, Michael. 2013. "Ex-CIA Chief: What Edward Snowden Did." CNN, July 19, 2013. cnn.com/2013/07/19/opinion/hayden-snowden-impact/index.html.

Heartney, Eleanor. 2009. "Shirin Neshat: an Interview." *Art in America*, June 16. www.artinamericamagazine.com/news-features/magazines/shirin-neshat/.

Heydari, Gholam. 1998. *Forough Farrokhzad and Cinema*. Tehran: Elm.

Hirsch, Marianne. 2004. "Editor's Column: Collateral Damage." *PMLA* 119 (5): 1209–15.

Holland, Patrick, and Graham Huggan. 1998. *Tourists with Typewriters: Critical Reflections on Contemporary Travel Writing*. Ann Arbor: Univ. of Michigan Press.

Kant, Immanuel. 2007. *Critique of Judgment*. Edited by Nicholas Walker. New York: Oxford Univ. Press.

Khayyam, Omar. *The Oxford Book of English Verse, 1250–1900*. Translated by Edward Fitzgerald; edited by Arthur Quiller-Couch. New York: Bartleby.

Kuzegar, Dorna. 2007. "From Silk Road to Nylon Road: The Story of an Iranian Designer in Switzerland." Translated by Mehraneh Ebrahimi Eshratabadi. *BBC Persian*, February 3, 2007. http://www.bbc.com/persian/arts/story/2007/02/070203_la-parsuabashi.shtml.

LaCapra, Dominick. 2001. *Writing History, Writing Trauma*. Baltimore: Johns Hopkins Univ. Press.

Lao-Tzu. 2001. *Tao Te Ching: The Definitive Edition*. Translated by Johnathan Star. New York: Penguin.

Levinas, Emmanuel. 1985. *Ethics and Infinity: Conversations with Philippe Nemo*. Pittsburgh: Duquesne Univ. Press.

———. 1989. "Ethics as First Philosophy." In *The Levinas Reader*. Edited by Sean Hand. Cambridge, UK: Basil Blackwell.

———. 1994. *Otherness than Being or Beyond Essence*. Norwell, MA: Kluwer.

Lorde, Audre. 2007. "Poetry Is Not a Luxury." In *Sister Outsider: Essays and Speeches*, 36–40. New York: Random House.

Lyotard, Jean-Francois. 2015. *Libidinal Economy*. New York: Bloomsbury USA Academic.

McCloud, Scott. 1994. *Understanding Comics: The Invisible Art*. New York: Harper Perennial.

McGrath, Charles. 2004. "Not Funnies." *New York Times Magazine*, July 11, 2004. nytimes.com/2004/07/11/magazine/not-funnies.html.

Michel, Serge, and Paolo Woods. 2010. *Marches sur mes yeux: Portrait de l'Iran aujourd'hui*. Paris: Grasset.

Milani, Farzaneh. 1991. *Stories by Iranian Women since the Revolution*. Texas: Univ. of Texas at Austin.

———. 1992. *Veils and Words: The Emerging Voices of Iranian Women Writers*. Syracuse, NY: Syracuse Univ. Press.

Miller, Nancy K. 2007. "Out of the Family: Generations of Women in Marjane Satrapi's *Persepolis*." *Life Writing* 4 (1): 13–29.

"Moving stories: Azar Nafisi." 2004. *BBC News*, January 2, 2004. http://news.bbc.co.uk/2/hi/middle_east/3322495.stm.

Mountford, Roxanne. 2001. "On Gender and Rhetorical Space." *Rhetoric Society Quarterly* 30 (1): 41–71.

Naghibi, Nima. 2007. *Rethinking Global Sisterhood: Western Feminism and Iran*. Minneapolis: Univ. of Minnesota Press.

———. 2009. "Revolution, Trauma, and Nostalgia in Diasporic Iranian Women's Autobiographies." *Radical History Review* (105): 79–91.

———. 2016. *Women Write Iran: Nostalgia and Human Rights from the Diaspora*. Minneapolis: Univ. of Minnesota Press.

Naghibi, Nima, and Andrew O'Malley. 2005. "Estranging the Familiar: East and West in Satrapi's *Persepolis*." *English Studies in Canada* 31 (2/3): 223–47. https://muse.jhu.edu/article/218786.

Neshat, Shirin. 2005. "In Movement: A Conversation between Shoja Azari and Shirin Neshat." In Shirin Neshat, *Shirin Neshat, 2002–2005*. Milan, Italy: Charta.

Nietzsche, Friedrich. 1940. *Thus Spake Zarathustra*. New York: Modern Library.

———. 1968. "On Truth and Lie in an Extra-moral Sense." In *The Viking Portable Nietzsche*. Translated by Walter Kaufmann. New York: Viking.

———. 2009. *Beyond Good and Evil*. Hamburg, Germany: Classic Books.

Owens, Craig. 1992. "Posing." In *Beyond Recognition: Representation, Power, and Culture*, Berkeley: Univ. of California Press.

Palmer-Mehta, Valerie. 2015. "The Rhetorical Space of the Garden in Shirin Neshat's *Women without Men*." *Women's Studies in Communication* 38 (1): 78–98.

Parsipur, Shahrnush. 1998. *Women without Men: A Novel of Modern Iran*. Translated by Kamran Talattof and Jocelyn Sharlet. New York: Feminist Press.

———. 2009. *Touba and the Meaning of Night*. New York: Feminist Press.

———. 2013. *Kissing the Sword: A Prison Memoir*. New York: Feminist Press.

Paxton, Robert O. 2004. *The Anatomy of Fascism*, 1st ed. New York: Alfred A. Knopf.

Plato. 1921. *The Republic*. New York: A. L. Burt.

Rahimi, Babak, and Elham Gheytanchi. 2008. "Iran's Reformists and Activists." *Middle East Policy* 15 (1): 46–59.

Rak, Julie. 2013. *Boom! Manufacturing Memoir for the Popular Market*. Waterloo, ON: Wilfrid Laurier Univ. Press.

Rancière, Jacques. 1999. *Dis-agreement, Politics, and Philosophy*. Minneapolis: Univ. of Minnesota Press.

———. 2006. *Hatred of Democracy*. New York: Verso.

———. 2009a. *Aesthetics and Its Discontents*. Cambridge, UK: Polity Press.

———. 2009b. *The Emancipated Spectator*. London: Verso.

Rancière, Jacques, and Steve Corcoran. 2015. *Dissensus: On Politics and Aesthetics*. London: Bloomsbury.

Rich, Adrienne. 2003. "Notes Toward a Politics of Location." In *Feminist Postcolonial Theory: A Reader*. Edited by Reina Lewis and Sara Mills. New York: Routledge.

Rondeau, James. 1999. "Shirin Neshat: Rapture." Focus series brochure. Chicago: The Art Institute of Chicago.

Rosenbaum, Jonathan. 2010. *Goodbye Cinema, Hello Cinephilia: Film Culture in Transition*. Chicago: Univ. of Chicago Press.

Rumi, Jalal al-Din, Maulana. 2013. *Masnavi: Book Three*. Oxford: Oxford Univ. Press.

Said, Edward W. 1978. *Orientalism*. New York: Pantheon.

———. 2002. *Reflections on Exile and Other Essays*. Cambridge, MA: Harvard Univ. Press.

———. 2005. "Homage to Joe Sacco." Introduction to *Palestine*, by Joe Sacco. Seattle: Fantagraphics.

Satrapi, Marjane. 2003. *Persepolis: The Story of a Childhood*. New York: Pantheon.

———. 2004. *Persepolis 2: The Story of a Return*. New York: Pantheon.

Saunders, Douglas. 2012. *The Myth of the Muslim Tide: Do Immigrants Threaten the West?* New York: Random House.

Scahill, Jeremy, and Glenn Greenwald. 2014. "The NSA's Secret Role in the U.S. Assassination Program." *The Intercept*, February 9, 2014. https://theintercept.com/2014/02/10/the-nsas-secret-role/.

Schiller, Friedrich von. 1967. *Letters on the Aesthetic Education of Man*. Oxford: Clarendon.

Sliwinski, Sharon. 2011. *Human Rights in Camera*. Chicago: Univ. of Chicago Press.

Sontag, Susan. 1977. *On Photography*. New York: Farrar, Straus and Giroux.

———. 2003. *Regarding the Pain of Others*. New York: Farrar, Straus and Giroux.

Spivak, Gayatri Chakravorty. 1999. *A Critique of Postcolonial Reason: Toward a History of the Vanishing Present*. Cambridge, MA: Harvard Univ. Press.

———. 2010. *Can the Subaltern Speak? Reflections on the History of an Idea*. Edited by Rosalind Morris. New York: Columbia Univ. Press.

———. 2013a. *An Aesthetic Education in the Era of Globalization*. Cambridge, MA: Harvard Univ. Press.

———. 2013b. *The Spivak Reader: Selected Works of Gayatri Chakravorty Spivak*. 2013. Donna Landry and Gerald MacLean, eds. Florence: Taylor and Francis.

Talebi, Shahla. 2011. *Ghosts of Revolution: Rekindled Memories of Imprisonment in Iran*. Stanford, CA: Stanford Univ. Press.

Trigg, Sarah. 2014. "SEEN in the Studio: Shirin Neshat." *Vulture*, December 17, 2014. www.vulture.com/2014/12/seen-in-the-studio-shirin-neshat.html.

Weber-Fève, Stacey. 2011. "Framing the 'Minor' in Marjane Satrapi and Vincent Paronnaud's *Persepolis*." *Contemporary French and Francophone Studies* 15 (3): 321–28.

Whitlock, Gillian. 2005. "The Skin of the Burqa: Recent Life Narratives from Afghanistan." *Biography* 28 (1): 54–76.

———. 2006. "Autographics: The Seeing 'I' of the Comics." *Modern Fiction Studies* 52 (4): 965–79.

———. 2007. *Soft Weapons: Autobiography in Transit*. Chicago: Univ. of Chicago Press.

———. 2008. "From Tehran to Tehrangeles: The Generic Fix of Iranian Exilic Memoirs." *ARIEL* 39 (1/2): 7–27.

Wilde, Oscar. 2008. *The Picture of Dorian Gray*. Harlow, UK: Pearson Education.

Wolf, Naomi. 2007. *The End of America: A Letter of Warning to a Young Patriot*. White River Junction, VT: Chelsea Green.

Wolpé, Sholeh, ed. and trans. 2010. *Sin: Selected Poems of Forugh Farrokhzad*. Fayetteville: Univ. of Arkansas Press.

Worth, Jennifer. 2007. "Unveiling *Persepolis* as Embodied Performance." *Theatre Research International* 32 (2): 143–60.

Index

Photos, figures, and tables are indicated by italicized page numbers.

ABC Africa, 145
Abrahamic cosmogony, 142
Abramović, Marina, 107
abstract expressionism, 60
Abtahi, Ali, 18
accountability, 48
aestextasy, xxii, xxiv, 17–18; Bashi and, 64; concepts connected through, 4; elements of, 63
aesthetico-political media, 49
aesthetic revolt, xiii, 10–11
aesthetics, 88; ethics, politics, and, xi–xiv, 3, 31, 37–38, 48, 87, 103, 157–58; Forough and, 148; playfulness of, 92; power of, xx; Rancière teaching, 159; resistance and, 44, 47–48
Aesthetics and Its Discontents (Rancière), 125
aesthetic sensitivity, 13
aesthetic uniqueness, 50
After the Revolution: Women Who Transformed Contemporary Art, 107
aggressions, 39
Ahmadinejad, Mahmoud, 18, 65
Ahmed, Sara, 156
alcohol ban, 11, 22, 22n19, 72, 74
alterity: connection, community, and, 14; engagement with, 158–59; proximity to, 160; radical, xi, 87, 103, 135, 166; transcendental, 7
Anatomy of Fascism, The (Paxton), xvn1
And Here My Troubles Began (Spiegelman), 33–34
anesthetization, xvi, 164n4
antagonism, 39
anticolonization, 17
arabesque (*tazhib* adornments), 129–30
Arendt, Hannah, xviii, 159
Aristotle, xvi–xvii
atomization, 6, 39
Atwood, Margaret, 60n2
audibility, xxii, 125n6, 135
authority, xxii
autobiographies, 13n12, 60; genre of, 13; as soft weapons, 12
autoimmunity, xii
avant-gardism, 44
Axis of Evil, 161n2

Babylon, conquest of, 32
Bakhtin, Mikhail, 48
banishment, 19
Barthes, Roland, 101

Bashi, Parsua, xii, xxiii, 7–8; aestextasy and, 64; comic technology used by, 66; three classes of people reviewed by, 75–79
Baudrillard, Jean, xiv
Beaujour, Michel, 80
Beckett, Samuel, 128
belonging, 106, 113, 135, 160, 166
Benjamin, Walter, 100–101
bi-ocularity, 29–30
birth control, 56
Birth of Biopolitics (Foucault), xvii
Blackmore, Tim, 22n18
Bloom, Harold, 1n1
body-writing, 129–34
Boom! Manufacturing Memoir for the Popular Market (Rak), 13n11
Borromean knots, xiii, 4, 10, 48, 160
Bourgeois, Louise, 107
Bresheeth, Haim, 141
Bush, George W., xvii, xix, 161n2
Butler, Judith, 4, 160

calligraphy, 70, 129–34
Can the Subaltern Speak? (Spivak), 150–51
capitalism, 51, 93, 163
cartoon avatars, 30
cartooning, xii, 34, 49
Caruth, Cathy, 89, 162
Central Intelligence Agency (CIA), 1n3, 47, 114, 136–37
characterization, 136–37
chauvinism, 72
childhood: end of, 44; rebellion in, 50; as untainted, 40
Churchill, Winston, 56
Chute, Hillary, 59–60
CIA. *See* Central Intelligence Agency
class apartheid, 105
classes, 7, 23; contested ideologies regarding, 83; double standards regarding, 44; segregation of, 62
cognitive ability, 10
Cold War, xviii
colonization, 15, 15n15, 23
comics, 29–30; as aesthetico-political media, 49; defining, 31; as facilitators, 42; as playful, 62
comic technology, 29, 161; contemplation facilitated through, 62; techniques in, 49–50; trauma transformed through, 34–35; as used by Bashi, 66
communication: classical techniques for, 94; ease in, 32, 117; mediums of, 6; visual, 89
communist activities, 75
community: alterity, connection, and, 14; belonging to, 135, 160, 166; created for fallen women, 162; decline, xvn1; poetry creating, 9; as shared, 12, 87, 110
compartmentalization, 6
compassion industry, 104
complicity, 3, 7, 50–51, 163
conceptualization, level of, 38
conformity, 104
Congo Free State, 5
Congo Reform Association, 89
"Conquest of the Garden," 126
Constitutional Revolution of 1905, xi
Corcoran, Steve, xvi
corruption, 15, 18
Courage of Truth, The (Foucault), xvii
Critique of Aesthetic Judgment (Kant), 10
cult assimilation, 79

Dabashi, Hamid, 9, 16, 112, 148, 156
Dadi, Iftikhar, 132–33

defamiliarization, 38
defense mechanisms, 2, 89–90, 92–94, 162
democracy, xii–xiv, 35, 165–66; desires toward, xxiv; dissensual, 6; fall of, 146; Foucault on, 5, 160; growth of, 2; as interrupted, 136–37; lack of, 74; lives lost fighting for, 39–40; pervertible power of, xix–xxiv; Rancière on, 17; ushering in, 84
democracy *a venir* (to come), xv, 16
democratic process, xiii, 161
demonization, 14, 84
Derrida, Jacques, xii, xvii, 16–17
Deyhim, Sussan, 111
Didi-Huberman, Georges, 3
displacement, xiv–xv, 19, 157
domination, xii, xxii, 163
dress codes, 51–56, 74, 83, 109–10

economic hegemony, 23
effacement, 59–61, 136
egoism, xxii
Egyptian tomb paintings, 31, *33*
elitism, xxi, 23, 44, 164
empathy, 56
End of America, The (Wolf), xix
Enlightenment, xiv, 3n5
Erfan (mysticism), 121, 138n4, 148
eroticism, 33, 103, 111
escapism, 33
essentialism, 165
estrangement (*ghorbat*), 5, 19, 21–23
ethical connectivity, xxiii
ethical repetitions, 59–60
ethical responsibility, 88, 99–100, 103, 123, 161; evading, 128; Spivak and, 48
ethics: dialectical, 64; notion of, 59; politics, aesthetics, and, xi–xii, 3, 31, 37–38, 48, 87, 103, 157–58; as problem of knowledge, xvii, 48; self-regulation and, 7, 83–84; Spivak on, 159
exile, 19–25, 38
exoticization, 14
expressivity, 30
extinction: war, humanity, and, xxiii
extremism, xv, 38, 64–65

fanaticism, 48, 56
Farah, Randa, 24
Farrokhzad, Forough (GENERAL), 8, 108–14, 143; aesthetics used by, 148; examples of style, 125–29; film talents of, 135; freedom alluded to by, 140; influence of, 117–24; sentiments of, 125–29
Farrokhzad, Forough (WORKS): "Conquest of the Garden," 126; "The House Is Black," 87, 113, 135–36, 143–46; "Let Us Believe in the Beginning of the Cold Season," 127; "My Heart Is Burning for the Garden," 154n10; "Rebirth," 126; "Standing on This Soil," 121; "Summer's Green Waters," 153
fascism, xiii–xv, xix–xx, 20
fashion, 53–56, 74, 80, 83
fashion cults, 7, 75
favoritism, 15
fear politics, xvi
feminism, 61, 137
Ferdowsi, 94
foreclosure, 3
foreign invasion, 22
Foucault, Michel, xv–xviii, xxii, 110; on body, 124, 156; on democracy, 5, 160; subjugated knowledges and, 35, 37–39, 49

freedom, 6–7; Forough alluding to, 140; lack of, 74; narratives of fighters for, 39–40; security and, xvii; women, nation, and, 138
French Revolution, 10
Freud, Sigmund, 2
fundamentalism, 6–7, 25, 162

Games of Desire, 108
Ganji, Ali Akbar, 18
gardens, symbolic, 120–34, 138, 140–43
gender norms, 106
genealogy, 47–59, 156
generalizations: double-sided blade of, 72–73; perils of, 84; by Satrapi, 54
Genette, Gérard, 69–70
genocide, xv, 5, 20, 91, 165
ghorbat (estrangement), 5, 19, 21–23
Ghosts of Revolution: Rekindled Memories of Imprisonment in Iran (Talebi), 44
globalization, xiv, 23, 152, 163
Golestan, Ebrahim, 144n7
Gramsci, Antonio, 12n10, 61
Greek mythology, 142–43
Green Movement of 2009, xi, 9
guns. *See* weapons

hallucinatory confusion, 2
Hart, Rebecca R., 139
Hayden, Michael, xvii–xviii
Heartney, Eleanor, 150
Heller, Dana, 40
heritage, xvi
hierarchies, 37; dismantling, 159; of domination, xxii; of gender, 122; readjusting, 103
Holocaust, 5, 91, 147
"House Is Black, The," 87, 113, 135–36, 143–46
humanism, 146
humanity: war, extinction, and, xxiii
human rights, 12, 14, 18, 22n19, 89
Hussein, Saddam, xi, 11, 47, 106, 114

idealism, 42–44
identity, 8; asserting sense of, 74; contested ideologies regarding, 83; ethnic, 105; negotiations of, 64; philosophical, 16; poetry as main part of sense of, 111–12; private and public sense of, 89; romanticizing, 21
images: characters' use of, 154; dissemination of, by news media, 93–94; hegemony of, 89; by Neshat, 88–89; philosophy of, 133; sequential, 30–31; terror brought through, 87; trauma depicted in, 88; truth in, 96–98; of violence, 32, 88–93; war over, 166
imagination, 31, 88–98
imperialism, 15
impoverishment, 22
innocence, 40
interdependence, of humankind, 4
ISIS. *See* Islamic State
Islamic Republic, 42, 44, 47, 48
Islamic Revolution of 1979, xi, 11–12, 23, 44, 47–48, 128
Islamic State (ISIS), xxiiin5, 1n2, 161n1
Islamophobia, xxiii
isolation, 15, 19, 159

Jacotot, Joseph, xxi–xxii
justice, 22n19, 54, 59, 161–62

Kafka, Franz, 113
Kant, Immanuel, 10, 90–93
Karroubi, Mehdi, 18
Khatami, Mohammad, 18, 137
Khayyam, Omar, 112
Khomeini, Ayatollah, 18
Kiarostami, Abbas, 113, 145
Kissing the Sword (Parsipur), 137n2
kitschiness, 104

Lacan, Jacques, 2
Lacanian Real, 91–92
LaCapra, Dominick, 146–47
Lao-tzu, 142
leadership, xiv, 16
leftist movement, genealogy of, 47–59
"Let Us Believe in the Beginning of the Cold Season," 127
Levinas, Emmanuel, 88, 98–100, 103–5, 145, 160–61
liberalism, xvii
Logic of the Birds, 111
Lorde, Audre, 103, 110–11
Lyotard, Jean-François, 156

magic, 129–34
magical realism, 136–39, 147–49
"Mahdokht," 139–40
Map of Misreading (Bloom), 1n1
Marx, Karl, 44
Marxism, 42
Mascia-Lees, Frances E., 124
massacres, 14n13
Maus: A Survivor's Tale: My Father Bleeds History (Spiegelman), 33–35
McCloud, Scott, 31
McGrath, Charles, 29
memory: collective, 38; freeze frames of, 87, 90, 133; national, 35; nature of, 30
metalepsis, xxiii, 1n1
metonymy, xviii, xxiii, 159, 165
Michel, Serge, 14
Milani, Farzaneh, 60, 116, 123, 156
Miller, Nancy K., 50–51
miniatures, use of, 61, 94, *95*, 130
Moaveni, Azadeh, 60
modernity, 6–7, 96, 104, 156
modernization, 15, 23, 155
Moebian-Labyrinthine skin, 156
monarchial tyranny, 15
Montazeri, Ayatollah, 18
Mossadegh, Mohammad, 127
Mountford, Roxanne, 122
Mousavi, Mir-Hossein, 18
Muhammad, Prophet, 53, 115–16
Mussolini, Benito, xvnn1–2
"My Heart Is Burning for the Garden," 154n10
mysticism (*Erfan*), 121, 138n4, 148

Nabavi, Ebrahim, 18
Nafisi, Azar, 20, 60–61, 105, 161
Naghibi, Nima, 40, 44, 137
narrators, children as, 39–42
nationalization, 9
National Security Agency (NSA), 1n3
native informant, 12, 12n10, 104–5
Nazis, 5
Nemat, Marina, 104–5, 161
neocapitalism, 1
Neshat, Shirin, xii, xxiii, 70; audience illuminated by, 156–57; awards for, 107n1; calligraphy used by, 130; characterization by, 136–40; curiosity of, 116–17; film strategies of, 149–50;

Neshat, Shirin (*cont.*)
images by, 87–89; interview with, 113–14; magic charms displayed by, *131*; minimalism of, 118; paradoxes used by, 148; poetic play in, 129–30; symbols searched for by, 132; transnational influences on, 155–56; tree references explained by, 141–42; use of symbolic garden, 121–23, 147–48; *Women of Allah* by, 8, 98, 103, 107–8, 114, 130; works by, 94, *95*, 96, 101–2, 105–8, 117–20, 129
news media, xi; awareness raised by, xiii; controlling, xix; desensitization of, 3, 89; dissemination of images by, 93–94
New World Order, 12, 158
Nietzsche, Friedrich, 97, 158–59, 163
9/11 terrorist attacks, 14, 18–19
NSA (National Security Agency), 1n3
Nylon Road (Bashi), xii, 7–8, 13, 159; audience for, 66–67; autocritique in, 74–79; common Western attitudes from, *73*; comparing types of cults in, *77*; comparison of covers for, *69*; first panel from, *82*; intimacy lacking in, 65; leftist fighter training in, *76*; as mediated, 64; outcomes for cult followers in, *78–79*; paratext for, 68–71; religion and politics in, 71–74; as self-therapeutic, 84

Obama, Barack, xviii
ocularcentrism, 89
oil industry, 9; economy based on, 74; management of wealth in, 17; theft within, 15
O'Malley, Andrew, 40
oppression, 13, 54; fighting against, 39; during monarchy, 47; women against, 106
Othering, 3n4, 33, 39, 161
Otherness, xi, xiv, 148
Owens, Craig, 70

Palmer-Mehta, Valerie, 122–23
parochialism, 3
parrhesia, xvii–xviii, xxii, 2–3
Parsipur, Shahrnush, 8, 87, 111, 121, 135, 139–43; character development by, 151–52; *Kissing the Sword* by, 137n2; *Touba and the Meaning of Night* by, 138
Paxton, Robert O., xvn1
Persepolis, palace of, 31, *32*
Persepolis: The Story of a Childhood (Satrapi), xii, 6, 13, 37, 159; aesthetic uniqueness in, 50; demise of idealists in, *43*; dichotomies and ambivalence in, *45*; end of childhood depicted in, *41*; first panel from, *81*; leftist movement genealogy in, 47–59; people categorized by dress code in, *55*; perpetuating violence in, *58*; revolution and menace in, *57*; torture envisioned in, *46*
Persepolis 2: The Story of a Return (Satrapi), xii, 6, 13, *52*
pesticization, 160
photography: as aesthetically pleasing, 97; authenticity of, 88, 98; as gift from technological advances, 100–101; installations and, by Neshat, 94, *95*, 96, 101–2, 105; safe distance contemplation provided by, 90
photo-poetry, 6, 8, 87–88, 110–11

Plato, xvii–xviii, xxi
Poetics of Literary Self-Portrait, The (Beaujour), 80
poetry, xi, 8, 61, 103; community created through, 9; flexibility within, 112–13; as main part of sense of identity, 111–12; as reviving, 120–21; tradition of, 156–57; violence, women, and, 116–17
policing, 125, 159
political literacy, 14
politics, 7, 23; contested ideologies regarding, 83; ethics, aesthetics, and, xi–xiv, 3, 31, 37–38, 48, 87, 103, 157–58; policing compared to, 125n6; Rancière on, 65; religion and, in *Nylon Road*, 71–74. *See also* fear politics; space politics
Prisoner of Tehran (Nemat), 105
proximity, xiii, xx, xxii, 93, 98–99, 103, 160
Pseudo-Longinus, 90
psychosocial development, 80
punctum, 101–2, 132

Qur'anic miniature pagination, 130
Qurratulayn, Tahereh, 124

racism, xi, 71–72
radicalism, xv, 65
Rak, Julie, 13n11
Rancière, Jacques, xii, xvi, xxi–xxii, 10; *Aesthetics and Its Discontents* by, 125; aesthetics taught by, 159; on democracy, 17; politics according to, 65; on violence, 91–94
Reading Lolita in Tehran (Nafisi), 105
"Rebirth," 126
Red Scare, xviii
refugees, 21
religion, 7; distinguishing between true and fake, 53; government distinguished from, 68; politics and, in *Nylon Road*, 71–74
religious beliefs, 23, 83
religious insurgency, 48
repartage, 65, 83, 89, 122
Republic VI (Plato), xxi
resilience, 38; bonding together for, 106; through flexibility, 142–43; resistance, revolt, and, 9, 155
resistance, 163; aesthetic and ecstatic, 44, 47–48; Iranian, 15–19; resilience, revolt, and, 9, 155
revolt, 104; as reactionary, 51; resilience, resistance, and, 9, 155; against transcendental, 121–22
revolution, 6, 15, 17, 38, *57*
Rich, Adrienne, 123–24, 164
Rosenbaum, Jonathan, 143–45
Rosler, Martha, 92
Roy, Oliver, 19
rule of law, xix, 2
Rumi, 113–14

Said, Edward, 21, 29, 109
Satrapi, Marjane, xii, xxiii, 6, 13; choice of techniques, 60; generalizations by, 54; skills of, 37; stereotypes and, 34; subjugated knowledges used by, 48–49; travels to Iran, 20n17; veiling and, 25
Saunders, Doug, 19
Sazegara, Mohsen, 18
Schiller, Friedrich von, 10

scopophilia, 29
self-argumentation, 64, 83–84
self-immunity, xix
self-presentation, visual, 79–83
self-regulation, 7, 83–84
sensory perception, xxii
Sepehri, Sohrab, 117
sexual liberation, 22
Shah, Reza, 25
Shahnameh (Ferdowsi), 94
Sharpe, Patricia, 124
Sherman, Cindy, 107
Shi'ism, 16
Shi'ite law, 7–8
sisterhood, global, 137n1
Sliwinski, Sharon, 89, 166
Smith, Kiki, 107
Snowden, Edward, xvii–xviii
social equality, 23
social normativity, 144, 147
Socrates, xviii
Soft Weapons: Autobiography in Transit (Whitlock), 12
Sontag, Susan, 87, 90, 100, 160
space politics, 120–34, 159
Spero, Nancy, 107
Spiegelman, Art, 33–34
Spivak, Gayatri, xxiii, 3n5, 12n10, 104, 155; ethical responsibility and, 48; ethics according to, 159; on ideology, 150–51
Stalinism, xv–xvi
"Standing in Awe," 117–20
"Standing on This Soil," 121
stereotypes, 60, 68; judgment according to, 37; reconfirming, 50; Satrapi and, 34; slippages in, 51; surrounding women, 54–55
stigmatization, 156
studium, 101–2
subaltern, 3n5, 59–61
subjecthood, 7, 104
subjugated knowledges, 35, 37–39, 48–49
sublime, 90–91
"Summer's Green Waters," 153
superstition, 104
supremacy, xiv
Symbolic Order, 2

taking turns (*tour à tour*), xvi, xix, xvin3
Talebi, Shahla, 44, 48
tattooing, religious, 133n10
tazhib adornments (arabesque), 129–30
terror, xii, 2, 161; brought through images, 87; combating, xxiii; pop, xiv; scopophilia and, 29; war on, 11n9, 14
terrorism, xiv, 161n2, 165–66
terrorists, 1n3, 19
theocracy, 16–17
thug caste, xix
tokenism, 104
torture, 15; as envisioned in *Persepolis: The Story of a Childhood*, 46; games of, 39; inhumanity of, 47; methods of, 59; recounting tales of, 44; as witnessed vicariously, 47
totalitarianism, xvn2, 14
Touba and the Meaning of Night (Parsipur), 138
tour à tour (taking turns), xvi, xix, xvin3
traditionalism, 8, 54
tragedy, depiction of, 34
trauma, xi, 115; comic technology transforming, 34–35; coming of age, 50; images depicting, 88; of Other, 7; reconciling, 66; repeating of, 39; representation of, 91; of war, 6
treason, xix

trees, 140–43
trivialization, 40
Trump, Donald, xviii
truth, xvii–xviii, 87–88; courage to voice, xvi; in images, 96–98; power of, 6
truth claims, 146–47

unemployment, 22
utopianism, 165

veiling, 7–8, 23–24, 25, 51, 62, 116
Velayati, Ali-Akbar, 113
victimization, 14, 145, 157
violence, xi, 13, 33, 162; in domestic sphere, 38–39, 62; exposure to, 40; images of, 32, 88–93; instinct for, 98–99; perpetuating of, in *Persepolis: The Story of a Childhood*, 58; poetry, women, and, 116–17; as political, 2; Rancière on, 91–94; sublime and, 91; symbols of, 3; used for control, 160; toward women, 84
visibility, 59; through art, 4, 8; audibility, belonging, and, 135; authority, audibility, and, xxii; of culture, 105; Islamic Republic erasing, 48; right to, 125–26; for women, 122
vulnerability, 88

"Waiting for Godot," 128
war, xi, 106; exile, revolution, and, 38; humanity, extinction, and, xxiii; over images, 166; methods of, xiv; on terror, 11n9, 14; trauma of, 6
weapons, xxiiin5; autobiographies as soft, 12; nuclear, 5; women and, 109
Weber-Fève, Stacey, 61
Westernization, 25
Whitlock, Gillian, 11n9, 11–12, 19, 23–24
Wilde, Oscar, 112–13
Wolf, Naomi, xix
women, xiii, 2; binaries between, 104; community created for fallen, 162; demands of, 24; education of, 110; empowering of, 70; freedom, nation, and, 138; guns and, 109; metamorphoses of, 139; occupation of voice, 124; against oppression, 106; physical segregation of, 25; poetry, violence, and, 116–17; stereotypes surrounding, 54–55; in symbolic garden, 129; trees and, 140–43; veiling of, 7–8, 23–25; as victimized, 13; violence toward, 84; visibility for, 122
Women of Allah, 8, 98, 103, 107–8, 114, 130, 159, 162–63
Women without Men, xii, 9, 87, 108, 135–39, 146–57, 159, 162
World Trade Center, xxiii
World War II, 20, 158
Worth, Jennifer, 59

xenophobia, 6, 38–39, 62

Zeynab, 115–17
Zinn, Howard, 163n3

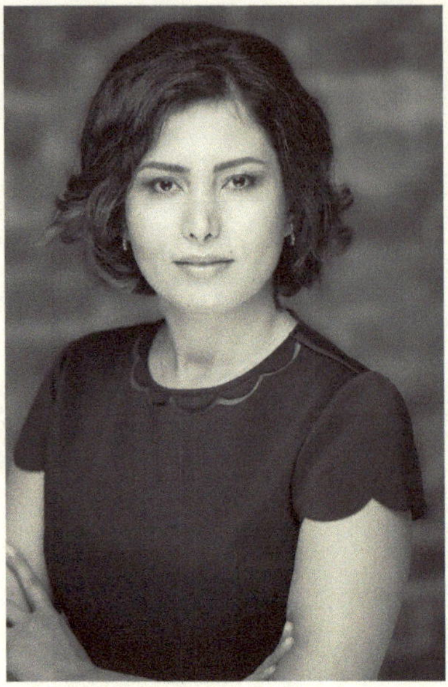

Edris Davarian

Mehraneh Ebrahimi has a PhD in Comparative Literature from Western University in London, Ontario, Canada, where she received numerous teaching awards. She was born into a traditional Muslim-Persian family and had the good fortune of growing up and studying in different countries around the world, including Italy, Pakistan, Iran, and Canada. This nomadic, fluid lifestyle colored her analytical perspective, in addition to helping her achieve fluency in four languages. Shuttling between home and elsewhere, between self and Other, and between the position of being a citizen and that of being an immigrant helped her understand that singling out a single enemy outside of the self as the sole cause of our misfortune is a defense mechanism to protect the weak self, that humanity is connected, and humans are responsible for each other's miseries. Instead of spending a lifetime living in different countries, sometimes the journey can be inward, like reading a story about a little girl faced with war, revolution, and immigration, as well as universal coming-of-age dilemmas. Reading about the tales of others can help create the shift in perspective that is so necessary to rescue humankind from the disastrous consequences of putting nations in binary opposition.

FSC
www.fsc.org
MIX
Papier | Fördert
gute Waldnutzung
FSC® C083411

Zeitfracht Medien GmbH
Ferdinand-Jühlke-Straße 7
99095 Erfurt, Deutschland
produktsicherheit@kolibri360.de